Photonics in Industrial IoT: Transforming Manufacturing and Beyond

The Role of IoT Innovation in Smart Factories and Connected

Dr. Preeta Sharan
Dr. Sandip Kumar Roy
Harshada J. Patil
Aryan Chaudhary
Dr. Deepak Kumar

Apress®

Photonics in Industrial IoT: Transforming Manufacturing and Beyond: The Role of IoT Innovation in Smart Factories and Connected

Dr. Preeta Sharan
Bengaluru, Karnataka, India

Harshada J. Patil
Vemana Institute of Technology
Bengaluru, Karnataka, India

Dr. Deepak Kumar
School of Electronic and Electrical Engineering
University of Leeds
Leeds, UK

Dr. Sandip Kumar Roy
Noida, Uttar Pradesh, India

Aryan Chaudhary
Chief Scientific Advisor
Bio Tech Sphere Research
Ghaziabad, Uttar Pradesh, India

ISBN-13 (pbk): 979-8-8688-2693-1
https://doi.org/10.1007/979-8-8688-2694-8

ISBN-13 (electronic): 979-8-8688-2694-8

Managing Director, Apress Media LLC: Welmoed Spahr
Acquisitions Editor: Spandana Chatterjee
Editorial Project Manager: Rachel Zhang
Desk Editor: James Markham

Cover designed by eStudioCalamar

Distributed to the book trade worldwide by Springer Science+Business Media New York, 1 New York Plaza, New York, NY 10004. Phone 1-800-SPRINGER, fax (201) 348-4505, e-mail orders-ny@springer-sbm.com, or visit www.springeronline.com. Apress Media, LLC is a Delaware LLC and the sole member (owner) is Springer Science + Business Media Finance Inc (SSBM Finance Inc). SSBM Finance Inc is a **Delaware** corporation.

For information on translations, please e-mail booktranslations@springernature.com; for reprint, paperback, or audio rights, please e-mail bookpermissions@springernature.com.

Apress titles may be purchased in bulk for academic, corporate, or promotional use. eBook versions and licenses are also available for most titles. For more information, reference our Print and eBook Bulk Sales web page at http://www.apress.com/bulk-sales.

Any source code or other supplementary material referenced by the author in this book is available to readers on GitHub. For more detailed information, please visit https://www.apress.com/gp/services/source-code.

If disposing of this product, please recycle the paper

The book is dedicated to Lord Ram and my beloved family.

Table of Contents

Chapter 3: Communication Systems in Industrial IoT 49

About the Authors

Dr. Preeta Sharan is a distinguished researcher and academician with extensive expertise in photonics, optical sensors, and quantum dots. Currently she is working in the Oxford College of Engineering, Bangalore. With over 26 years of experience, Dr. Sharan has done a Ph.D. from IIT BHU and a postdoctorate from IIT Kharagpur. She made significant contributions to education, research, and student mentorship. Dr. Sharan's work continues to shape advancements in medical health care devices and photonic sensors, making her a leading figure in scientific innovation and technological development, including Industrial IoT application development. Her research spans optical networks and biosensors, leading to over 250 research publications and multiple patents. She has received significant government funding to execute real-time projects. She is a recipient of many awards from state government and international agencies. She has guided 17 Ph.D. scholars in the area of photonics and optoelectronics.

Dr. Sandip Kumar Roy is a dedicated professor, researcher, and consultant specializing in artificial intelligence, IoT, photonics, and cybersecurity. With over 20 years of experience in both industry and academia, he has made significant contributions to cutting-edge research, technological innovation, and digital transformation. His expertise spans AI-driven healthcare solutions, cybersecurity strategies, embedded systems, and data analytics, with a strong focus on solving real-world problems through interdisciplinary research. He is a recipient of multiple awards, including the IEEE, USA HCI Best Design, Geospatial Excellence, and Leadership Awards in the United States. Dr. Roy has published extensively in peer-reviewed journals, delivered international keynote speeches, and led industry collaborations for AI-powered solutions.

Harshada J. Patil is an academician with 20 years of experience, currently working as an associate professor at Vemana Institute of Technology, Bengaluru, and an emerging researcher in the field of photonic sensors and integrated photonic circuits. She is actively involved in academic leadership and professional body activities such as IEEE. She is a senior member of the IEEE Photonics Society.

Aryan Chaudhary is the Director and Chief Scientific Advisor at BioTech Sphere Research, India. Aryan continues to make groundbreaking contributions to the industry. Having served as the Research Head at Nijji HealthCare Pvt Ltd, he has demonstrated his expertise in leveraging revolutionary technologies such as artificial intelligence, deep learning, IoT, cognitive technology, and blockchain to revolutionize the healthcare landscape. His relentless pursuit of excellence and innovation has earned him recognition as a thought leader in the industry. His dedication to advancing healthcare is evident through his vast body of work. He has authored several influential academic papers on public health and digital health, published in prestigious international journals. His research primarily focuses on integrating IoT and sensor technology for efficient data collection through one-time and ambulatory monitoring. As a testament to his expertise and leadership, he is not only a keynote speaker at numerous international and national conferences but also serves as the series editor of a CRC book series and is the editor of several books on biomedical science. His commitment to the advancement of scientific knowledge extends further, as he acts as a guest editor for special issues in renowned journals. Recognized for his significant contributions, he has received prestigious accolades, including the "Most Inspiring Young Leader in Healthtech Space 2022" by *Business Connect* and the title of the best project leader at Global Education and Corporate Leadership. Moreover, he holds senior memberships in various international science associations, reflecting his influence and impact in the field. Adding to his accomplishments, Aryan Chaudhary is currently serving as a guest editor for a special issue in the highly regarded journal, *EAI Endorsed Transactions on AI and Robotics*, and he has joined the editorial board of Biomedical Science and Clinical Research (BSCR). Additionally, he is a respected professional member of the Association for Computing Machinery (ACM).

Dr. Deepak Kumar completed B.Sc. Hons. Physics from Ramjas College, University of Delhi, and M.Sc. Physics from the Department of Physics, Kurukshetra University, India. He worked at the Institute for Plasma Research (IPR) Gujarat and the Indian Institute of Technology (IIT) Ropar, India, during his research internships. Thereafter, he joined as Junior Research Fellow at the Department of Physics, Indian Institute of Technology (IIT) Guwahati, India. He completed his PhD from the Department of Physics, Panjab University, Chandigarh, India. Further, he worked as guest faculty at the Department of Physics, Guru Jambheshwar University of Science and Technology, Hisar, Haryana, and as Project Scientist I at CSIR CSIO, Chandigarh, India. He is currently working as a research fellow at the School of Electronic and Electrical Engineering, University of Leeds, United Kingdom. His scientific contributions involve featured article, coverage of research as the cover picture of journal, book chapters, and patents. He has interests in broadly exploring metamaterials, terahertz photonics, green composites, and laser and light-matter interaction.

About the Technical Reviewer

 **Atonu Ghosh** is a Ph.D. research scholar in the Department of Computer Science and Engineering at the Indian Institute of Technology Kharagpur, West Bengal, India. He also has an M.Tech. and a B.Tech. in Computer Science and Engineering. Atonu's research domain includes the Internet of Things (IoT), edge computing, low power networks, and Industry 4.0. Atonu has built IoT solutions for over a decade and has executed several research and consulting projects. He is also an active reviewer of research journals and books. Find out more about Atonu or reach him through his personal website: `https://www.atonughosh.com/`.

Acknowledgments

"Presentation, inspiration, and motivation have always played an important role in the success of any venture."

First, we thank the Almighty for his inspiration, benevolence, and for giving me the opportunity to design this book.

We want to acknowledge the help of all the people involved in this project, specifically, the reviewers who took part in the review process. Without their support, this book would not have become a reality. I want to thank each one of them.

We pay our sincere gratitude to our mentors, who always told us to aim high and said, "do not aim low; otherwise, we will miss the mark." I wish to thank the staff at Springer Nature for their invaluable efforts, great support, and valuable advice toward the successful publication of this book.

We sincerely acknowledge the valuable contributions of Sonam Rani (Department of Physics, Guru Jambheshwar University of Science and Technology, Hisar, Haryana, India), Mamta Dahiya (Department of Physics, Indian Institute of Technology Delhi, New Delhi, India), Vinita Sharma (Department of Environmental Science and Engineering, Guru Jambheshwar University of Science and Technology, Hisar, Haryana, India), Naveen Kumar Baskaran (Department of Computer Science and Engineering, Faculty of Engineering and Technology, JAIN (Deemed-to-be University), Bengaluru, India), Vivek Kumar (Laboratoire Kastler Brossel, ENS-Université PSL, CNRS, Sorbonne Université, Collège de France, Paris, France), and Sushil Kumar (Om Sterling Global University, Hisar, Haryana, India) to help in preparing the content.

Introduction

Industrial systems are evolving from isolated automation into connected, data-driven, and increasingly autonomous environments. The industrial Internet of Things (IIoT) enables this shift by linking machines, sensors, and software so that industrial operations can be monitored and optimized in real time. However, as Industry 4.0 scales, traditional sensing and connectivity methods are often stressed by industrial realities—electromagnetic interference, long-distance signal transmission, harsh operating conditions, high-speed data streams, and the need for reliable low-latency decision-making. This is where photonics—the science and engineering of light—becomes a critical enabler.

Photonics in Industrial IoT explores how photonics technologies strengthen IIoT from the sensing layer to the communication backbone and analytics pipeline. Optical fiber networks support high-bandwidth, low-latency data transfer and remain resilient in electrically noisy environments. Photonic sensors and imaging systems deliver high precision for metrology, condition monitoring, inspection, and safety applications. When integrated into IIoT platforms, these capabilities improve visibility across operations, increase quality control effectiveness, reduce downtime through predictive maintenance, and support safer, more energy-efficient industrial processes.

This book is written for engineers, researchers, graduate students, solution architects, and industrial practitioners working across smart manufacturing, industrial automation, sensing and instrumentation, industrial networking, and digital transformation. It is also useful for technology leaders evaluating modern sensing and connectivity strategies for factories, utilities, and critical infrastructure. Readers do not need deep prior expertise in photonics; the book introduces core concepts before moving into applied industrial use cases.

A recurring theme throughout the book is that industrial adoption is driven by outcomes, not novelty. Photonics is not presented here as "technology for technology's sake," but as a set of tools that can deliver measurable operational advantages when engineered thoughtfully into IIoT systems. The chapters are written to help readers understand what to use, where to use it, and how to integrate it reliably—so that photonics-enabled IIoT solutions can move from lab concepts to robust industrial deployments.

We hope this book provides a clear, practical pathway for understanding and building photonics-driven IIoT systems that advance the next generation of connected industry.

CHAPTER 1

Introduction to Photonics and Industrial IoT

This chapter addresses fiber optics and optical communication and introduces photonics and emerging trends in photonics, including future prospects, in the first part. In the second part, it introduces Industrial IoT (IIoT) and discusses key components of IIoT, technologies enabling IIoT, and future trends in IIoT. The third part discusses convergence of photonics and Industrial IoT.

Photonics: Reshaping the 21st Century

People often say that light is important, but… is it *really* that significant in our everyday lives? More than you might imagine. Light shapes almost everything around us—construction, telecommunications, transportation, entertainment, and even the clothes we wear. Modern society is built on our ability to use and control light. That sounds huge, so some of the examples are given here. Consider data transmission: optical fibers send information using light. Optoelectronic devices rely on it too. Take a compact disc player—when a laser beam reflects off the CD's surface, the returning light signal becomes music. Light also powers laser printing, digital photography, and the fiber-optic cables connecting computers and phone networks. So it's in communication, entertainment, and even everyday machines? Exactly. And beyond that, we use light in fiber lasers, interferometers, modulators, sensors—tools found in research, industry, and medicine. In hospitals, light produces diagnostic images, and lasers enable precise eye surgeries. People always think of light as something simple. But it is actually complex. It's made of electromagnetic waves, yet it behaves like particles under certain conditions. It covers a broad range of wavelengths—the electromagnetic spectrum, which is shown in Figure 1-1.

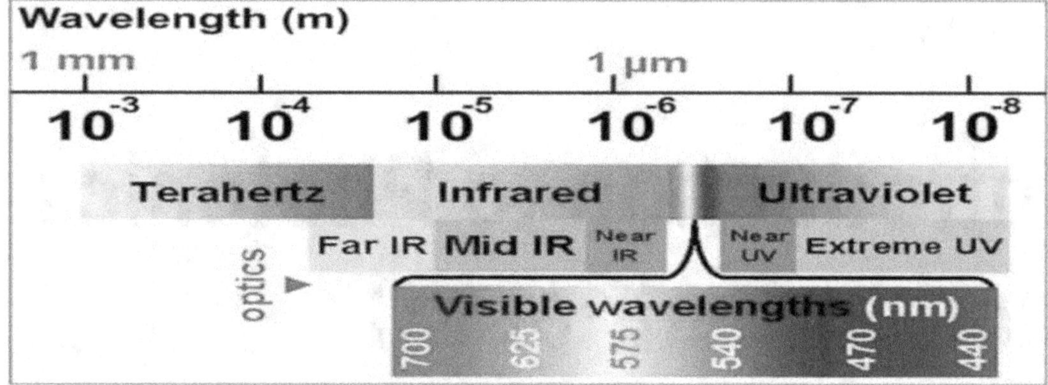

Figure 1-1. *The Electromagnetic Spectrum*

This makes me wonder—what exactly is *photonics*? Photonics is the scientific field focused on generating, detecting, and manipulating photons—light particles. It includes transmission, emission, signal processing, modulation, switching, amplification, and sensing. In short, photonics turns light into a powerful tool for human progress. Photonics deals with the entire electromagnetic spectrum, but most photonics research concentrates on visible and near-infrared light. The word itself comes from "photon," the smallest unit of light—just as an electron is the smallest unit of electricity. So, photonics is becoming as big as electronics. The 20th century was transformed by electronics, and photonics is reshaping the 21st. It includes optical fibers, lasers, detectors, quantum electronics, and advanced materials.

A Brief History of Photonics

Its roots go back to 1960 with the invention of the laser. Then came optical fibers for data transmission, the laser diode in the 1970s, and erbium-doped fiber amplifiers. These breakthroughs set the stage for the telecommunications revolution and the rise of the internet. Although the concept existed earlier, the term "photonics" gained traction in the 1980s when telecom companies adopted fiber-optic communication. Photonics became recognized as a distinct field when the IEEE Lasers and Electro-Optics Society launched *Photonics Technology Letters*. I would like to give more clarity over here about what happened after the early telecom boom. Before the dot-com crash of 2001, research focused heavily on fiber-optic telecommunications. Afterwards, photonics expanded into diverse areas: chemical and biological sensors, laser manufacturing, medical diagnostics and treatments, optical computing, and display technologies. Today, silicon photonics is accelerating this progress even further.

Photonics and Related Fields

Photonics intersects with opto-mechanics, electro-optics, quantum electronics, and quantum optics. But each term means something different. Quantum optics explores fundamental theory, while photonics emphasizes applied research. Optoelectronics refers to devices combining electrical and optical components. Historically, "electro-optics" described nonlinear electrical-optical interactions, like crystal modulators and advanced surveillance imaging sensors. So why do people call photonics an "all-pervasive" technology? Because it offers capabilities electronics simply can't match. Light travels faster than electrons in computer chips. This opens the door to optical computers that may someday compute thousands of times faster. Optical fibers carry many wavelengths simultaneously, giving them enormous bandwidth. And unlike copper wires, optical fibers are immune to electromagnetic interference. So, photonics isn't just about light—it's about the future. Precisely. Photonics is transforming how we communicate, heal, manufacture, sense, compute, and perceive the world.

Evolution of Photonics

The evolution of photonics is a fascinating journey, spanning several decades and intertwined with advancements in physics, materials science, and engineering. The concise summary of its key milestones is explained here. Photonics, in its earliest conceptual form, stems from the study of light and optics, which dates back to ancient times. The study of light as an electromagnetic phenomenon began with scientists like Isaac Newton (who studied the nature of light and color) and Thomas Young (who conducted the double-slit experiment in the early 1800s, establishing the wave theory of light). During the early 20th century, significant advancements in quantum theory laid the foundation for modern photonics. In 1905, Albert Einstein introduced the photon theory of light through his explanation of the photoelectric effect, demonstrating that light can exist as discrete packets of energy, or photons. Throughout the 1920s and 1930s, the development of quantum mechanics and the formalization of quantum theory further deepened our understanding of light at a fundamental level. This period also saw the emergence of key concepts like quantum electrodynamics (QED) and the principle of stimulated emission, both of which would later play crucial roles in the development of lasers. In the 1950s, the foundation for the laser (light amplification by stimulated emission of radiation) was established based on Albert Einstein's earlier work on stimulated emission. In the early 1960s, Charles Townes and Arthur Leonard Schawlow further explored the theoretical concept of the laser, ultimately leading to the creation of the first laser. In 1960, Theodore Maiman successfully developed the first working laser using a ruby crystal, marking a major milestone in the history of photonics. This groundbreaking invention opened up a wide range of new possibilities for applications in fields such as communication, medicine, and manufacturing. In the 1960s and 1970s, research into optical fibers began, focusing on their potential for communication purposes. A significant breakthrough occurred in 1970 when researchers at Corning Glass Works developed the first low-loss optical fiber, which enabled light to be transmitted over long distances with minimal signal loss. In the 1970s, the development of laser diodes further advanced fiber-optic communication by providing an efficient light source for transmitting data through optical fibers, revolutionizing telecommunications. By the 1980s, fiber-optic cables became widely adopted, facilitating high-speed data transmission and forming the backbone of the growing internet infrastructure. In 1987, the introduction of the erbium-doped fiber amplifier (EDFA) enhanced the efficiency of fiber-optic networks by amplifying signals over long distances without the need for electronic regeneration, further improving the capabilities of optical communication. The 1990s saw the rapid growth of fiber-optic networks, especially in telecommunications and the internet, as photonics technologies became essential to high-speed communication systems. These innovations allowed data to be transmitted at much higher speeds and over longer distances compared to traditional copper wires. The introduction of optical switches, multiplexing, and wavelength division multiplexing (WDM) enabled multiple signals to travel simultaneously through a single optical fiber, significantly increasing network capacity. In the late 1990s, advances in silicon photonics began to gain attention. This emerging technology combined the high-speed capabilities of photonics with the scalability and cost-efficiency of silicon, paving the way for the development of integrated photonics circuits. Since the 2000s, photonics has become central to several emerging technologies. In the field of quantum photonics, there has been significant progress, particularly in quantum computing and quantum communication. Photonics plays a crucial role in developing quantum systems that can perform operations beyond the capabilities of classical computers. In silicon photonics, research has made great strides in integrating photonics onto silicon chips, allowing for the creation of low-cost, high-performance photonic devices. These innovations are benefiting fields like telecommunications, data centers, and even quantum computing. In medicine, photonics has led to major advancements in medical imaging, diagnostics, and treatments. Techniques like optical coherence tomography (OCT), laser-based surgery, and biomedical sensors highlight the impact of photonics on healthcare. Looking ahead, the future of photonics is likely to involve terabit communication networks and light-based processors that operate at ultra-high speeds, with innovations such as multi-core fibers, nonlinear optical devices, and advanced photonic crystals further enhancing data transmission capabilities. Additionally, photonics is being used for environmental monitoring, with sensors helping to detect pollution, monitor air quality, and study climate change. Photonics is rapidly expanding beyond its traditional applications, branching into new and innovative areas such as autonomous vehicles (through LIDAR systems), artificial intelligence, the Internet of Things (IoT), augmented reality (AR), and virtual reality (VR). Research is also ongoing into the development of optical computers, which use photons rather than electrons to perform calculations. This shift has the potential to significantly enhance computational speeds and energy efficiency, opening up exciting possibilities for the future of computing and technology. Figure 1-2 illustrates the evolution of photonics year-wise.

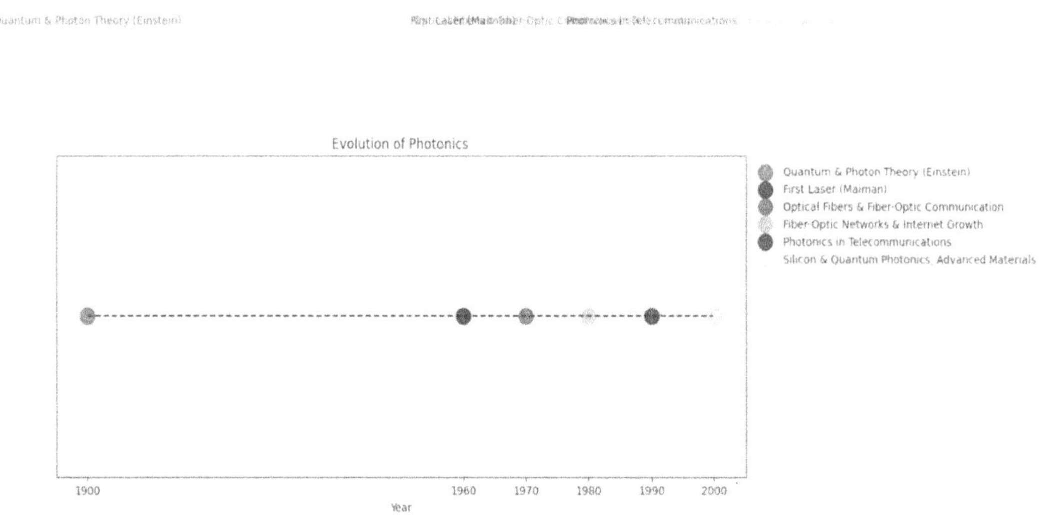

Figure 1-2. Evolution of Photonics

Emerging Trends in Photonics

Several groundbreaking advancements are shaping the future of photonics. Silicon photonics is paving the way for high-speed data transfer by integrating optical components onto silicon chips. Meanwhile, AI and machine learning are enhancing optical systems, enabling automated decision-making and improving high-resolution imaging. Additionally, integrated photonic circuits are combining multiple optical functions onto a single chip, fueling progress in quantum computing and communication technologies. The artistic impression of trends in photonics in the area of Si photonics, AI-ML in photonics and PICs is depicted in Figure 1-3.

Figure 1-3. *Artistic Impression of Trends in Photonics in the Area of Si Photonics, AI-ML in Photonics and PICs*

The Future of Photonics: Opportunities and Prospects

The future of photonics holds immense potential, with applications spanning across communication, computing, energy, healthcare, and space exploration. One of the most exciting prospects is quantum communication, which is poised to revolutionize cybersecurity. By using quantum encryption, it promises secure transmission and the creation of unbreakable cryptographic systems, making data theft nearly impossible. In the field of space exploration, advanced optical sensors will enhance deep-space exploration, while high-speed optical communication between satellites and laser-based propulsion systems could significantly transform space travel. Another key area of progress is the development of next-generation photonic devices, such as ultrafast and energy-efficient photonic chips. These will accelerate advancements in AI, computing, and high-speed data processing, supporting the growth of applications from data centers to edge computing. Furthermore, photonics is also positioning itself as a solution for sustainability. Eco-friendly lighting technologies, solar energy harvesting, and energy-efficient optical devices are all contributing to reducing carbon footprints and mitigating the effects of climate change. Neuromorphic photonics, which involves creating brain-inspired optical processors, will lead to rapid, low-power AI systems capable of solving complex problems in real time. Additionally, terahertz photonics is gaining attention for its potential in ultra-fast wireless communication, biomedical imaging, and security screening, with its ability to penetrate materials while maintaining high resolution. The development of integrated photonic circuits, which miniaturize and optimize optical systems, will pave the way for breakthroughs in telecommunications, quantum computing, and data processing at unprecedented speeds. In the realm of healthcare, biophotonic advancements are already transforming medical diagnostics. New laser therapies, non-invasive diagnostic tools, and advanced imaging techniques are enabling more personalized and efficient treatments for patients. Photonics will also play a role in the next generation of holographic displays and augmented/virtual reality technologies, promising ultra-realistic visual experiences for gaming, training, and remote collaboration. In environmental monitoring, photonic sensors are poised to play a pivotal role in detecting pollutants, tracking climate change, and improving agricultural efficiency by providing real-time data on environmental conditions. The development of optical metamaterials is enabling the manipulation of light in ways previously thought impossible, leading to innovations such as invisibility cloaks and extremely high-resolution imaging systems. Finally, the integration of deep learning and AI in photonics will drive automated decision-making systems, advance autonomous vehicles, and enhance intelligent imaging capabilities, creating smarter, more efficient systems.

As research continues to evolve in these areas, photonics is poised to reshape the future of technology, industry, and society, influencing everything from global communication networks to healthcare innovations and environmental sustainability.

The Industrial Internet of Things (IIoT): Transforming Industries

The Industrial Internet of Things (IIoT) is a subset of the broader Internet of Things (IoT) ecosystem, specifically designed for industrial applications. IIoT refers to the interconnection of devices, sensors, machinery, and systems within industrial environments through the internet and communication technologies. These devices collect, exchange, and analyze data in real time, enabling machines to autonomously monitor, communicate, and make intelligent decisions based on the data they collect. The central idea behind IIoT is to optimize industrial processes by enabling intelligent systems that can make real-time decisions, improving efficiency and reducing human intervention. The application of IIoT is transforming industries across the globe by improving operational efficiency, reducing downtime, increasing production capacity, and enhancing safety and quality control in ways that were once unimaginable.

For example, real-time monitoring systems and predictive analytics are allowing manufacturers to identify and address issues before they lead to costly breakdowns. Through advanced data analytics, IIoT systems can assess machinery conditions, optimize performance, and automate maintenance processes, ultimately reducing operational costs and enhancing productivity. IIoT plays a significant role in achieving the digital transformation of traditional industries such as manufacturing, energy, agriculture, logistics, and healthcare. By facilitating automation, predictive maintenance, and data analytics, IIoT systems are driving better decision-making and enabling optimized use of resources. In manufacturing, for instance, IIoT allows for greater automation of production lines, which not only enhances productivity but also reduces human error, ensuring higher consistency and quality control. Similarly, in energy management, IIoT applications help in the real-time monitoring and optimization of energy consumption, contributing to significant cost savings and more sustainable operations. In agriculture, IIoT solutions are enabling precision farming, where sensors collect environmental and soil data to optimize irrigation, fertilizer usage, and pest control, leading to higher crop yields and reduced environmental impact. Logistics companies are also benefiting from IIoT by implementing smart sensors and GPS tracking to improve supply chain efficiency, reduce delivery times, and track inventory in real-time. In healthcare, IIoT devices are enhancing patient monitoring and diagnostics, contributing to better patient outcomes and more personalized treatment plans. Furthermore, IIoT allows industries to tap into previously untapped data, unlocking new value streams and insights. The ability to collect and analyze data at the edge (near the point of generation) is providing companies with the means to not only optimize existing operations but also to create entirely new business models. The wealth of data generated by IIoT systems offers companies a competitive edge by enabling them to understand and predict market demands, track customer preferences, and innovate more effectively. In summary, IIoT is not only a catalyst for digital transformation but also a powerful tool for improving operational efficiencies, reducing costs, and generating new opportunities across various industries. As technologies evolve and more industries adopt IIoT solutions, its impact will continue to reshape how businesses operate, driving innovation and accelerating growth.

Evolution of IIoT

The evolution of the Industrial Internet of Things (IIoT) is closely linked to advancements in sensor technology, computing power, wireless connectivity, and cloud storage capabilities. In its early stages, IIoT primarily focused on the basic connectivity of machinery, allowing devices to communicate over networks. However, over time, the scope has expanded to include advanced automation, real-time data processing, and predictive analytics. The key technologies driving these advancements include machine learning (ML), which is leveraged for predictive analytics to forecast equipment failures and optimize operations; edge computing, enabling real-time data processing at the source, reducing latency and improving decision-making speeds; 5G networks, which provide faster and more reliable communication, facilitating real-time data exchange in environments requiring high-bandwidth connections; and cloud computing, which offers vast storage capabilities and scalable data processing, allowing organizations to analyze and store large volumes of data generated by IIoT systems. These technologies have not only made IIoT feasible but also scalable across various industries, including complex operations in sectors like automotive, aerospace, and energy, where real-time insights and automation are crucial for efficiency and innovation.

Key Components of IIoT

The Industrial Internet of Things (IIoT) is built on a network of interconnected components, each playing a crucial role in ensuring the efficient operation of the system. At its core are sensors and devices, which are the fundamental building blocks of IIoT systems. These sensors collect real-time data from machines, equipment, and environments, measuring various parameters such as temperature, pressure, humidity, motion, vibration, and energy consumption. For example, vibration sensors in manufacturing plants can detect early signs of machine malfunction, while temperature sensors monitor sensitive equipment like engines or electrical circuits. Once the data is collected, it must be transmitted to processing systems, and this is where connectivity comes into play. Connectivity ensures that devices and systems can share data efficiently, with common communication methods including Wi-Fi for general connectivity; Bluetooth and Zigbee for short-range communication; LPWAN (low power wide area networks) for long-range communication; and 5G networks for ultra-low latency, high bandwidth, and fast data transmission. The choice of connectivity depends on specific application needs, such as range, energy efficiency, or speed of data transfer. Another key component is edge computing, which involves processing data near its source rather than sending it all to the cloud. By analyzing data at the edge of the network in real time, IIoT systems reduce latency, which is critical for applications that require quick decisions, like autonomous vehicles or factory robots. Additionally, edge computing reduces bandwidth costs by processing data locally and only sending relevant or summarized data to the cloud. Cloud computing further enhances IIoT by providing the infrastructure to store vast amounts of data from IIoT devices and offering powerful analytics capabilities to process and analyze this data on a large scale. The cloud allows companies to scale their IIoT operations quickly, providing virtually unlimited storage and processing power. Popular platforms like Amazon Web Services (AWS), Microsoft Azure, and Google Cloud are widely used in IIoT applications. To transform raw data into actionable insights, analytics and artificial intelligence (AI) play a pivotal role. Big data analytics tools process large amounts of data in real time to identify patterns, trends, and correlations. Machine learning models can predict future outcomes based on historical data, such as predicting machine failures or suggesting optimizations for production lines, thus enhancing operational efficiency. Finally, control systems enable IIoT systems to take autonomous actions based on data insights. These systems can adjust machine settings, initiate maintenance processes, or alert human operators to critical changes in machine behavior. Industrial control systems, such as programmable logic controllers (PLCs) and supervisory control and data acquisition (SCADA) systems, are commonly used to monitor and control machinery and equipment in industrial settings. Each of these components plays an essential role in making IIoT systems efficient, responsive, and capable of driving intelligent automation across various industries. Figure 1-4 depicts the key components of IIoT.

Top of Form

Bottom of Form

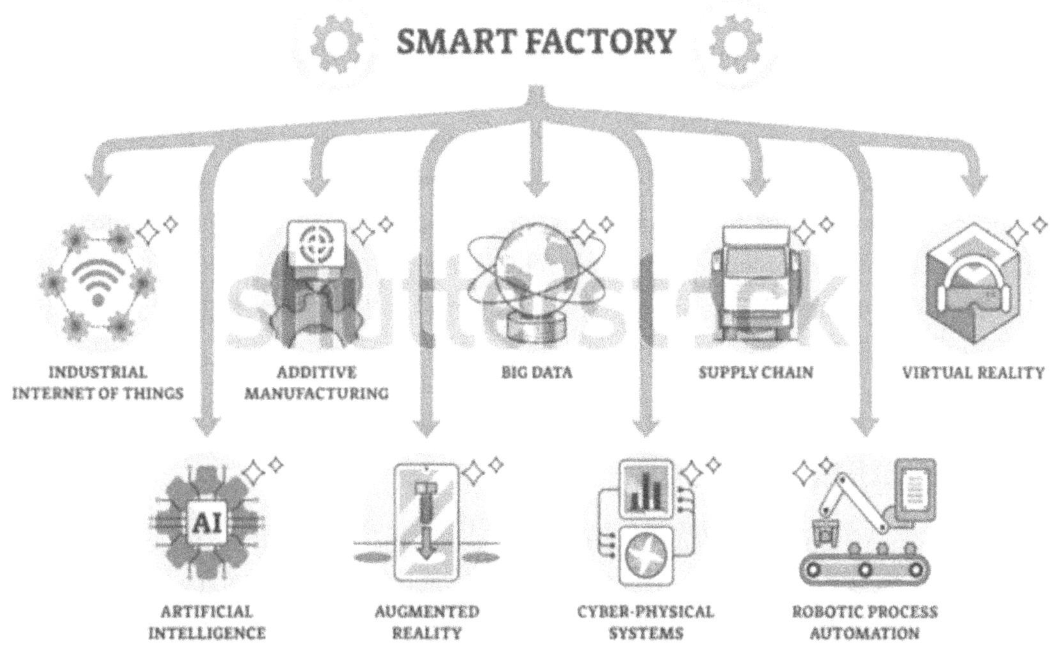

Figure 1-4. *Key Components of Industrial IoT*

Figure 1-4 illustrates the key technologies that make up a **Smart Factory**. At the top, the Smart Factory acts as the central concept, supported by several interconnected technologies. These include the Industrial Internet of Things (IIoT), additive manufacturing, big data, supply chain integration, and virtual reality. Each of these main components is further supported by advanced technologies such as artificial intelligence, augmented reality, cyber-physical systems, and robotic process automation. Together, these elements enable factories to operate more efficiently, intelligently, and autonomously through real-time data, automation, and digital connectivity.

Working Mechanism of IIoT

The working mechanism of an Industrial Internet of Things (IIoT) system involves several key steps, starting with data collection and culminating in intelligent actions or decisions. First, data collection occurs through sensors attached to industrial machinery, equipment, and infrastructure, which continuously gather data such as machine temperature, humidity levels, or energy consumption. This data is then transmitted across communication networks to local servers or cloud platforms, often in real-time, to facilitate immediate analysis. Once the data reaches its destination, it undergoes data processing and analytics, where advanced algorithms, including artificial intelligence (AI) and machine learning models, analyze the data to detect patterns, identify anomalies, and predict future behavior. For example, machine learning models can forecast when a machine is likely to fail based on its historical performance data. Finally, the analysis produces real-time actionable insights. These insights prompt actions, such as alerting a maintenance team about an impending machine failure or adjusting production speeds in a factory based on real-time energy consumption data. These steps allow for proactive management and decision-making, optimizing efficiency and reducing downtime.

Technologies Enabling IIoT

The effective functioning of the Industrial Internet of Things (IIoT) ecosystem is underpinned by several advanced technologies. One of the most crucial advancements is the deployment of 5G networks, which offer ultra-fast data transfer speeds, low latency, and the ability to connect millions of devices simultaneously. This is especially beneficial for applications such as smart factories, autonomous vehicles, and real-time monitoring systems, where rapid and reliable communication is essential. Cloud computing also plays a pivotal role by providing scalable, on-demand storage and computing power, enabling businesses to manage and analyze the vast amounts of data generated by IIoT systems with greater efficiency. Complementing this is edge computing, which processes data locally, near the source of generation, allowing for quicker decision-making and reducing dependence on cloud infrastructure. This is particularly important for time-sensitive applications, such as safety-critical systems in industrial settings. AI and machine learning further enhance IIoT capabilities by enabling predictive analytics, helping systems anticipate future events or behaviors based on historical data. For instance, predictive maintenance algorithms can analyze sensor data from machines to forecast when parts are likely to need replacement. Finally, big data analytics tools help companies manage the overwhelming amount of data generated by IIoT systems, sorting through it to extract actionable insights that drive operational efficiency and informed decision-making. Together, these technologies enable IIoT to deliver significant value across industries.

Benefits of IIoT

The benefits of implementing IIoT systems are substantial. They lead to increased operational efficiency by automating tasks and optimizing processes through real-time data analysis, reducing bottlenecks, and boosting productivity. Additionally, IIoT helps achieve cost savings by predicting failures and minimizing downtime through predictive maintenance, which cuts repair costs and prevents unplanned halts in production. It also enhances safety by providing real-time alerts about unsafe conditions, allowing workers to take preventive action. For example, gas sensors in chemical plants can trigger alarms if hazardous gas levels are detected. Finally, IIoT enables better decision-making by providing businesses with access to real-time data and predictive insights, which can be used to make more informed decisions about resource allocation, machine use, and workforce management.

Unlocking the Potential and Overcoming the Challenges of Industrial Internet of Things (IIoT)

While the implementation of Industrial Internet of Things (IIoT) systems offers numerous benefits, it also presents several significant challenges. One of the primary concerns is data security, as the massive influx of data raises the risk of cyber-attacks, data breaches, and unauthorized access to sensitive information. Protecting IIoT systems from these threats is critical. Integration with legacy systems is another challenge, as many industries still rely on traditional machinery and software that may not be compatible with newer IIoT technologies. Though this integration can be both costly and complex, requiring significant investment in upgrading infrastructure, it will be a long-time solution for future IoT devices. Scalability also poses a challenge, as IIoT systems generate enormous volumes of data, and ensuring that systems can scale effectively to accommodate growing storage, processing power, and connectivity needs can be difficult. Additionally, interoperability between different devices, sensors, and software is crucial for smooth operation, but ensuring that all these elements work seamlessly together can be technically challenging. Key strategies to ensure security include data encryption, which protects sensitive information during transmission, and authentication and access control mechanisms to ensure that only authorized users and devices can access critical systems. Network security also involves implementing firewalls, intrusion detection systems, and secure communication channels to protect against cyber threats. Regular audits are essential to identify vulnerabilities and ensure the ongoing security of IIoT systems. Looking to the future, several trends are poised to shape IIoT. Edge AI is expected to play a significant role by enabling real-time decision-making at the edge of the network, reducing reliance on centralized cloud systems. Blockchain technology offers potential for securely storing and tracking data through an immutable ledger, enhancing the transparency and security of IIoT transactions. Additionally, the rise of autonomous systems will likely lead to fully autonomous machines capable of performing tasks without human intervention. Finally, augmented reality (AR) is expected to complement IIoT by providing real-time data visualizations to assist workers in maintenance tasks and enhance user experiences.

Convergence of Photonics and Industrial IoT

The integration of photonics with Industrial IoT (IIoT) has revolutionized industrial automation, manufacturing, and smart industries. Photonics involves the generation, transmission, and detection of light, while IIoT refers to the interconnection of industrial devices to optimize production and efficiency. Their convergence is transforming industries by improving sensing, communication, and control mechanisms. This document explores the fundamentals, applications, benefits, challenges, and future of this integration.

Fundamentals of Photonics and IIoT

Photonics is the science of manipulating light, and it plays a critical role in many industrial applications, particularly in high-speed data transmission and precise environmental sensing. Key principles of photonics include optical waveguiding, which involves guiding light through optical fibers or integrated photonic circuits for efficient signal transmission, and laser technology, which uses coherent light sources for material processing, sensing, and optical communication. Light-based sensing utilizes optical sensors to detect real-time changes in parameters like temperature, pressure, and chemical composition, enabling accurate monitoring in industrial environments. Additionally, photonic integrated circuits (PICs) integrate miniaturized photonic components that enhance industrial automation and telecommunication capabilities. These photonic technologies are essential in the context of the Industrial Internet of

Things (IIoT), a subset of the broader IoT focused on industrial applications such as smart factories, predictive maintenance, and real-time monitoring. IIoT systems rely on interconnected sensors, actuators, and analytics platforms to improve operational efficiency. Key components of IIoT include edge computing, which reduces latency by processing data closer to its source; cloud integration, which enables centralized data storage and analytics for better decision-making; artificial intelligence (AI), which enhances automation and predictive maintenance; and cybersecurity, which ensures the protection of industrial networks from potential cyber threats. Together, photonics and IIoT are driving the next generation of industrial advancements, offering enhanced communication, automation, and real-time insights.

Synergies Between Photonics and IIoT

The integration of photonics with the Industrial Internet of Things (IIoT) is driving significant advancements across industries by enhancing data transmission, sensing capabilities, and overall system efficiency. Enhanced data transmission through optical fibers enables faster and more efficient communication, a crucial requirement for IIoT systems that rely on real-time data exchange. Photonics also contributes to precision sensing, as optical sensors provide highly accurate measurements that are essential for real-time monitoring and predictive maintenance, ensuring optimal performance of IIoT devices. Additionally, low power consumption in photonics technologies makes them ideal for IIoT applications, especially in remote or energy-limited environments where energy efficiency is critical. The ability of photonics to support high bandwidth communication allows IIoT systems to handle large volumes of data, which is vital in applications such as smart factories and industrial automation. Furthermore, miniaturization of photonics components leads to smaller, more compact devices, facilitating scalable and flexible deployment in diverse IIoT settings. Finally, improved security through optical encryption technologies ensures that IIoT systems can safeguard sensitive data from cyber threats, providing an added layer of protection to critical industrial networks. Together, these synergies between photonics and IIoT are transforming industries by enabling faster, more efficient, and secure systems. Figure 1-5 presents a comprehensive overview of **intelligent photonics** and its wide range of applications across multiple fields. At the center is the concept of intelligent photonics—systems that combine photonic technologies with intelligent processing. Surrounding this core are different domains where photonics plays a major role, including VR/

AR, biomedical imaging, microscopy, optical communications, astronomical observation, adaptive optics, target detection, precision instrumentation, and advanced manufacturing. The outer ring highlights practical implementations such as holographic displays, diffractive layers, photonic sensors, metamaterials, optical devices, and fiber lasers. Overall, the diagram illustrates how intelligent photonics integrates sensing, imaging, communication, and computation technologies to enable innovations across science, engineering, and industry.

Bottom of Form

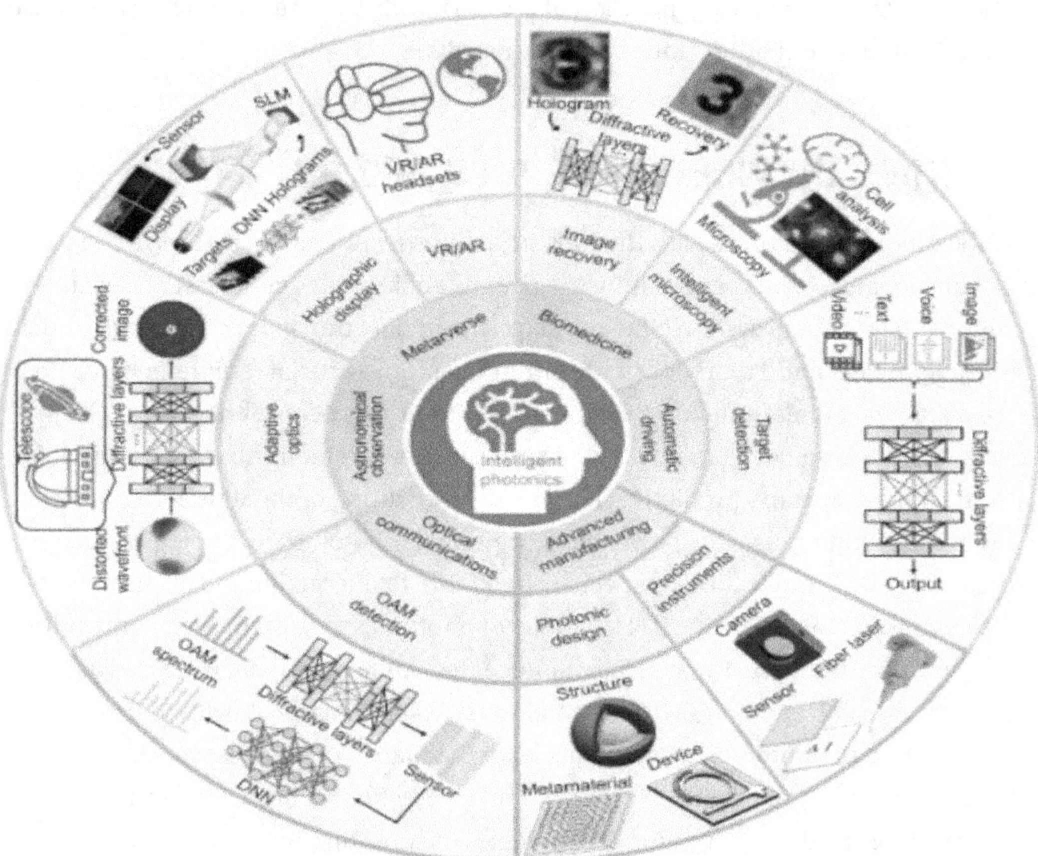

Figure 1-5. *Applications of Intelligent Photonics Across Diverse Fields: Metaverse, Biomedicine, Autonomous Driving, Advanced Manufacturing, Optical Communications, and Astronomy*

Applications and Benefits of Photonics in Enhancing IIoT Systems

Photonics plays a critical role in enhancing the functionality and efficiency of Industrial Internet of Things (IIoT) systems. It enables high-speed optical communication, with optical fibers facilitating ultra-fast, low-latency data transmission across industrial networks, a vital feature for real-time applications. Optical sensors are integral to process monitoring, detecting environmental changes such as temperature, pressure, and chemical composition with exceptional precision. In machine vision and imaging, photonic technologies in cameras support defect detection, robotics, and automation, driving quality control in manufacturing. Additionally, LiDAR (light detection and ranging) systems are employed for industrial navigation, providing precise mapping and navigation capabilities for autonomous machinery and automated warehouses. Quantum photonics further enhances security through quantum key distribution (QKD), ensuring ultra-secure communication channels in industrial environments. Photonics also contributes to predictive maintenance, where optical sensors monitor machinery wear and tear, reducing downtime and optimizing operations. Beyond these applications, the integration of photonics in IIoT systems offers several key benefits: high-speed data transmission with optical fibers enables rapid, interference-free communication; enhanced sensing and monitoring provide real-time insights with high sensitivity; energy efficiency is achieved as photonic devices typically consume less power than traditional electronic components; improved precision and accuracy in measurements help optimize industrial processes; scalability and flexibility are supported, enabling large-scale automation; and reduced maintenance costs are realized as optical sensors and fiber optics require less upkeep compared to conventional electronic sensors. These combined applications and benefits make photonics a cornerstone technology for advancing IIoT systems.

Challenges, Limitations, and Future Trends of Photonics in Industrial IoT

While the convergence of photonics and the Industrial Internet of Things (IIoT) offers significant benefits, several challenges and limitations hinder its widespread adoption. High initial costs associated with deploying photonic infrastructure can be a barrier for many industries, particularly in terms of investment in advanced optical technologies. Complex integration is another challenge, as combining photonics with existing IIoT frameworks requires specialized expertise and can involve significant technical hurdles. Additionally, maintenance and durability of optical components are concerns, as they can be sensitive to environmental factors such as temperature and humidity, which may impact their performance over time. The lack of standardization in optical technologies creates fragmentation in the market, slowing down the adoption of photonics in IIoT systems. Cybersecurity risks also persist, as the secure communication capabilities of photonic systems are still in the early stages of development. Moreover, data overload from the vast amounts of high-speed data generated by photonics systems demands advanced processing power and storage solutions. However, the future of photonics in IIoT is promising, with exciting trends on the horizon. The integration of 5G and optical networks is set to enhance industrial connectivity, while AI-powered photonic systems will enable smarter analytics for predictive maintenance. Quantum technologies are advancing in photonics to provide ultra-secure communication channels for industrial networks. Additionally, the miniaturization of photonic devices will make optical components more compact and cost-effective, facilitating broader deployment. Sustainable photonics, using eco-friendly optical materials, will contribute to energy-efficient IIoT solutions, and the development of smart optical grids will allow for dynamic, self-adjusting optical networks to meet the changing demands of industrial environments.

Case Studies and Real-World Implementations of Photonics in IIoT

Photonics is being successfully integrated into IIoT systems across various industries, demonstrating its versatility and impact. In smart manufacturing, fiber optic sensors are widely used for real-time process monitoring, allowing factories to optimize production lines and reduce downtime. The oil and gas industry has deployed photonic sensing technologies for pipeline monitoring and leak detection, providing early warnings that prevent costly accidents and environmental hazards. In healthcare, optical biosensors enable remote diagnostics and ensure the sterilization of medical equipment, improving patient safety and operational efficiency. The automotive industry utilizes LiDAR-based systems for autonomous vehicle navigation, enhancing the safety and efficiency of operations within smart warehouses. In telecommunications, high-speed fiber-optic networks support industrial automation, ensuring seamless data transmission for critical IIoT applications. Finally, the aerospace industry relies on optical gyroscopes and sensors for real-time aircraft monitoring, providing accurate data to ensure the safety and performance of aviation systems. These real-world examples highlight the transformative potential of photonics in IIoT, improving efficiency, safety, and productivity across diverse sectors.

The ongoing pursuit of photonic materials with unique optical properties has led to significant advancements in photonic devices capable of overcoming certain limitations inherent in electronic systems. To date, a remarkable array of photonic signal processors has been developed to perform reconfigurable signal processing tasks, including temporal integration, temporal differentiation, Hilbert transformation, and nonlinear photonic activation. Silicon-based materials and thin-film lithium niobate platforms have also been successfully demonstrated to generate and control optical quantum states, paving the way for scalable photonic quantum computing in the future.

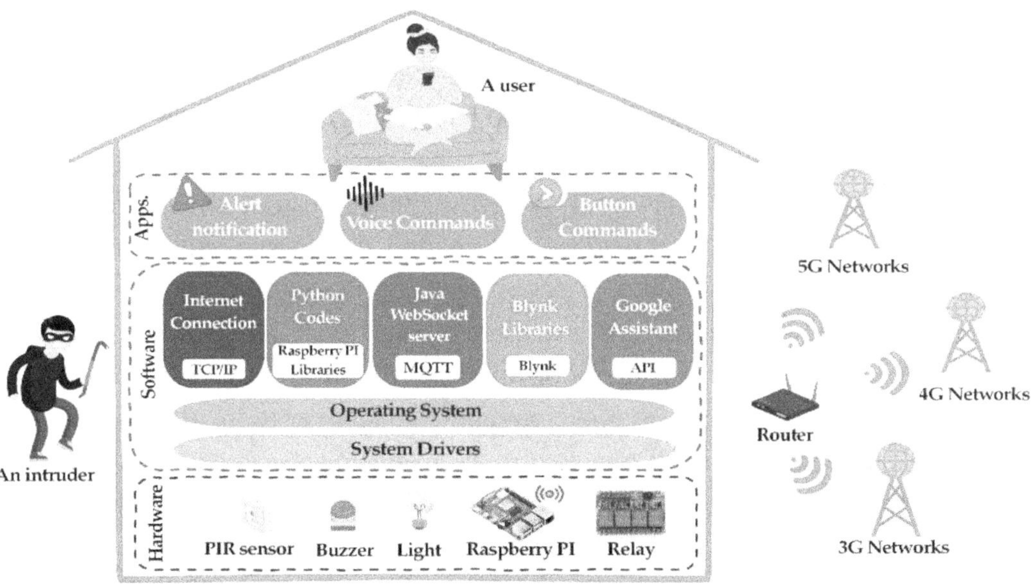

Figure 1-6. *IoT-Enabled Smart Home System Using PIR Intruder System*

Figure 1-6 illustrates the architecture of an IoT-based smart home security system that integrates hardware, software, and user interaction layers. At the hardware level, components such as the PIR sensor, buzzer, relay, lights, and Raspberry Pi function as the core detection and control units. These devices are managed by system drivers and the Raspberry Pi operating system, which support higher-level software modules including Python scripts, MQTT-based Java WebSocket servers, Blynk libraries, and Google Assistant APIs. These software components enable real-time communication, device automation, and cloud connectivity through TCP/IP. At the application level, the user interacts with the system via alert notifications, voice commands, and button-based controls on a smartphone. External network support—through 3G, 4G, 5G, or Wi-Fi routers—ensures remote access and seamless data transmission. Together, the layers enable the detection of an intruder and allow the user to receive alerts and manage home devices from anywhere.

Conclusion

Photonics has grown into a foundational technology driving major innovations in communication, computing, healthcare, and aerospace. Its ability to enable ultra-fast data transmission, high-precision sensing, and energy-efficient processing is opening new frontiers in AI, quantum technologies, and advanced manufacturing. At the same time, the Industrial Internet of Things (IIoT) is reshaping industries through connected devices, real-time analytics, and intelligent automation, despite challenges such as security, integration, and scalability. The convergence of photonics and IIoT represents a powerful shift toward smarter, faster, and more secure industrial systems. Photonic sensors enhance monitoring accuracy, optical communication boosts network speed, and advanced photonic security methods strengthen data protection. Although high costs and infrastructure demands remain obstacles, ongoing research and technological progress are rapidly reducing these barriers. Together, photonics and IIoT will drive the next generation of smart factories, sustainable operations, and highly autonomous industrial environments, ultimately transforming global industry and shaping the technological landscape of the future.

CHAPTER 2

Fundamental Technologies in Photonics for IIoT

The future of photonics is poised for exciting advancements, driven by emerging trends that promise to reshape industries and technologies. One significant trend is the **integration with electronics**, where photonics and electronics are converging to enhance performance in devices such as optoelectronic circuits and photonic integrated circuits (PICs). This integration is set to enable faster, more efficient data processing and communication. Another cutting-edge area is **nanophotonics**, which focuses on manipulating light at the nanometer scale, unlocking possibilities for miniaturized lasers, sensors, and new materials with applications in electronics, energy, and more. Additionally, **photonics in artificial intelligence (AI)** is creating new opportunities, particularly in machine vision, smart sensors, and data processing, allowing for enhanced automation and decision-making. As photonics continues to expand across various technological sectors, its role in shaping the future is undeniable, especially with advancements in optics, materials science, and quantum mechanics. With its broad scope and interdisciplinary applications, photonics remains one of the most dynamic and promising fields in modern science and engineering, offering solutions to complex challenges and driving innovation across industries.

Light Sources

Light sources can be categorized based on their physical mechanisms for generating light. Here's a brief overview of the most common types of light sources given in Table 2-1.

© Dr. Preeta Sharan, Dr. Sandip Kumar Roy, Harshada J. Patil, Aryan Chaudhary, and Dr. Deepak Kumar 2026
Dr. P. Sharan et al., *Photonics in Industrial IoT: Transforming Manufacturing and Beyond,*
https://doi.org/10.1007/979-8-8688-2694-8_2

Table 2-1. *Commonly Used Light Sources in Optical Communication*

	Type of Light Source	Principle	Characteristics	Examples	Figure
1.	Incandescent Light Sources	Light is produced by heating a tungsten filament until it glows.	Emits warm, yellowish light; energy-inefficient; much energy is released as heat.	Traditional light bulbs (household lighting).	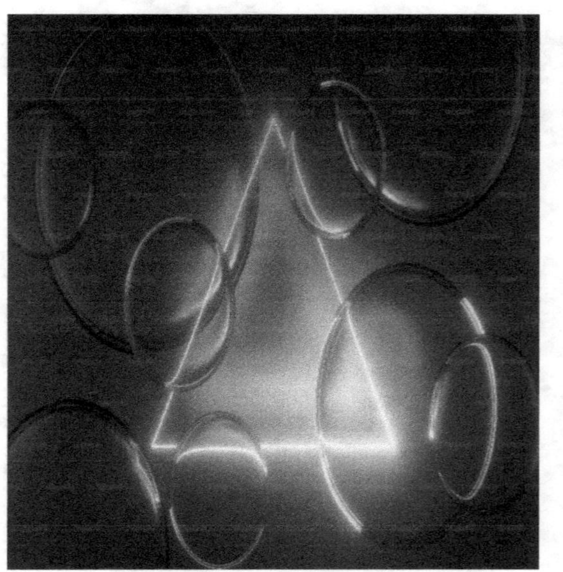
2.	Fluorescent Light Sources	Electricity passes through mercury vapor gas, emitting UV light, which excites a phosphor coating to emit.	More energy-efficient than incandescent bulbs; cooler, bluish-white light; contains mercury.	Fluorescent tube lights (office, industrial settings).	

No.	Light Source	Description	Characteristics	Applications	
3.	LED (Light Emitting Diode) Light Sources	Light is generated by the movement of electrons in semiconductor materials, releasing photons.	Highly energy-efficient; long lifespan; emits light in various colors without filters.	LED bulbs, displays, streetlights, electronic devices.	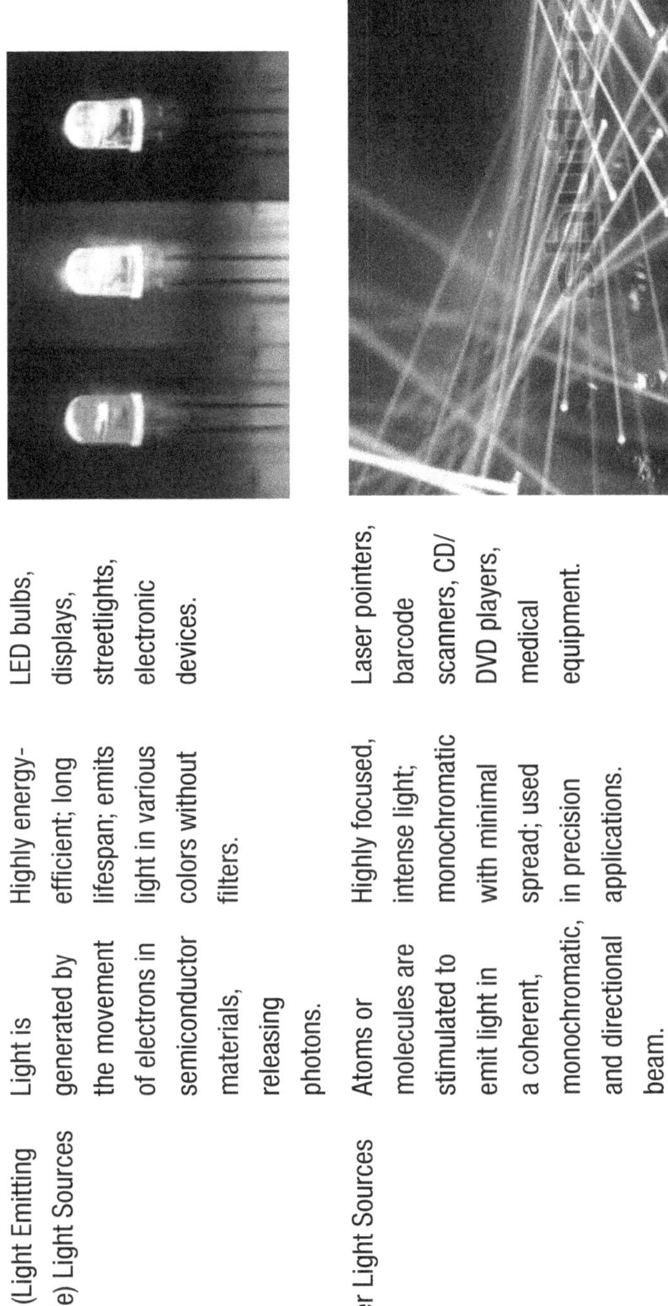
4.	Laser Light Sources	Atoms or molecules are stimulated to emit light in a coherent, monochromatic, and directional beam.	Highly focused, intense light; monochromatic with minimal spread; used in precision applications.	Laser pointers, barcode scanners, CD/DVD players, medical equipment.	

(continued)

Table 2-1. *(continued)*

	Type of Light Source	Principle	Characteristics	Examples	Figure
5.	Halogen Light Sources	A halogen gas (like iodine or bromine) is used to increase the filament lifespan and enhance light output.	Brighter and whiter light than incandescent bulbs; operates at a higher temperature; more efficient.	Car headlights, floodlights, stage lighting.	

| 6. | Gas Discharge Light Sources | Electric current ionizes gas, emitting light depending on the gas type. | More energy-efficient than incandescent bulbs; produces light in a range of colors. | Neon lights, sodium vapor lamps, metal-halide lamps (streetlights). | |

(continued)

Table 2-1. *(continued)*

Type of Light Source	Principle	Characteristics	Examples	Figure
7. OLED (Organic Light Emitting Diode) Light Sources	Organic compounds emit light when an electrical current is applied.	Thin, flexible; large-area light emission; excellent color accuracy; used in displays and lighting panels.	TV screens, smartphone displays, flexible lighting panels.	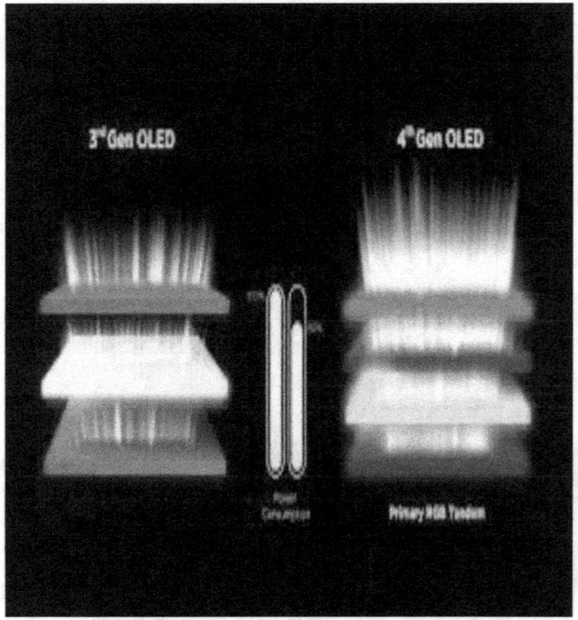 3rd Gen OLED · 4th Gen OLED · Power Consumption · Primary RGB Tandem

8.	Xenon Light Sources	Xenon gas is ionized by electricity, producing bright white light.	Produces bright, daylight-like light; high intensity.	Movie projectors, automotive headlights, flash photography.	
9.	Phosphor-Converted LED (PC-LED) Light Sources	Blue LED light is converted into a broad spectrum using phosphors.	Energy-efficient; mimics natural daylight with a balanced color temperature.	White LEDs (home lighting, TV backlighting, automotive lights).	

(continued)

Table 2-1. *(continued)*

	Type of Light Source	Principle	Characteristics	Examples	Figure
10.	Supercontinuum Light Sources	Nonlinear interaction of light in specially engineered optical fiber generates a broad spectrum.	Wide range of wavelengths (UV to infrared); highly tunable for specific applications.	Scientific research, spectroscopy, optical sensing.	

Light Detectors

Light detectors are the devices that convert light energy into electrical signals, enabling the measurement and analysis of light. A summary of different types of optical light detectors is presented in Table 2-2.

Table 2-2. *Optical Light Detectors*

Type	Structure/Working Principle	Advantages	Disadvantages/ Limitations	Applications/ Notes
p-n Photodiode	Simple p-n junction that generates electron-hole pairs upon illumination	Simple design, low cost	Limited performance at longer wavelengths	Basic optical detection tasks
p-i-n Photodiode	Includes intrinsic (i) layer between p and n regions for a wider depletion region	Better performance at longer wavelengths, lower capacitance	Slightly more complex than p-n photodiodes	Optical communication, biomedical sensing
Avalanche Photodiode (APD)	Uses impact ionization for internal gain	High sensitivity	Higher noise, temperature dependence, complex biasing	LIDAR, range finding, low-light imaging
Phototransistor	Transistor structure where light hits the base-collector junction, modulating collector current	Higher sensitivity than photodiodes	Slower response time, nonlinear output	Consumer electronics, ambient light detection
Photomultiplier Tube (PMT)	Photoelectric effect followed by electron multiplication via dynodes	Extremely high sensitivity, fast response	Bulky, high-voltage operation, expensive	Nuclear medicine, scientific instrumentation

(continued)

Table 2-2. *(continued)*

Type	Structure/Working Principle	Advantages	Disadvantages/ Limitations	Applications/ Notes
Photoconductive Detector	Light changes the material's electrical conductivity	Simple mechanism	Slow response, requires bias voltage	Infrared sensing, imaging
Phototube	Early vacuum tube device using the photoelectric effect	Basic light detection	Obsolete, low sensitivity compared to modern devices	Historically, used before photodiodes became common
MSM Phototector	Metal-semiconductor-metal structure with fast transit time	High-speed response, planar fabrication compatible	Lower sensitivity than APDs or PMTs	High-speed optical communication, integrated photonic circuits

Applications of Photodiodes and Detectors in IIoT

Photosources and photodetectors play a critical role in advancing Industrial
IoT applications by enabling fast, accurate, and non-contact sensing in diverse
environments. In industrial automation, these devices are used for object detection,
position sensing, and process control. For example, laser diodes and LEDs serve as
illumination sources in systems like optical encoders, safety light curtains, and robotic
vision systems, while photodiodes, phototransistors, and avalanche photodiodes (APDs)
detect reflected or transmitted light to monitor object presence, speed, or alignment on
assembly lines. These optoelectronic systems significantly enhance productivity and
safety by offering precise and real-time feedback to control systems. In environmental
monitoring, photosources and detectors are essential for analyzing air and water
quality, detecting gases, and measuring light intensity. Infrared (IR) and ultraviolet (UV)
LEDs, along with laser diodes, are commonly used to emit light at specific wavelengths,
which interact with environmental substances such as dust, pollutants, or gases. The
resulting signals are captured by photodetectors like PIN photodiodes, photoconductors,
and spectral sensors, enabling systems to assess particulate concentration, detect
leaks or flames, and monitor atmospheric conditions. These photonic-based sensors

provide critical data for early warning systems and regulatory compliance in industrial settings. In the realm of smart manufacturing, photosources and photodetectors are integrated into advanced inspection systems and additive manufacturing processes. Optical sources like structured light lasers and LEDs illuminate components during inline inspection to detect defects, verify dimensions, or analyze surface properties. High-resolution CMOS or CCD image sensors, along with photodiodes and spectral detectors, collect visual and spectral data that can be processed using AI for real-time quality control. Furthermore, in fiber-optic sensing systems used for structural health monitoring, broadband laser sources and photodetectors like fiber Bragg gratings (FBGs) are deployed to measure strain, vibration, and temperature across critical infrastructure. These applications highlight how photonics technologies are transforming traditional manufacturing into smart, self-aware systems that are more efficient, sustainable, and responsive.

Fundamentals of Optical Fibers

Optical fibers work based on total internal reflection (TIR). They consist of the following: Core—The central part through which light travels. Cladding—Surrounds the core and has a lower refractive index to facilitate TIR. Buffer Coating—Protects the fiber from moisture and physical damage. Light entering the fiber at a suitable angle reflects along the length of the core, remaining confined due to TIR. Optical fibers are classified based on modes: Single-mode fibers (SMF) have a core diameter of ~8–10 µm. It supports only one propagation mode (fundamental mode). It typically operates at a wavelength range between 1310 nm and 1550 nm. Single-mode fibers are useful in long-distance communication, high-bandwidth internet, and cable TV. Advantages include lower attenuation and dispersion and suitability for long-distance, high-speed transmission. The second type of fiber is multimode fibers (MMF), having a core diameter of ~50 µm or 62.5 µm. It supports multiple modes of light, and the operating wavelength range is typically between 850 nm and 1300 nm. The applications of MMF are in LANs, data centers, and short-distance transmission. Advantages of MMF are easier to couple light into (from LEDs or lasers) and cheaper connectors and sources. Disadvantages include modal dispersion due to different paths taken by modes and limited bandwidth over long distances. There are some specialty fibers such as photonic crystal fibers. Their structure is different than conventional fibers. They have microstructured air holes running along their length, forming a periodic structure around a solid or hollow core.

They exist in two types: Index-Guiding PCF: Light is guided by TIR using an effective refractive index difference and Photonic Bandgap PCF: Light is guided by the photonic bandgap effect, not TIR. The key features are (1) high birefringence and nonlinearity, (2) controllable dispersion and mode area, and (3) can guide light in air (hollow-core PCF). Specialty fibers have applications in supercontinuum generation, high-power lasers, sensing (temperature, pressure, chemical), and nonlinear optics. Table 2-3 gives the comparative study of fundamental optical fibers.

Table 2-3. *Comparison of Fundamental Optical Fibers*

Feature	Single-Mode Fiber	Multimode Fiber	Photonic Crystal Fiber
Core Size	8–10 μm	50–62.5 μm	Variable
Light Modes	One	Many	Tailored (single or few)
Transmission Distance	Long (>100 km)	Short (<2 km)	Application-specific
Dispersion	Low	High	Tunable
Applications	Telecom, Internet	LANs, data centers	Sensing, lasers, nonlinear optics

Optical Waveguides: Fundamentals and Types

An optical waveguide is a physical structure that guides light waves in the desired direction, typically by total internal reflection (TIR) or optical confinement. These are essential in integrated photonic circuits, sensors, and optical communication systems.

Planar Waveguide: The structure is flat and layered, made up of a core layer (higher refractive index) and cladding layers (above and below, lower refractive index). The mechanism of light involves that light is confined in the vertical direction via TIR, and in the horizontal direction, confinement is weak unless laterally patterned. It is typically fabricated using techniques like ion exchange, chemical vapor deposition (CVD), or lithography. Planar waveguides are useful in optical filters, modulators, switches, and interconnects in photonic integrated circuits (PICs).

Rib Waveguide: The structure is a raised "rib" or ridge etched on top of a planar slab. The rib defines the lateral boundaries for light confinement. There is a strong confinement of light in both vertical and lateral directions. It supports single-mode or few-mode propagation based on rib dimensions. It has advantages of reduced scattering losses, better mode confinement compared to planar, and compatibility with silicon photonics platforms. Rib waveguides are applicable in high-density photonic integration.

Slot Waveguide: The structure consists of two high-index rails separated by a narrow low-index slot (e.g., silicon–air–silicon or silicon–silica–silicon). The light is guided despite the slot being low-index; a significant portion of the optical mode is confined within the slot due to discontinuity of the electric field. Also light exploits strong field enhancement in the low-index region. Slot waveguides are advantageous for high sensitivity to environmental changes in the slot (ideal for sensing) and enhanced nonlinear interaction due to tight confinement and compact size. They have various applications in biosensors, electro-optic modulators, lab-on-chip photonic circuits, and nonlinear optics. Table 2-4 gives the comparative study of optical waveguides.

Table 2-4. *Comparison of Study of Optical Waveguides*

Feature	Planar Waveguide	Rib Waveguide	Slot Waveguide
Structure Type	Layered slab	Etched ridge on slab	Two high-index rails separated by a low-index gap
Confinement	Vertical only	Vertical lateral	High confinement in low-index slot
Fabrication Ease	Easiest	Moderate	More complex
Mode Control	Weak lateral	Strong	Strong with a high field in slot
Applications	Passive components	PICs, sensors, SOI	Biosensors, nonlinear optics

Integration of Optical Fibers and Waveguides with Industrial IoT

The Industrial Internet of Things (IIoT) involves interconnecting industrial machines and processes through sensors, actuators, and communication networks for real-time monitoring and control. Optical fibers and waveguides enable (1) high-speed, interference-free data transmission, (2) precision sensing in harsh environments, and (3) miniaturized photonic circuits for embedded applications. The Industrial Internet of

Things (IIoT) aims to interconnect industrial machines, sensors, and processes through intelligent networks for real-time monitoring, analysis, and control. In this context, photonic devices—particularly optical fibers and waveguides—play a vital role by offering unique advantages over traditional electronic systems.

Role of Photonic Devices in IIoT

Optical fibers enable high-speed and interference-free data transmission, which is crucial in electrically noisy industrial environments where electromagnetic interference (EMI) can degrade signal quality. Moreover, their inherent robustness and ability to function under extreme temperature, pressure, and chemical conditions make them ideal for precision sensing in harsh environments such as oil fields, power plants, or chemical processing units. Additionally, miniaturized photonic circuits, often based on integrated optical waveguides, allow the development of compact, efficient, and highly sensitive sensor modules that can be embedded directly into industrial equipment, facilitating smarter, more responsive, and predictive industrial operations. Table 2-5 explains optical fiber-based IIoT applications.

Table 2-5. *Examples of Fiber-Based IIoT Applications*

Application Area	Role of Optical Fiber
Smart Manufacturing	Machine condition monitoring, precision alignment
Energy Sector	Power line monitoring, substation automation
Oil and Gas	Pipeline leakage detection, pressure/temperature sensing
Transportation	Structural monitoring of bridges, tunnels, railways
Environmental Monitoring	Sensing pollutants, seismic activity, temperature trends

Optical Waveguides in IIoT

Optical waveguides play a crucial role in advancing Industrial IoT (IIoT) technologies by enabling compact, high-performance photonic systems. Integrated waveguides, particularly those fabricated on-chip, are ideal for applications such as miniaturized sensor arrays, on-chip signal processing, and field-deployable photonic sensor platforms. Different types of waveguides are employed based on specific requirements:

planar waveguides serve as the backbone for photonic integrated circuits; rib waveguides offer strong mode confinement suitable for compact layouts; and slot waveguides are particularly effective for biosensing and chemical detection due to their ability to confine light within low-index regions.

Waveguide-based sensors are widely used in IIoT for various monitoring tasks. Refractive index sensors detect chemical changes in industrial processes, while interferometric sensors measure critical parameters like temperature, pressure, and strain in machinery. Absorption spectroscopy systems integrated within waveguides help monitor gas compositions and emissions. Furthermore, biophotonic sensors are integrated into lab-on-chip platforms for process-level contamination monitoring, particularly in industries dealing with fluids and biohazards.

The integration of optical waveguides into IIoT systems brings several advantages. These include immunity to electromagnetic interference **(EMI)**, ensuring reliable operation in high-voltage or RF-noisy industrial environments; high bandwidth for supporting real-time monitoring and control; distributed sensing capabilities, enabling multi-point measurements over long distances using a single fiber; and a small footprint, allowing seamless integration into embedded and space-constrained environments. Additionally, waveguides support multiparameter detection, enabling the simultaneous monitoring of parameters such as temperature, strain, and pressure. However, several challenges must be addressed for widespread adoption. These include ensuring robust packaging to withstand harsh industrial conditions, achieving cost-effective and scalable fabrication, managing the complexity of hybrid photonic-electronic interfaces, and establishing standardized protocols for photonic IIoT integration. Looking forward, the future of optical waveguides in IIoT is promising. Advancements are expected in photonic integrated circuits **(PICs)** for edge computing, AI-enhanced optical sensing for predictive maintenance, and quantum-enhanced sensing and communication over fiber networks. Additionally, the use of photonic crystal waveguide sensors will enable the detection of trace gases and chemicals with unprecedented sensitivity, opening up new frontiers in industrial diagnostics and automation. Waveguide-based sensor types and their IIoT applications are summarized in Table 2-6.

Table 2-6. *Waveguide-Based Sensors in IIoT*

Sensor Type	Description and Application
Refractive Index Sensors	Detect chemical changes in industrial processes
Interferometric Sensors	Measure temperature, pressure, and strain on machinery
Absorption Spectroscopy	Monitor gas composition and emissions

An overview of the benefits of optical integration in IIoT is given in Table 2-7, while Table 2-8 lists several challenges that must be addressed to successfully integrate photonic devices within IIoT infrastructures.

Table 2-7. *Benefits of Optical Integration in IIoT*

Feature	Benefit
EMI Immunity	Reliable in high-voltage or RF-noisy environments
High Bandwidth	Supports real-time monitoring and control
Distributed Sensing	Long-range, multi-point measurements with one fiber
Small Footprint	Fits into embedded systems and harsh industrial setups
Multiparameter Detection	Simultaneous temperature, strain, and pressure monitoring

Table 2-8. *Integration Challenges with IIoT*

Challenge	Description
Packaging and Robustness	Optical components must survive extreme industrial conditions
Cost and Scalability	Need for low-cost manufacturing for widespread adoption
Interface with Electronics	Hybrid photonic–electronic integration is complex
Standardization	Lack of unified protocols for photonic IIoT networks

Photonic Sensors and Actuators

Photonic sensors detect changes in light properties—such as intensity, phase, wavelength, or polarization—to measure physical, chemical, or biological parameters like temperature, pressure, strain, or gas concentration. They are valued for their high sensitivity, EMI immunity, and suitability for harsh environments. Photonic actuators use light to trigger a mechanical, thermal, or chemical response in materials or systems. They are used in precision positioning, microfluidics, and optomechanical systems, enabling remote and fast control with minimal interference.

Fiber Optic Sensors

Fiber optic sensors are advanced sensing devices that utilize optical fibers to detect and measure variations in physical, chemical, or biological conditions. These sensors operate by transmitting light through a fiber and analyzing changes in the light's properties—such as intensity, phase, wavelength, or polarization—caused by external environmental influences. Based on their design, fiber optic sensors can be classified as intrinsic or extrinsic. Intrinsic sensors detect changes directly within the fiber, while extrinsic sensors transmit light to and from an external sensing element. Common types include fiber Bragg grating **(FBG)** sensors, which reflect specific wavelengths that shift in response to strain or temperature, and interferometric sensors, which measure very small changes through light wave interference. Distributed sensors, which use backscattering mechanisms like Raman or Brillouin scattering, allow for continuous sensing along the entire length of a fiber. These sensors offer several advantages: they are immune to electromagnetic interference (EMI), lightweight, non-conductive, and capable of operating in remote or harsh environments. They support both distributed and multipoint sensing and provide high sensitivity and precision. As a result, fiber optic sensors are widely used across various sectors, including structural health monitoring of bridges and buildings, pipeline and pressure monitoring in the oil and gas industry, temperature and fault detection in smart grids, biomedical diagnostics, and industrial process control involving chemical and gas detection.

Surface Plasmon Resonance Sensors

Surface Plasmon Resonance (SPR) sensors are highly sensitive optical sensors widely used for detecting molecular interactions in real time without the need for labels. They operate based on the excitation of surface plasmons, which are coherent oscillations of electrons that occur at the interface between a thin metallic film—usually gold or silver—and a dielectric medium. When polarized light is directed at the metal film at a specific angle, it can excite these surface plasmons, resulting in a measurable drop in the intensity of reflected light. This phenomenon, known as resonance, is extremely sensitive to changes in the refractive index of the medium near the metal surface. As molecules bind or interact on the sensor surface, the refractive index changes, leading to a shift in the resonance angle, which can be precisely measured. SPR sensors offer several key advantages, including label-free detection, real-time monitoring, and high sensitivity to minute changes in the surrounding environment. They are non-destructive and suitable for repeated use, making them ideal for applications that require continuous monitoring. These sensors are extensively used in biosensing for detecting proteins, antibodies, DNA, and viruses, as well as in medical diagnostics, environmental monitoring, food safety, and pharmaceutical research, where they help analyze the kinetics and affinity of drug-target interactions. Despite their many strengths, SPR sensors also have some limitations. They can be sensitive to temperature fluctuations and bulk refractive index changes and require clean, smooth surfaces for accurate measurements. Additionally, they are typically limited to detecting surface-bound interactions. Nevertheless, ongoing advancements such as nanoplasmonic and integrated photonic SPR are enabling more compact, efficient, and high-throughput sensing platforms, making SPR technology a cornerstone in modern optical sensing and lab-on-chip diagnostics.

Photonic Crystal Sensors

Photonic crystal sensors are a class of optical sensors that utilize the unique light-guiding properties of photonic crystals—materials with periodic dielectric structures that create a photonic bandgap. This bandgap prevents certain wavelengths of light from propagating through the material, allowing for highly controlled light manipulation. When a photonic crystal is designed with a defect or cavity within its structure, it can localize and enhance light at specific wavelengths, making it extremely sensitive to changes in the surrounding environment. These sensors detect variations in refractive index, chemical composition, or biological activity by observing shifts in the resonant wavelength or changes in transmission/reflection characteristics. Even small changes in the analyte near the defect region can significantly affect the optical response, enabling high sensitivity and label-free detection. Photonic crystal sensors are widely used in biosensing, gas and chemical detection, environmental monitoring, and medical diagnostics. Their ability to be miniaturized, integrated on chips, and fabricated using CMOS-compatible techniques makes them ideal for lab-on-chip platforms and portable sensing devices. Furthermore, their tunability and design flexibility allow for multiparameter sensing and selectivity by tailoring the structure to specific applications. Overall, photonic crystal sensors offer a powerful combination of compactness, sensitivity, and integration potential, making them a promising technology in the next generation of optical sensing systems.

Photonic Actuators

Photonic actuators are devices that convert light energy into mechanical, thermal, or chemical motion, enabling controlled physical responses triggered by optical signals. These actuators operate based on the interaction of light with responsive materials, such as photostrictive, thermo-optic, or photochromic substances, which undergo structural or dimensional changes when exposed to specific wavelengths or intensities of light. By using light as a stimulus, photonic actuators allow remote, contactless, and precise control of actuation without the need for electrical wiring or mechanical input. Photonic actuators are especially valuable in applications requiring high-speed switching, miniaturization, or operation in hazardous or electromagnetically sensitive environments. They are commonly used in fields such as micro-electromechanical systems **(MEMS)**, microfluidics, optical switching, biomedical devices, and soft robotics. For instance, light-triggered actuators can control fluid flow in lab-on-chip devices, move micromechanical parts in precision instruments, or drive artificial muscles in soft robots. The advantages of photonic actuators include fast response times, minimal mechanical wear, and the potential for seamless integration with photonic and optoelectronic systems. As materials science advances, the development of low-power, highly responsive, and biocompatible photonic actuators is paving the way for innovative applications in industrial automation, healthcare, and smart materials.

Electro-Optic Modulators

Electro-optic modulators **(EOMs)** are devices that control the properties of light—such as its amplitude, phase, frequency, or polarization—by applying an electric field to an electro-optic material. These materials exhibit the electro-optic effect, where their refractive index changes in response to an external voltage. By altering the refractive index, EOMs can precisely modulate how light passes through or reflects within the device, enabling dynamic control of optical signals. EOMs are essential components in optical communication systems, where they encode data onto a light wave for high-speed transmission through optical fibers. They are also used in laser systems, quantum optics, lidar, and signal processing. Common types include phase modulators, intensity modulators, and Mach–Zehnder interferometers, often based on materials like lithium niobate **($LiNbO_3$)**, gallium arsenide **(GaAs)**, or emerging silicon photonics platforms. These modulators offer benefits such as high speed, broad bandwidth, and low signal distortion, making them ideal for modern optical networks and integrated photonic circuits. As photonics continues to evolve, electro-optic modulators play a critical role in enabling faster, more efficient, and scalable optical systems across telecommunications, sensing, and computing applications.

Micro-Opto-Electro-Mechanical Systems

Micro-opto-electro-mechanical systems **(MOEMS)** are miniaturized devices that integrate optical, electrical, and mechanical **components** on a single chip or platform using microfabrication techniques. These systems are an extension of MEMS **(Micro-Electro-Mechanical Systems)**, with the added capability to manipulate or interact with light. MOEMS components typically include micromirrors, micro-lenses, gratings, or optical shutters, which can move or change their properties in response to electrical signals, allowing for precise control of light paths or intensity. MOEMS play a vital role in a wide range of applications, including optical communication, projection displays **(such as DLP technology)**, optical switches, lidar systems, spectroscopy, and biomedical imaging. For example, in telecommunications, MOEMS-based optical switches can dynamically reconfigure light paths in fiber networks. In biomedical fields, they enable compact, high-resolution imaging and diagnostic devices. The major advantages of MOEMS include miniaturization, low power consumption, fast response times, and the ability to integrate with electronic and photonic systems. These features make MOEMS highly suitable for use in portable, wearable, and embedded systems.

As technology advances, MOEMS continue to drive innovation in fields requiring compact and agile optical control, particularly within the expanding domains of smart sensors, autonomous systems, and industrial photonics.

Photonic Integrated Circuits

Photonic integrated circuits **(PICs)** are compact devices that integrate multiple photonic components, such as lasers, modulators, waveguides, detectors, and filters, onto a single chip to manipulate and transmit light signals. Analogous to electronic integrated circuits (ICs), PICs use light instead of electrical signals, enabling high-speed, high-bandwidth, and low-power data transmission and processing. These circuits are typically fabricated using materials like silicon (silicon photonics), indium phosphide (InP), or silicon nitride, which support efficient optical signal manipulation at various wavelengths. PICs are a key technology in optical communication, particularly in data centers and telecommunications networks, where they dramatically reduce size, cost, and energy consumption compared to discrete optical components. Beyond communications, they are also used in biosensing, quantum computing, lidar systems, and microwave photonics. The integration of multiple photonic functions on a single chip enhances reliability, scalability, and signal fidelity while allowing mass production using CMOS-compatible fabrication processes. As the demand for faster, more energy-efficient data processing and sensing systems grows, PICs are becoming central to next-generation technologies. Their ability to support dense, high-performance optical functionality in compact form factors makes them ideal for applications in 5G, AI hardware acceleration, autonomous vehicles, and Industrial IoT **(IIoT)**. With continued research and innovation, PICs are expected to revolutionize photonic system design much like microelectronics transformed computing.

Photonic Sensors and Actuators in Industrial IIoT Applications

Photonic sensors and actuators are increasingly vital components in **Industrial Internet of Things (IIoT)** environments due to their ability to offer **high-precision, real-time, and robust monitoring and control** capabilities. In industrial settings, where accuracy, reliability, and resilience to harsh conditions are essential, photonic technologies enable smarter and more responsive systems by leveraging the interaction of light with materials to sense or trigger changes.

Precision Measurement

In IIoT applications, precision measurement is critical for monitoring critical parameters such as temperature, strain, pressure, displacement, and vibration in real time. Photonic sensors, particularly fiber Bragg grating (**FBG**) sensors and interferometric sensors, are widely used because of their high resolution and accuracy (down to micrometer or nanometer scale), immunity to electromagnetic interference (EMI), and compactness and ability to be embedded in equipment. In smart manufacturing, photonic sensors monitor machine alignment, tool wear, and material deformation, ensuring product quality and minimizing downtime. In metrology systems, integrated photonic interferometers enable sub-nanometer resolution for position and distance measurements in high-precision machining or robotics.

Structural Health Monitoring (SHM)

Structural health monitoring involves continuously assessing the integrity of infrastructure like bridges, pipelines, tunnels, wind turbines, and industrial machinery. Photonic sensors, particularly distributed fiber optic sensors (using Rayleigh, Brillouin, or Raman scattering), offer unmatched capabilities for SHM, such as distributed sensing over tens of kilometers with a single fiber, multipoint and multiparameter sensing (strain, temperature, corrosion, cracks), and remote monitoring in real time, ideal for hazardous or inaccessible locations. FBG arrays can be embedded into concrete or steel to detect early-stage cracks, load changes, and thermal stress, allowing predictive maintenance and reducing the risk of catastrophic failure.

Photonic Actuators in Intelligent Control Systems

In intelligent IIoT systems, photonic actuators are used to dynamically respond to sensor input. These actuators convert light into mechanical motion, enabling functions such as micro-positioning in robotic assembly lines, valve control in microfluidic or chemical systems, and light-driven switches in optical communication networks within smart factories. Integrated into feedback control systems, photonic actuators work alongside sensors to create closed-loop systems that adjust operations based on environmental or structural conditions.

Integration with Intelligent Control Systems

Photonic sensors and actuators, when combined with edge computing, AI, and real-time analytics, form the backbone of intelligent IIoT control systems. These systems can (1) analyze sensor data on-site for rapid decision-making, (2) predict equipment failure before it occurs, and (3) automatically adjust machine parameters to optimize performance and energy usage. For example, in a wind turbine, photonic sensors can monitor blade stress and temperature, while actuators adjust pitch angles or damping mechanisms to minimize fatigue and extend operational life. Key benefits in IIoT applications are given in Table 2-9.

Table 2-9. *Key Benefits in IIoT Context*

Feature	Benefit in IIoT Applications
High Sensitivity	Accurate micro- and nano-scale measurements
EMI Immunity	Reliable operation in electrically noisy environments
Distributed Sensing Capability	Continuous monitoring over large infrastructure
Harsh Environment Resistance	Suitable for extreme temperatures, chemicals, or pressure
Compactness and Integrability	Embeddable in structures and smart devices
Real-Time Feedback	Enables automated and intelligent decision-making

Advanced Photonic Materials

Advanced photonic materials are at the core of next-generation optical technologies, enabling faster, smaller, and more efficient devices for applications ranging from communication to sensing. Silicon photonics is one of the most mature platforms, leveraging the well-established CMOS fabrication infrastructure to integrate optical components such as waveguides, modulators, and detectors directly onto silicon chips. It offers high scalability, cost-effectiveness, and compatibility with electronic circuits, making it ideal for data centers, optical interconnects, and photonic integrated circuits (PICs). In parallel, III-V semiconductor materials, such as gallium arsenide (GaAs) and indium phosphide (InP), are essential for active photonic components like lasers, amplifiers, and high-speed modulators due to their direct bandgap and excellent light-emission properties. These materials are crucial for high-performance optical communication and optoelectronic integration, often used in hybrid platforms combining III-V layers with silicon substrates. Emerging materials like two-dimensional (2D) materials, such as graphene and transition metal dichalcogenides (TMDs), offer remarkable optical and electronic properties at the atomic scale. Their ultra-thin nature enables strong light-matter interaction, making them suitable for applications in ultrafast modulators, photodetectors, and flexible photonics. Additionally, quantum dots—nanoscale semiconductor particles—exhibit size-tunable emission wavelengths and high quantum efficiency. These are used in quantum photonics, bio-imaging, and low-threshold lasers, offering new capabilities for miniaturized and highly sensitive photonic systems. Together, these advanced materials are pushing the boundaries of photonic integration, enabling innovations in telecommunications, industrial sensing, quantum technologies, and next-generation IIoT systems.

Role of Advanced Photonic Materials in Enhancing IIoT Devices

Advanced photonic materials play a transformative role in enhancing the performance, functionality, and integration of Industrial Internet of Things (IIoT) devices. Materials such as silicon photonics, III-V semiconductors, and emerging platforms like 2D materials and quantum dots are driving the development of compact, energy-efficient, and high-speed photonic components that are essential for smart industrial systems. Silicon photonics enables the large-scale integration of photonic and electronic circuits on a single chip, supporting high-bandwidth, low-latency communication between IIoT nodes and edge computing platforms. Meanwhile, III-V semiconductor materials, with their superior light-emitting properties, enable the fabrication of efficient lasers, detectors, and modulators that are critical for real-time sensing and data transmission in industrial environments. The use of 2D materials, such as graphene and MoS_2, further enhances IIoT capabilities by enabling ultra-sensitive and flexible photonic sensors that can be embedded into machinery, pipelines, and infrastructure for continuous structural health monitoring. Similarly, quantum dots offer high sensitivity and tunable optical properties, making them suitable for trace chemical detection, biosensing, and compact optical sources in IIoT applications. These materials support the creation of photonic sensors and actuators with enhanced accuracy, reliability, and environmental resistance, ensuring optimal performance even in harsh industrial conditions. Overall, advanced photonic materials are key enablers in the evolution of IIoT, enabling smarter, faster, and more adaptive industrial systems through next-generation photonic integration.

Challenges and Future Directions in Photonics for IIoT: Technical Perspective

As photonics continues to integrate with the Industrial Internet of Things **(IIoT)**, it faces a range of technical challenges that must be addressed to realize its full potential. One of the primary challenges is the scalability and integration of photonic components with existing electronic systems. While photonic devices offer high-speed, low-loss communication and sensing, integrating them with CMOS electronics requires complex hybrid fabrication processes, precise alignment, and efficient interfacing methods. Packaging and miniaturization also remain critical issues, especially when photonic sensors and actuators need to be embedded in harsh industrial environments where they must endure temperature extremes, vibrations, and chemical exposure. Another key technical hurdle is the lack of standardized platforms and protocols for photonic components in IIoT systems.

Unlike electronics, photonics lacks universally adopted design and testing frameworks, which hampers interoperability and widespread adoption. Moreover, power consumption and thermal management in densely integrated photonic systems pose significant design constraints, particularly in edge devices where compactness and energy efficiency are essential. There are also challenges in achieving low-cost manufacturing, as many advanced photonic materials and processes (such as those involving III-V semiconductors or 2D materials) are still expensive and not yet scalable for mass production. Looking ahead, future directions in photonics for IIoT will focus on the development of photonic integrated circuits **(PICs)** that combine sensing, processing, and communication on a single chip. Innovations in materials science—including silicon photonics, hybrid plasmonics, and quantum photonic platforms—will enable more compact and versatile components. The adoption of AI-driven design automation, open-source photonic **CAD tools**, and modular system architectures will accelerate the development and deployment of photonic IIoT solutions. Moreover, advances in standardization, self-calibrating systems, and low-power photonic interfaces will support the deployment of large-scale, intelligent IIoT networks.

Ultimately, overcoming these technical challenges will pave the way for resilient, high-performance photonic systems that are deeply embedded in the industrial fabric of smart factories, energy grids, and infrastructure.

The integration of photonics into IIoT systems is a rapidly evolving research domain, driven by the need for high-speed communication, real-time sensing, and enhanced data processing in complex industrial environments. However, several research challenges continue to shape the trajectory of this field. One major concern is the limited maturity of photonic integration technologies, especially in terms of achieving compact, multifunctional devices that can be mass-produced using cost-effective methods. Research is ongoing to develop scalable photonic integrated circuits **(PICs)** that can reliably perform sensing, signal processing, and data transmission on a single chip. Another key challenge is the need for novel photonic materials and fabrication techniques that are compatible with harsh industrial environments and capable of ultra-sensitive measurements. While materials such as silicon, III-V semiconductors, and emerging 2D materials offer great promise, research is still required to optimize their performance, long-term stability, and environmental resistance. Moreover, innovations in hybrid integration—combining photonics with electronics, MEMS, and microfluidics—pose complex design and fabrication issues that require interdisciplinary collaboration across optics, materials science, and nanofabrication. From an innovation standpoint, future research will focus on developing self-powered and autonomous photonic sensors, enabled by energy harvesting and ultra-low-power operation. The use of machine learning and AI algorithms to interpret photonic sensor data in real time is also gaining attention, especially for predictive maintenance and anomaly detection in IIoT systems. Another promising direction is the advancement of quantum photonics and nanophotonic platforms, which could revolutionize secure communication and ultra-precise sensing in industrial applications. Additionally, there is a growing research interest in the standardization of photonic design platforms, including open-source software tools and modular components that can accelerate innovation and deployment. Collaboration between academia, industry, and government bodies will be critical to create testbeds, pilot projects, and funding programs that push photonic IIoT technologies from lab-scale prototypes to industrial-scale implementation. Overall, sustained research and innovation will be essential to overcome existing barriers and unlock the full potential of photonics in the future of intelligent, interconnected industrial systems.

Summary

The integration of photonics into IIoT systems has the potential to revolutionize future industrial infrastructures by enabling ultra-fast communication, highly sensitive sensing, and energy-efficient operation. However, realizing this vision comes with several challenges that could directly influence the structure and capabilities of future IIoT systems. One of the foremost challenges is the need for scalable and reliable deployment of photonic technologies across large, complex industrial networks. As IIoT systems grow in scale, incorporating thousands of interconnected devices, the performance, durability, and interoperability of photonic components will become critical factors in system design. Another significant hurdle is the integration of photonic systems with conventional electronic infrastructure, which dominates current IIoT architectures. This requires advanced hybrid platforms capable of seamless communication between optical and electrical domains, as well as new protocols and standards for managing data transmission, synchronization, and power distribution. Additionally, cost and manufacturing scalability will heavily influence adoption. Photonic devices, particularly those involving advanced materials or precision fabrication, must become more affordable and easier to mass-produce if they are to be widely adopted in future IIoT ecosystems. Despite these challenges, the future impact of photonics on IIoT systems is profound. Photonic sensors and communication systems will enable real-time, high-bandwidth data acquisition and transmission over long distances with minimal signal loss, supporting advanced applications like predictive maintenance, remote diagnostics, and autonomous industrial operations. As photonic technologies mature, they will also contribute to the development of ultra-low-latency industrial networks, crucial for robotics, automation, and closed-loop control systems. In the long term, emerging technologies such as quantum photonics, photonic neural networks, and on-chip light-based computing could redefine how IIoT systems process information, offering new paradigms in secure communication, AI-driven decision-making, and distributed intelligence. The convergence of photonics with edge computing, 5G/6G, and AI will ultimately shape the next generation of smart factories, energy grids, and infrastructure systems. Therefore, overcoming current limitations and investing in photonic innovation will be essential to building future-proof, high-performance IIoT platforms.

Top of Form

Bottom of Form

CHAPTER 3

Communication Systems in Industrial IoT

The Industrial Internet of Things (IIoT) represents the integration of physical machines, sensors, and systems with the internet, enabling real-time data exchange and analytics. IIoT improves operational efficiency, predictive maintenance, and decision-making in industries like manufacturing, logistics, energy, and more. A critical component of IIoT is the communication systems that support seamless, reliable, and secure data transfer between devices. This chapter explores key communication systems in IIoT, with a particular focus on optical wireless communication.

Overview of IIoT Communication Requirements

IIoT enables the networking of intelligent machines, advanced analytics, and the human workforce. By integrating machines and devices via the Internet, you can collect and exchange comprehensive data in real time. This data provides you with deeper insights into production processes, improves automation, and optimizes operational procedures. IIoT increases productivity, reduces costs, and opens up new business models. The Industrial Internet of Things, or IIoT, is a term used to describe the application of Internet of Things (IoT) technology in industrial settings. It encompasses the integration of advanced sensors, software, and machinery with internet connectivity to collect, analyze, and act upon vast amounts of data. This data-driven approach enables real-time decision-making and predictive analytics, leading to improved operational efficiency, reduced costs, and improved product quality. IIoT is a key component of Industry 4.0, the fourth industrial revolution, characterized by the fusion of digital, physical, and biological technologies. It's revolutionizing traditional industries, facilitating the transformation from manual and labor-intensive processes to automated, data-driven operations. IIoT is not just about technology; it's about leveraging data to drive business results for manufacturers. With IIoT, you can monitor equipment performance, predict failures, optimize logistics, improve product quality, and more. It's about creating a smarter, more efficient, and more profitable industrial operation. The following sections review some of the communication requirements.

Sensors and Devices

Sensors and devices form the foundation of IIoT. These are the tools that capture data from the physical environment and convert it into digital format. They can monitor a wide range of parameters, including temperature, pressure, humidity, light, sound, and motion. This data is then transmitted to a central system for analysis and action. For instance, in a manufacturing plant, sensors can monitor machine performance, detecting any abnormalities or signs of potential failure. In the energy sector, sensors can measure power consumption, helping to optimize energy usage and reduce waste.

Connectivity Technologies

Connectivity is a critical component of IIoT, enabling the transfer of data from sensors and devices to a central system. Various technologies can be used for connectivity, including Wi-Fi, cellular networks, satellite communication, and low-power wide-area networks (LPWANs). The choice of connectivity technology depends on factors such as the volume of data, transmission range, power consumption, and cost. For example, a logistics company might use cellular networks to track its vehicles in real-time, while a smart factory might use Wi-Fi for internal communication and control.

Messaging Protocols

Messaging protocols are the language that devices use to communicate and exchange data within the IIoT system. They define the format and rules for data exchange between devices, ensuring that all parts of the system can understand and process the data effectively. Different protocols are used depending on the use case, as each one has its unique features, advantages, and disadvantages. For example, MQTT (message queuing telemetry transport) is a commonly used messaging protocol in IIoT systems due to its lightweight design and reliable data delivery, even under unreliable network conditions.

Edge Computing

Edge computing is a key technology in IIoT architecture, addressing the challenges of data volume, latency, and connectivity. It involves processing data at the edge of the network, close to the source, rather than sending it to a central cloud for processing. This reduces the amount of data that needs to be transmitted, saving bandwidth and improving response times. For instance, in a smart factory, edge computing can enable real-time control of machinery, reducing downtime and improving efficiency.

Cloud Platforms

Cloud platforms play a crucial role in IIoT, providing the infrastructure for data storage, processing, and analysis. They offer scalable, flexible, and cost-effective solutions for managing vast amounts of data. Moreover, cloud platforms enable advanced data analytics, machine learning, and artificial intelligence, unlocking valuable insights from the data. For example, a healthcare provider might use a cloud platform to store and analyze patient data, facilitating early disease detection and personalized treatment.

Data Analytics and AI

Data analytics and AI are at the heart of IIoT, turning raw data into actionable insights. Data analytics involves examining, cleaning, and modeling data to discover useful information, draw conclusions, and support decision-making. AI, on the other hand, involves creating systems that can learn from data, make decisions, and improve over time. For instance, in the energy sector, data analytics and AI can be used to predict equipment failures, optimize energy usage, and reduce costs.

Role of Photonics in Addressing Communications Challenges

Collaborative efforts in the field of photonics have resulted in the widespread adoption of Wavelength-Division Multiplexing (WDM) in communication systems. WDM allows multiple data streams to be transmitted simultaneously over a single optical fiber, each using a different wavelength. This technology, developed through collaborations between physicists and communication experts, significantly increases the overall capacity of optical communication networks. Coherent optical communication, a product of collaborations between researchers in optics and communication, has revolutionized long-distance data transmission. By employing advanced modulation formats and signal processing techniques, coherent communication systems enable the transmission of high-speed data over thousands of kilometers of optical fiber. This section explores how coherent communication has become a key technology in submarine cables and high-capacity terrestrial networks. Silicon photonics, a result of collaboration between experts in silicon technology and photonics, is transforming communication systems. The integration of photonic components on silicon chips allows for compact, energy-efficient, and cost-effective devices. Silicon photonics is playing a crucial role in data centers, telecommunications, and high-performance computing, enabling the development of faster and more efficient communication systems. From addressing technical challenges to ensuring network scalability, enhancing security, and promoting sustainability, collaborations are essential for the continued evolution of communication technologies. As photonics-based communication systems advance, ongoing collaborative initiatives will play a pivotal role in unlocking new possibilities, addressing emerging challenges, and ushering in an era of communication systems that are faster, more secure, and environmentally sustainable. The future of photonics-based communication holds exciting possibilities. Collaborative research is expected to focus on pushing the limits of data transmission rates, exploring novel materials for photonics components, integrating photonics with emerging technologies, and addressing the global challenges of digital connectivity. The ongoing collaboration between researchers, engineers, policymakers, and industry stakeholders will continue to drive innovations, ensuring that photonics-based communication systems remain at the forefront of technological advancements in the years to come.

Optical Wireless Communication: Key Systems in IIoT

Effective communication systems are vital to the success of Industrial IoT applications. Traditional wireless technologies like Wi-Fi, Bluetooth, and 5G continue to dominate IIoT, but newer communication systems like Optical Wireless Communication (OWC) offer unique benefits in specific environments, particularly in settings where RF-based systems may face interference or limitations. As IIoT evolves, so too will the communication technologies that underpin it, enabling more efficient, secure, and high-performance industrial systems. The key to successful IIoT deployment will lie in selecting the most appropriate communication system for the specific needs of the application, whether it's high-speed, low-power, or interference-resistant communication.

Wireless Communication Technologies

Wireless communication is central to IIoT, offering flexibility in connectivity without the need for extensive wiring. Several wireless technologies are commonly used in IIoT applications:

- **Wi-Fi:** Common in many industrial environments for short- to medium-range communication, Wi-Fi supports high data throughput and is suitable for applications where mobility and high-speed data transfer are required.

- **Bluetooth and BLE (Bluetooth Low Energy):** Ideal for short-range communication, Bluetooth and BLE are frequently used for connecting sensors and small devices in IIoT systems, where power consumption is a key concern.

- **Zigbee:** A low-power, low-data-rate communication protocol designed for sensor networks and industrial control systems. It operates in the 2.4 GHz frequency band and is highly suitable for short-range wireless communication in IIoT environments.

- **LoRaWAN (Long Range Wide Area Network):** LoRaWAN supports long-range, low-power communication, ideal for applications requiring wide-area coverage with minimal energy consumption. It's widely used in agriculture, logistics, and other remote industrial applications.

- **5G:** With ultra-low latency, high-speed data transfer, and massive connectivity capabilities, 5G is set to play a significant role in IIoT, particularly for applications requiring high-throughput, such as autonomous vehicles and industrial automation.

Optical Wireless Communication

Optical wireless communication (OWC) is an emerging technology that uses light (infrared or visible) for wireless data transmission. It offers an alternative to traditional radio-frequency communication and is particularly valuable in environments where radio interference is a concern or where high-speed, high-capacity communication is required.

Types of Optical Wireless Communication:

- **Li-Fi (Light Fidelity):** Li-Fi is a form of wireless communication that uses visible light to transmit data. It operates by modulating the intensity of light emitted from LEDs to carry data. Li-Fi can provide high-speed data transfer, even up to 100 Gbps in some cases. Its use in IIoT is especially relevant in environments like factories, warehouses, and industrial plants where traditional wireless signals (Wi-Fi, etc.) might face interference from metallic structures or other obstacles.

- **Infrared Communication (IR):** Infrared communication uses light in the infrared spectrum (above the visible range) to transmit data. It is often used in short-range applications due to its line-of-sight requirements but is useful in IIoT environments where high-speed, secure communication is necessary in controlled settings.

- **Free-Space Optics (FSO):** FSO is a form of optical communication that uses light beams to transmit data between devices through free space (air). FSO is often used in industrial settings for high-bandwidth communication between fixed nodes. It offers an advantage over radio frequency-based systems, especially in situations where electromagnetic interference could be problematic.

Advantages of OWC in IIoT:

- **High Bandwidth:** Optical communication can provide data rates much higher than traditional RF-based wireless systems.

- **No Interference:** Since optical communication is immune to radio-frequency interference, it is ideal for environments with heavy electromagnetic interference, such as industrial plants.

- **Security:** The directionality of optical signals makes them more secure than conventional wireless communication, as the signal is confined to a narrow beam, reducing the risk of interception.

- **Energy Efficiency:** Optical communication systems can be more energy-efficient, especially when using LED lighting for Li-Fi communication.

Challenges of OWC:

- **Line-of-Sight Requirement:** Optical systems typically require a clear line of sight between the transmitter and receiver, which may be challenging in dynamic industrial environments where obstructions are common.

- **Environmental Sensitivity:** Factors like fog, dust, and rain can impact the reliability of optical communication, especially for free-space optics.

- **Limited Range:** Optical communication systems generally have a shorter range compared to traditional RF-based systems.

Industrial Protocols and Edge Computing in IIoT Communication

Protocols for Industry (e.g., the foundations of IIoT include edge computing (local data processing) and OPC UA, MQTT, and Modbus, which allow for safe, low-latency, and compatible communication between IT and operational technology (OT). By processing data close to the source, edge computing minimizes bandwidth consumption, and protocols guarantee dependable, real-time connectivity.

- **MQTT (Message Queuing Telemetry Transport):** A lightweight messaging protocol widely used in IIoT for efficient communication between devices and cloud platforms. It is particularly well-suited for environments with limited bandwidth and where real-time data transmission is required.

- **OPC UA (Open Platform Communications Unified Architecture):**
  A communication standard for secure and reliable data exchange in
  industrial automation systems. OPC UA supports both real-
  time communication and data modeling, making it ideal for IIoT
  applications.

- **Edge Computing:** Edge computing is integral to IIoT as it involves
  processing data closer to the source of the data (i.e., on edge devices)
  rather than transmitting all data to centralized cloud platforms. This
  reduces latency, bandwidth usage, and reliance on cloud-
  based services, ensuring faster response times and more efficient
  communication.

Security in IIoT Communication

Security is a significant concern in IIoT, given the sensitive nature of industrial data
and the risks posed by cyber threats. Communication systems in IIoT must be secure
to protect against data breaches, unauthorized access, and other vulnerabilities. Some
common security measures include:

- **Encryption:** Ensuring that data is encrypted during transmission and
  storage to prevent unauthorized access.

- **Authentication:** Verifying the identity of devices and users to ensure
  that only authorized entities can access the system.

- **Firewalls and Intrusion Detection Systems (IDS):** Protecting
  the network from malicious attacks and unauthorized access by
  monitoring and controlling network traffic.

Applications and Use Cases

Let's discuss the use cases of IIoT in photonic systems, such as indoor positioning
systems, secure data transmission, authentication and authorization controls, data
encryption, hardware security models, and many more.

Indoor Positioning System

Indoor target localization has gained significant importance across various fields, such as smart buildings, industrial automation, and security systems. The capacity to effectively monitor and follow targets within indoor settings is crucial for enhancing operations, maintaining safety, and improving overall efficiency. Conventional localization techniques often encounter difficulties in restricted indoor environments due to signal interference and environmental barriers. Nevertheless, with the progress of technologies like the Internet of Things (IoT) and wireless sensor networks (WSNs), there is an increasing potential to address these challenges and create more effective indoor target localization systems. This paper emphasizes the developments in direction monitoring for indoor target localization through the use of IoT and WSN technologies. By integrating IoT devices and strategically placing wireless sensors throughout indoor areas, this method aims to deliver real-time and precise tracking of targets in confined spaces. The use of IoT allows for smooth communication and data interchange between sensors, while WSNs enable the gathering of accurate directional data essential for localization. The suggested system utilizes intelligent sensors outfitted with advanced signal processing abilities to capture and interpret directional information pertaining to the target's movement. A centralized processing unit compiles and processes this information using complex algorithms to identify the target's exact location within the indoor environment. Furthermore, machine learning algorithms are included to progressively enhance localization accuracy over time, taking into account factors such as environmental shifts and signal fluctuations.

Secure Data Transmission

In a time shaped by digital advancement, the Industrial Internet of Things (IIoT) signifies a significant leap forward for enhancing industrial automation and intelligent manufacturing. By utilizing interconnected sensors and devices to improve efficiency and productivity, organizations are conserving time, resources, and financial assets. Nevertheless, the demand for strong cybersecurity strategies becomes increasingly vital to maintain and safeguard operational excellence. Industrial operations encounter a range of potential threats, from device hijacking to data breaches and device impersonation. With security incidents frequently making news, businesses must implement proactive strategies to mitigate these threats. A recent study conducted by HiveMQ and IIoT World revealed that cybersecurity was identified as a key issue, with

35% of participants voicing concerns about adopting new IIoT technologies. Gaining insight into best practices and methods can assist development teams in ensuring the integrity, confidentiality, and availability of essential industrial systems. Best practices for IIoT cybersecurity includes the following methods to proactively reduce risk within your IIoT systems.

Authentication and Authorization Controls

To build a secure foundation for your IIoT strategy, focus on implementing strong authentication and authorization controls. Select vendors that provide robust authentication for users and devices accessing the IIoT network. This should include secure management of credentials, multi-factor authentication, and strict authorization measures. Ensuring that only permitted entities can access critical systems significantly lowers the risk of unauthorized access.

Data Encryption

Protecting sensitive data is crucial in IIoT settings. Apply end-to-end data encryption, both while in transit and at rest, to shield information from interception and unauthorized access. This is especially important for securing data exchanged between IoT devices, edge devices, and cloud services. Employing encryption protocols introduces an additional layer of protection against potential cyber threats.

Hardware Security Modules

Enhance the physical security of hardware components by integrating Hardware Security Modules (HSM). These specialized devices provide an extra layer of security by protecting cryptographic keys and sensitive information. By securing the hardware itself, organizations can prevent unauthorized access and tampering, thereby decreasing the risk of compromise.

Regular Security Audits

Establish a routine schedule for conducting security audits to evaluate the effectiveness of current cybersecurity measures. Regular assessments ensure that the IIoT infrastructure complies with industry standards and regulatory requirements. In highly regulated sectors, like healthcare or finance, compliance with security protocols is particularly vital. Security audits help identify weaknesses and allow for prompt remediation before they can be exploited.

MQTT and Other Secure Messaging Protocols

Think about utilizing secure messaging protocols, such as MQTT, for IIoT communication. MQTT's architecture promotes security by permitting only clients subscribed to specific topics to receive messages. Furthermore, employing transport layer security (TLS) encryption bolsters data confidentiality and integrity in transit, creating a secure channel for communication.

Tailored Security Approaches for Deployment

Acknowledge that the security strategy may differ based on the deployment setting. Whether implementing IIoT solutions in the cloud or on-premise, organizations should customize their security approaches to address the specific risks associated with each scenario. Cloud deployments present distinct challenges compared to on-premise setups, requiring a nuanced and adaptive cybersecurity strategy.

Keeping IIoT Systems Secure

As IIoT continues to transform industrial environments, cybersecurity remains a critical issue. By adopting strong authentication, encryption, hardware security, regular audits, and customized security strategies, organizations can strengthen their IIoT systems against potential threats. Securing industrial operations not only protects vital systems but also builds trust, ensuring customer loyalty and corporate accountability in an increasingly interconnected landscape. With IIoT deployments rising year after year, organizations must grasp the trends, challenges, and opportunities that this approach presents.

Industrial Automation

Industrial automation focuses on enhancing productivity, optimizing operational costs, improving product quality, minimizing routine inspections, and increasing safety levels. Embedded systems used in industrial automation involve the application of data-driven control mechanisms like PLC controllers, robotic systems, and industrial computers, all of which help decrease the reliance on human operators for machinery. The rise of IoT applications is significant, as they play an essential role in industrial automation. The Industrial Internet of Things (IIoT) establishes systems that are cost-effective, efficient, and adaptable to customer requirements.

The following sections and Figure 3-1 detail practical applications of IIoT in industrial automation.

Remote Access to Industrial Machines

In conventional factory environments, diagnosing a faulty machine typically necessitates engineers traveling to the location, which can result in wasted time and resources. This downtime can elevate expenses. With industrial remote access, engineers can connect to machines from afar, examine PLC or robot log files, and even reset devices when needed. This process can be completed in just minutes, significantly cutting downtime and enhancing operational efficiency.

Enhanced HMI Functionalities

In our modern digital age, regular updates to technology and equipment are crucial. Gaining access to a dependable embedded software development company is vital for sustaining performance, boosting security, and incorporating new features after delivery. Consistent updates to human-machine interface (HMI) software facilitate smooth integration of additional functionalities. Through secure internet connections, these updates can be executed remotely. Furthermore, HMI capabilities can be assessed through web-based virtual networks on IIoT platforms, providing convenience and efficiency in industrial automation.

Predictive Maintenance

Predictive analytics is essential for the upkeep of industrial machines. By tracking machinery deterioration over production cycles, businesses can effectively forecast maintenance timetables. Data amassed and stored in cloud systems offers invaluable insights, while automatic alerts inform personnel when maintenance is required. This proactive strategy extends equipment lifespan and diminishes unexpected downtime.

Practical Applications of IIoT in Industrial Automation

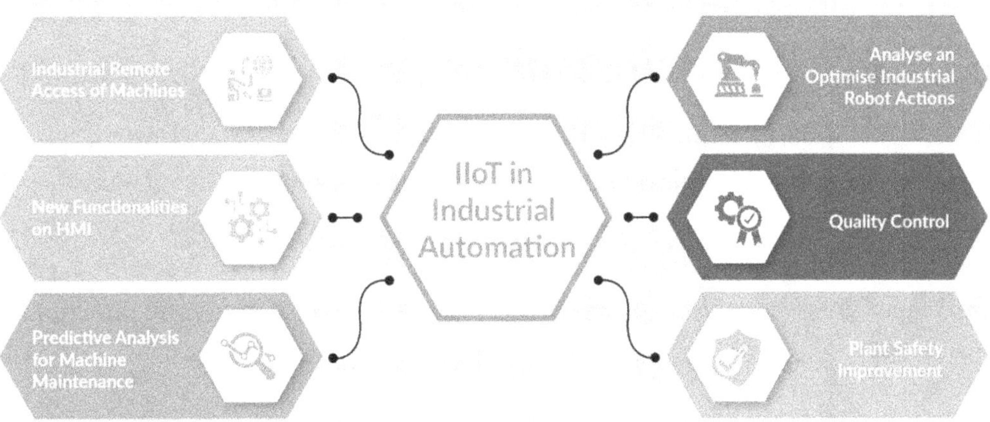

Figure 3-1. *Practical Applications of IIoT in an Industrial Automation*

Optimizing Industrial Robot Actions

Industrial robots streamline repetitive processes, and IIoT-enabled remote access allows for deeper insights through log file evaluation. Video analytics improve robot performance, while IP camera footage and live streams enable rapid assessments. Secure VPN connections permit straightforward access to devices associated with robots, facilitating prompt optimization.

Quality Control

IIoT applications assist in monitoring product quality during each stage of the production process, beginning with raw materials. Intelligent tracking applications pinpoint problems within the production chain, allowing for swift resolution. This not only identifies defects but also mitigates risks in sectors such as food and pharmaceuticals, ensuring superior product quality and safety.

Plant Safety Improvements

Machinery equipped with IIoT technology delivers real-time information regarding plant conditions. Continuously monitoring equipment health and air quality helps avert dangerous situations, creating a safer work environment. This proactive approach to safety minimizes risks and improves overall plant operations.

IIoT in industrial automation revolutionizes manufacturing practices, providing smarter, safer, and more efficient solutions for industries around the globe.

Fiber Optic Communication Network

In fiber optic communication systems, the core network, also known as the backbone network, is a high-capacity, permanent, and frequently used network that links significant network nodes and enables traffic transmission among them. It serves as the support structure, guaranteeing effective and dependable data transmission. Core networks play an essential role in connecting various areas or nations and directing traffic to external networks such as the internet and cloud services.

Core Networks

Optical core networks, referred to as wide area networks (WAN) or interchange carrier (IXC) public networks, are extensive networks that cover significant physical distances. These networks deliver advanced, enterprise-level speed and data capacity to meet the highest operational demands. This enables organizations to swiftly transfer data across long distances with substantial data transmission capabilities. Optical/WAN networks frequently utilize radio or telephone connections instead of dedicated lines. They employ optical fiber cables or satellite transmissions alongside packet switching or message switching techniques. These networks are commonly set up using leased communication circuits. They are utilized by businesses, educational institutions, and government agencies to transmit data to clients, suppliers, students, staff, and customers across various global locations. Long-distance networks connect major urban centers within continents, covering distances that typically range from 1,000 km to over 2,500 km.

Metropolitan Networks

Optical metro networks, also referred to as edge/regional/metropolitan networks, encompass optical networks that cover distances of up to several hundred kilometers and primarily serve densely populated metropolitan regions. These networks connect long-haul and access networks, linking a diverse array of client protocols from enterprise/private users in access networks to backbone service provider infrastructures. Optical metro networks utilize synchronous digital hierarchy (SDH) or synchronous optical network (SONET) ring architectures, in which smaller rings consolidate traffic into larger core inter-office (IOF) rings that link central offices. The defining features of these networks include extended transmission distances and rapid transmission rates. They harness the capabilities of optical fiber to convey data over metropolitan and regional territories. The terminals of an optical metro network can include urban locations, office computers, or global telecommunication systems. Optical metro networks are essential for linking different parts of the telecommunications framework, facilitating uninterrupted data transmission and communication across various networks and geographic areas.

Access Networks

Optical access networks (OANs) serve as the connecting bridge for subscribers to the network provider's outermost switching office/exchange, often referred to as the "last mile" or "first mile" networks. These networks are tailored to support a range of bidirectional interactive services typically provided to residential customers and small to medium-sized businesses by local exchanges. The optical access method comprises two primary technologies:

- **Single Star (SS) Technology (Point-to-Point)**: This method directly links the service node to the user with a dedicated optical fiber connection.

- **Passive Optical Network (PON) Technology (Point-to-Multipoint)**: This is the more prevalent technology found in OANs, where a service node connects to several users through a shared optical fiber infrastructure.

OANs utilize optical fiber for data transmission, enabling them to deliver high-quality, interactive services that operate in both directions for their users.

The networks consist of an optical line terminal (OLT) that is set up by the telecommunications carrier or service provider and an optical network unit (ONU) that is placed in the subscriber's home or office. In certain instances, particularly with DSL, the OAN is divided into optical distribution and access for customers, where the optical distribution connects to the ONU and customer access utilizes copper-based twisted pairs. The main objective of OANs is to offer bidirectional interactive services to residential customers and businesses within the subscriber loop, facilitating high-quality two-way switched voice or data communication in a local calling area.

Key Technologies in Fiber Optic Communication Networks

Key technologies in fiber optic communication networks enable high-speed, reliable, and long-distance data transmission through optical fibers by using advanced components such as optical transmitters, receivers, amplifiers, and multiplexing techniques. Innovations such as Wavelength Division Multiplexing and optical amplifiers significantly enhance network capacity and efficiency, making fiber optics a critical backbone for modern communication systems and the Internet of Things. Let's discuss one by one in brief.

Dense Wavelength Division Multiplexing

Dense wavelength division multiplexing (DWDM) is a fiber optics technology designed to connect several channels over a dark fiber pair utilizing a multiplexer (Figure 3-2). This approach optimizes fiber use and assists organizations in accommodating increasing demands without the need to lay or lease additional fiber until it becomes absolutely necessary. DWDM utilizes multiplexed channels that operate in the 1550nm wavelength range, which is where fiber experiences the least loss, maintaining a separation of only 0.8nm between them. Typically, DWDM supports around 40 channels at speeds of 100G. Nonetheless, incorporating an interleaver can double the channel count by halving the speed. An interleaver takes DWDM signals spaced at 50GHz and combines them onto a channel plan spaced at 100GHz. The signals at 50GHz and 100GHz are often called odd and even signals, respectively, and these signals are interleaved together, usually resulting in an increase from 40 to 80 channels operating at 50GHz.

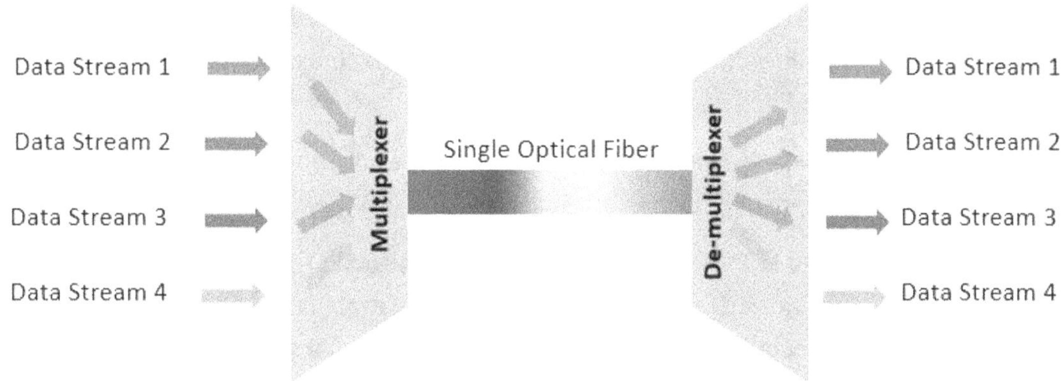

Figure 3-2. *Dense Wavelength Division Multiplexing (DWDM)*

Passive Optical Networks

A passive optical network (PON) refers to a fiber-optic telecommunications system that utilizes unpowered devices for signal transmission, specifically in the final stretch connecting service providers to consumers (Figure 3-3). It depends on fiber optic cabling and passive optical splitters to convey data from one source to several endpoints. Key characteristics of PON include:

- **Fiber Optic Based**: PONs employ fiber optic cables for data transmission, providing high bandwidth and minimal signal degradation.

- **Passive Components**: The central element of a PON is the passive optical splitter, which divides the optical signal into several branches without requiring any external power.

- **Point-to-Multipoint Architecture**: A single fiber from the central office is divided to connect multiple subscribers, minimizing the necessity for separate fiber connections for each user.

- **Efficiency and Cost-Effectiveness**: PONs are efficient in their use of bandwidth and are often more economical to implement and maintain compared to traditional copper-based networks.

- **Reliability**: The reliance on passive components within PONs enhances their reliability, as they have a lower likelihood of failing than powered active components.

- **Scalability**: PONs can be easily expanded by incorporating additional optical network terminals (ONTs) into the network.

- **Components of Passive Optical Network (Optical Line Terminal (OLT)):** Positioned at the service provider's central office, the OLT transforms electrical signals into optical signals and transmits them through the fiber optic cable.

- **Optical Network Unit (ONU)/Optical Network Terminal (ONT)**: Located at the customer's location, the ONU/ONT receives the optical signals, converts them back into electrical signals, and manages both downstream and upstream data communication.

- **Passive Optical Splitter**: A device that splits the optical signal from the OLT into several branches, enabling it to reach multiple ONUs/ONTs.

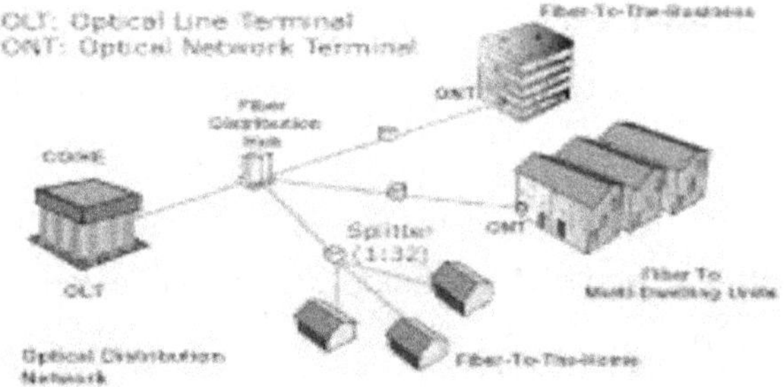

Figure 3-3. *Passive Optical Network*

Fiber to the X (FTTx) Solutions

Fiber to the X (FTTx) refers to a broadband network structure that incorporates fiber optic cables for at least a portion of the last mile connectivity to end-users. This term broadly encompasses various configurations such as fiber to the home (FTTH), fiber to the building (FTTB), and fiber to the curb (FTTC). The primary goal of FTTx is to enhance existing copper-based networks, delivering faster, more dependable, and higher-capacity internet, television, and telephone services.

Key Aspects of FTTx

FTTx is not a singular technology, but rather an overarching concept. It includes different methods of utilizing fiber for last-mile connections, with "X" denoting the location where fiber ends before connecting to the user's device (Figure 3-4). FTTx is vital for next-generation access (NGA). It plays a crucial role in modernizing broadband infrastructure to accommodate the growing demand for enhanced speed and quality of service. It provides various advantages: it offers quicker speeds, increased bandwidth, reduced latency, and greater reliability compared to conventional copper-based networks. FTTx is essential for facilitating emerging technologies: it is important for supporting applications such as 5G, the Internet of Things (IoT), smart cities, and cloud computing, which depend on high-speed, low-latency networks.

FTTx is available in several configurations:

- **FTTH (Fiber to the Home)**: fiber is installed directly to individual residences or buildings.

- **FTTB (Fiber to the Building)**: fiber reaches the building, and the final connection to individual units is completed using alternative methods.

- **FTTC (Fiber to the Curb)**: fiber is installed at a curb or pole close to the user's location, with a short copper connection covering the final distance.

FTTx is considered a "future-proof" technology: fiber optic networks are highly adaptable and can meet future increases in bandwidth requirements.

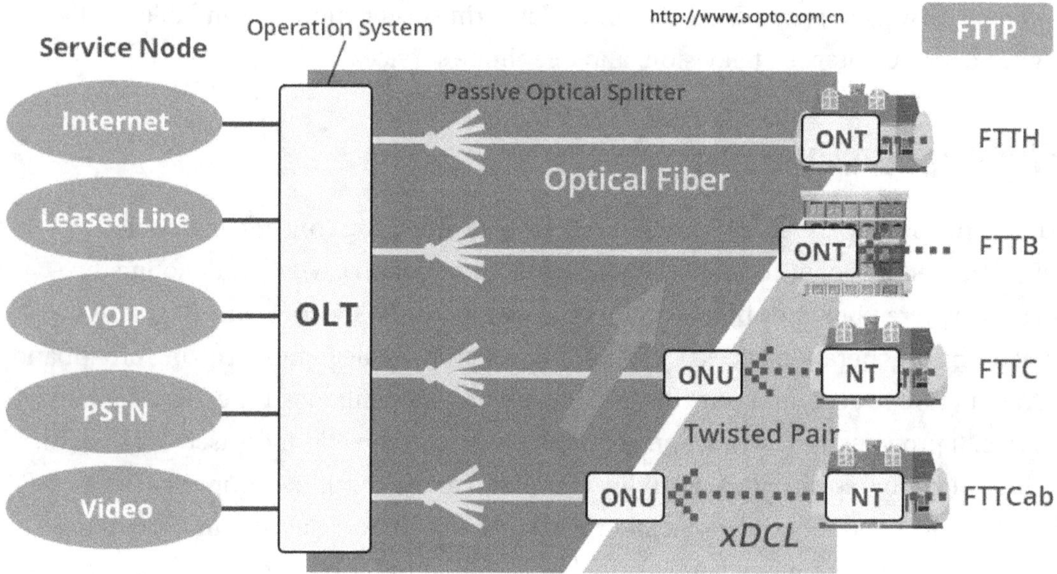

Figure 3-4. *FTTx System*

Integration with IIoT

The integration of fiber optic communication networks with the Industrial Internet of Things (IIoT) presents substantial benefits for industrial applications that demand high-speed, dependable, and secure data transmission. Fiber optics delivers enhanced speeds, broader bandwidth, and resistance to interference, making it particularly suitable for IIoT settings where immediate data analysis and control are essential. Advantages of fiber optic integration in IIoT are as follows:

- **High Speed and Bandwidth**: Fiber optic cables provide significantly superior data transmission speeds and bandwidth compared to conventional copper cables, allowing for the swift transfer of large volumes of data produced by IIoT devices.

- **Low Latency**: Fiber optics guarantees minimal delays in data transmission, which is critical for time-sensitive applications such as automated manufacturing and robotics.

- **Reliability and Interference Resistance**: Fiber optic cables are immune to electromagnetic interference, ensuring consistent data transmission even in challenging industrial environments.

- **Long-Distance Data Transmission**: Fiber optics facilitates long-range communication, enabling the connection of IIoT devices across extensive industrial sites and even between different geographical locations.

- **Enhanced Security**: Fiber optic communication offers superior protection against eavesdropping and tampering compared to wireless or copper-based networks, safeguarding sensitive industrial information.

- **Scalability and Future-Proofing**: Fiber optic networks are designed to be scalable, accommodating growing bandwidth requirements and ensuring adaptability for future IIoT developments.

- **Power Over Fiber (PoF)**: Fiber optics can also transmit power, allowing for the creation of wireless sensor nodes within IIoT systems, which minimizes the need for traditional wiring and enhances flexibility.

- **Illustrations of Fiber Optic Integration in IIoT (Smart Manufacturing)**: Fiber optics supports high-speed communication among sensors, actuators, and control systems in automated manufacturing facilities, enabling real-time monitoring and management.

The use of optical fiber in the Internet of Things environment has several limitations despite its advantages in high-speed communication:

- **High Installation Cost**: Deploying fiber infrastructure requires optical cables, transmitters, receivers, connectors, and specialized installation equipment. This also involves trenching, cable routing, and testing, resulting in slower deployment compared to wireless solutions. For these reasons, optical fiber is typically used as a high-speed backbone or backhaul network, while IoT edge devices commonly communicate using lightweight protocols such as MQTT.

- **Limited Flexibility and Mobility**: Since fiber communication relies on physical cabling, it is unsuitable for mobile or widely distributed IoT devices. Optical fibers are also fragile, as the glass strands can be damaged by excessive bending, mechanical stress, or environmental factors. Maintenance and repair are complex and costly, requiring skilled technicians and specialized tools for splicing and fault detection.

- Optical communication components such as lasers and photodetectors often require higher power, which makes them less suitable for battery-powered IoT sensor nodes.

- Deploying fiber to thousands of distributed sensors is also impractical and difficult to scale, especially in applications like smart agriculture or environmental monitoring.

High-Speed Data Transfer

Fiber optic communication networks play a vital role in facilitating high-speed data transfer for Industrial Internet of Things (IIoT) applications. They support the swift and dependable transmission of substantial data volumes, which is critical for the real-time monitoring, control, and analysis of industrial operations. This integration provides benefits such as minimal latency, immunity to interference, and the capability for long-distance data transmission, rendering them highly suitable for IIoT implementations.

Fiber optics facilitates high-speed data transmission in IIoT with high bandwidth, low latency, reliability, resistance to interference, long-distance transmission, and WDM. All these facilities are explained briefly here:

- **High Bandwidth**: According to HFCL, fiber optic cables can achieve data transmission speeds of up to 100 gigabits per second, far surpassing the capabilities of traditional copper cables. This exceptional bandwidth is essential for managing the substantial data volumes produced by IIoT devices.

- **Low Latency**: The low latency associated with fiber optics guarantees minimal delays in data transmission, which is critical for real-time control applications in sectors such as manufacturing and automation.

- **Reliability and Resistance to Interference**: Fiber optics are unaffected by electromagnetic interference, a significant advantage in industrial settings where such disturbances are prevalent.

- **Long-Distance Transmission**: Fiber optics can effectively transmit data over extensive distances with minimal signal degradation, making them ideal for scenarios where devices are dispersed across large industrial sites or even across different locations.

- **Wavelength Division Multiplexing (WDM)**: WDM technology enables the transmission of multiple data channels through a single fiber optic cable, thereby enhancing the overall bandwidth capacity.

Scalability and Reliability

In an environment characterized by the Industrial Internet of Things (IIoT) and supported by fiber optic communication networks, the importance of scalability and reliability cannot be overstated. These factors are essential for managing the growing volumes of data and ensuring uninterrupted communication among devices. Fiber optic networks are particularly advantageous for IIoT applications due to their high bandwidth and minimal latency, which are critical for real-time data transmission and processing. The scalability of fiber optic networks allows for the easy expansion to support an increasing number of IIoT devices and data streams. This can be achieved by adding additional fibers or employing Wavelength Division Multiplexing (WDM) to enhance bandwidth. By processing data closer to its source, edge computing minimizes latency and alleviates network congestion, thereby further improving scalability. Cloud-based platforms for IIoT are capable of managing substantial data volumes and offer flexible scaling solutions to adapt to changing requirements.

Fiber optic networks are renowned for their high reliability; fiber optic networks exhibit low signal attenuation and are resistant to electromagnetic interference, making them ideal for industrial applications. The implementation of redundant network pathways and backup systems guarantees that data transmission remains consistent, even in the event of failures.

To safeguard data and systems against unauthorized access and cyber threats, which are particularly critical in IIoT environments, robust security protocols are essential. Ongoing monitoring and proactive maintenance are vital for detecting and resolving potential issues before they disrupt operations. In conclusion, the integration of fiber optic networks, edge computing, and cloud infrastructure equips IIoT applications with the necessary scalability and reliability, facilitating efficient communication, data processing, and decision-making within industrial environments.

Industrial Connectivity Solutions

Industrial Connectivity Solutions, particularly when combined with IIoT and fiber optic communication networks, aim to facilitate uninterrupted communication and data transfer among industrial devices, machinery, and systems. This integration supports real-time data analysis, remote monitoring, and the management of industrial operations, ultimately resulting in improved efficiency, productivity, and safety. Key features of industrial connectivity solutions in fiber optic networks are:

- **Fiber Optic Communication**: Fiber optics offer high bandwidth, minimal latency, and dependable data transmission, which are essential for real-time data exchange in industrial settings.

- **IIoT Integration**: Devices such as sensors, actuators, and industrial robots are linked to the fiber optic network, allowing for effective data collection, monitoring, and control.

- **Industrial Ethernet**: Industrial Ethernet serves as a prevalent protocol for connecting IIoT devices to the network, ensuring robust and reliable communication.

- **Data Analytics and Edge Computing**: The data gathered through the IIoT network is analyzed using sophisticated analytics and edge computing techniques to derive valuable insights and facilitate real-time decision-making.

These solutions find applications across various sectors, including smart manufacturing, energy and utilities, transportation, and healthcare. The primary advantages of these solutions include enhanced efficiency, minimized downtime, increased productivity, improved safety, and optimized resource utilization.

Examples of industrial connectivity solutions include the following:

- **Smart Manufacturing**: Overseeing production lines, optimizing energy use, and executing predictive maintenance.

- **Energy Management**: Tracking and managing energy consumption, optimizing distribution networks, and implementing smart grid technologies.

- **Transportation and Logistics**: Monitoring the location and condition of vehicles and cargo, optimizing routes, and enhancing delivery efficiency.

Photonics in Data Centers

Photonics technology presents a viable solution to the challenges faced by data centers by utilizing light rather than electrons for the transmission and processing of information. This method offers several significant benefits, such as:

- **Increased Speed**: Data transmission using light can reach speeds that are up to 100 times greater than conventional electronic techniques.

- **Reduced Power Consumption**: Photonic systems produce less heat and require minimal energy for operation, leading to a substantial decrease in power requirements.

- **Enhanced Signal Integrity**: Optical signals are more resistant to electromagnetic interference, facilitating more dependable data transmission over extended distances.

- **Compact Architecture**: Integrated photonics allows for the development of densely arranged optical components on a single chip, optimizing physical space within data centers.

One of the most prominent uses of photonics in data centers is the implementation of optical interconnects. These light-based connections serve as a replacement for conventional copper wiring, facilitating quicker data transfer between servers and minimizing energy loss caused by heat generation. Companies such as Intel have already introduced silicon photonic transceivers that can transmit data at speeds of 100 gigabits per second, with even greater speeds anticipated in the future.

Photonic integrated circuits (PICs) signify a major advancement in data center technology. These compact devices consolidate multiple photonic functions onto a single chip, allowing for rapid data transmission at light speed. PICs are especially effective for high-frequency data transmission over distances greater than 10 meters, making them well-suited for extensive data center operations. Optical switches are increasingly replacing traditional electronic switches in data centers, providing faster data routing without the delays associated with electronic systems. This transition enhances network scalability and decreases resource contention within the data center.

Newly developed photonic processors promise significantly improved processing speeds and reduced power consumption compared to their electronic equivalents. These processors utilize light for computational tasks, potentially transforming AI model training and data analysis. Central to these innovations is photonics epitaxial wafer technology. This cutting-edge manufacturing technique allows for the production of high-performance optical components that are crucial for the next generation of data centers and AI systems (Figure 3-5).

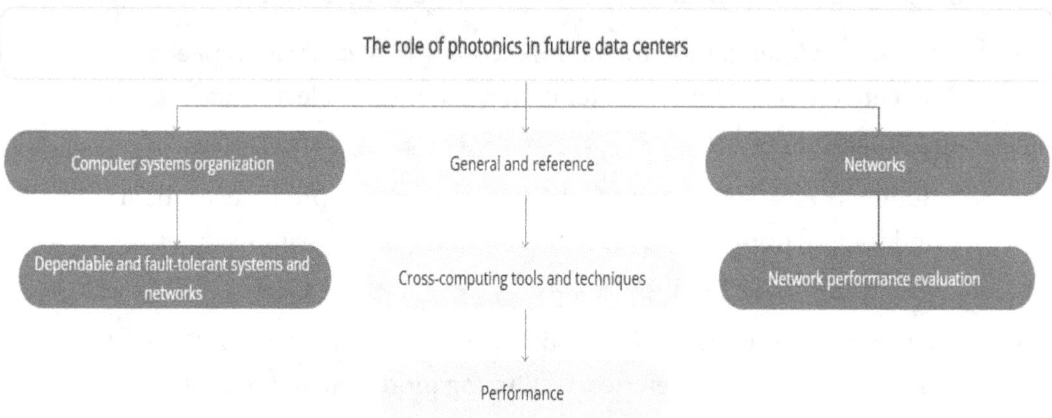

Figure 3-5. *Role of Photonics in Future Data Centers*

Specific IIoT applications benefiting from fiber optic networks include the following:

- **Smart Factories**: Fiber optics support real-time data communication among sensors, actuators, and control systems in smart factories, promoting efficient automation and process optimization.

- **Remote Monitoring and Control**: In sectors such as oil and gas or power generation, fiber optics facilitates remote monitoring and control of equipment, thereby enhancing safety and operational efficiency.

- **Connected Vehicles:** In the automotive sector, fiber optics are utilized to transmit data between vehicles and infrastructure, enabling features such as autonomous driving and advanced driver-assistance systems. Data collected from vehicles, such as speed, location, traffic conditions, and safety alerts, is transmitted to roadside infrastructure through wireless links and then forwarded through high-capacity fiber optic cables to centralized control systems.

- **Smart Cities**: Fiber optics play a crucial role in developing smart city infrastructure, allowing for the collection and analysis of data from various sensors, including those monitoring traffic, environmental conditions, and security.

Emerging Communication Technologies

The Internet of Things (IoT) has found applications across diverse sectors such as agriculture, healthcare, defense, transportation, and manufacturing. This shift from tangible objects in the physical realm to the Internet of Things has led to the rise of the Industrial Internet of Things (IIoT). IIoT applications are designed to facilitate automation within the manufacturing sector, a concept often referred to as Industry 4.0. Additionally, the growing demand for personalized experiences from end-users has contributed to the increasing prominence of Industry 5.0. This new phase aims to integrate artificial intelligence (AI) into everyday life to enhance capabilities and productivity. For Industry 5.0 to succeed, IIoT must deliver improved efficiency, heightened productivity, and superior asset management. In this regard, device-to-device communication is crucial. IoT devices need to be equipped with seamless communication technologies that function across diverse networks. This paper reviews communication standards, technologies, and various research contributions in the field. It also presents an analysis to identify the challenges and opportunities associated with developing communication methods for IIoT. Furthermore, the paper outlines general guidelines for advancing communication techniques in the context of Industry 5.0.

Terahertz Communication

Advancements in communication technologies, especially terahertz (THz) communication, are set to transform Internet of Things (IoT) applications by facilitating extremely high data rates, minimal latency, and extensive connectivity. Operating within the 0.1-10 THz frequency range, THz communication provides significantly greater bandwidth than 5G, thereby enabling innovative applications such as real-time digital twins, immersive virtual reality, and telemedicine surgeries. Nevertheless, obstacles such as substantial propagation loss and the design of transceivers must be overcome to ensure effective implementation. Figure 3-6 illustrates the diverse application areas of quantum computing within the ecosystem of the Internet of Things. As IoT systems continue to generate vast volumes of data and require advanced computational capabilities, quantum computing has emerged as a promising technology to address challenges related to processing speed, security, optimization, and intelligent decision-making. Figure 3-6 presents several key domains where quantum computing can enhance IoT functionalities, including network optimization, faster computation at IoT end points, secure IoT communication using quantum cryptography, quantum-enabled sensors, digital marketing analytics, and secure smart lock systems. Each section highlights specific applications such as dynamic pricing, environmental monitoring, fraud detection, and access security systems.

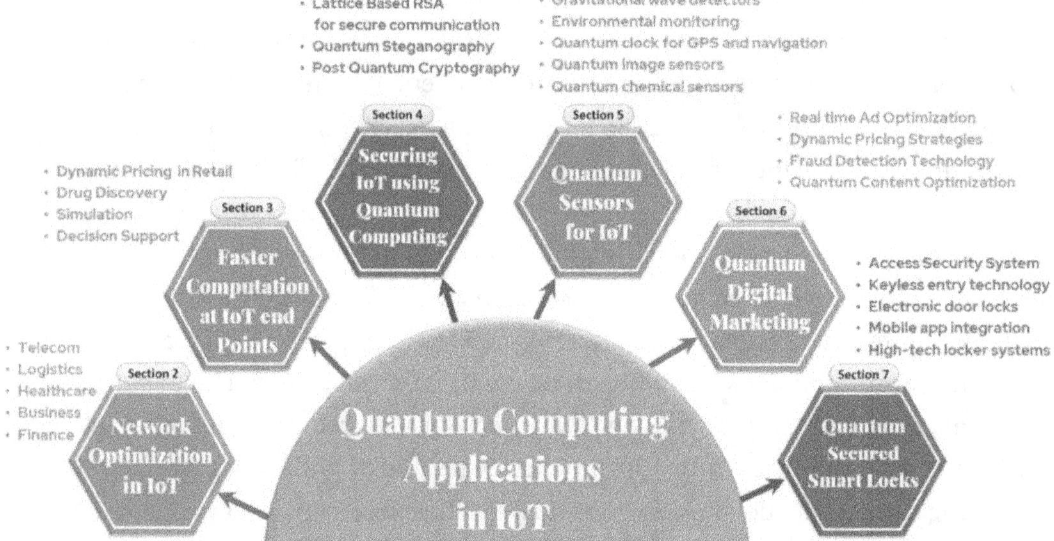

Figure 3-6. *Quantum Computing and Internet of Things Based on Different Sections*

Quantum Communication Technologies

IIoT presents numerous pertinent applications where quality control (QC) can enhance IoT operations, which have arisen from advancements in technology facilitating machine-to-machine communication and the broader IoT ecosystem. The IIoT spans all industrial domains, including manufacturing facilities, storage warehouses, shipbuilding yards, and transportation sectors. Its applications are diverse, covering areas such as supply chain management, quality assurance, maintenance and control, and resource optimization. However, a significant challenge arises from the substantial volume of sensor data, which can lead to latency and storage complications, rendering cloud-based data processing and analytics inadequate for managing IIoT effectively. To address these issues, IIoT systems must ensure enhanced connectivity, interoperability, and data security while being robust and energy-efficient to alleviate network strain and utilize cloud resources effectively. Nonetheless, certain heterogeneous strategies pose challenges concerning overall energy efficiency, network connectivity, and time sensitivity. In this context, quantum-inspired optimization techniques can be employed for effective routing, with quantum particle swarm optimization being one viable method that meets the necessary criteria. By improving overall connectivity and intelligent automation, the application of quantum computing-inspired technologies can significantly accelerate technological advancements, industrial evolution, and shifts in social dynamics in the 21st century. This suggests that the onset of Industry 4.0 may occur sooner than anticipated.

As a result, manufacturing processes are likely to become more flexible and responsive to customer needs, enabling the production of highly customized products without necessitating extensive reconfiguration of the manufacturing infrastructure. Nevertheless, several challenges remain in the implementation phase, such as effectively translating quantum technology solutions into commercial applications. A comprehensive understanding of quantum technology, along with expertise in the relevant domains and integration processes, is essential. The other challenge may be the quantum computing landscape and market are varied. Current benchmarks primarily focus on low-level hardware performance, failing to accurately represent application performance. The absence of community-driven, application-focused benchmarks hinders users from easily assessing the performance they can expect from available solutions.

Potential Impact on IIoT Communication System

Integrating communication technologies with the Industrial Internet of Things (IIoT) will greatly improve operational efficiency, foster new business models, and stimulate innovation, especially within the manufacturing sector and its associated industries. This progress is largely facilitated by advancements such as 5G, which provides rapid data transmission and minimal latency, thus supporting real-time analysis and decision-making. Nonetheless, challenges persist in areas such as security, data management, and the integration of these technologies with existing systems. The IIoT, enhanced by communication technologies, enables the real-time collection and analysis of data from interconnected devices and machinery. This capability supports predictive maintenance, optimized production scheduling, and enhanced product quality, resulting in greater efficiency and lower costs. Additionally, it encourages innovation by paving the way for the creation of new products and services, as well as the establishment of novel business models. The advent of 5G networks, characterized by their exceptional speed, reliability, and reduced latency, is set to transform the IIoT landscape. 5G facilitates more sophisticated applications and enhances real-time data analysis, particularly in manufacturing, where timely data is essential.

Challenges and Future Directions

The rise of communication technologies within the Industrial Internet of Things (IIoT) brings forth considerable challenges as well as encouraging prospects for the future. Key challenges encompass security weaknesses, concerns regarding data privacy, elevated costs, and issues related to interoperability. Future developments aim to tackle these obstacles by enhancing cybersecurity measures, advancing edge computing capabilities, and establishing standardized communication protocols. The next section discusses some of the technical and regulatory challenges.

Security and Privacy

Industrial Internet of Things (IIoT) devices face significant risks from various cyber threats, such as malware, unauthorized access, and data breaches. Additionally, the collection and transmission of large volumes of sensitive information raise serious concerns regarding data privacy. As technology evolves at a pace faster than expected, numerous industry professionals are expressing apprehension regarding the associated risks. The increasing integration of generative AI in decision-making processes has raised concerns among manufacturers about the clarity of its reasoning. Concurrently, the extensive data collection and dissemination by industrial IoT systems prompt some companies to reflect on their data protection strategies. As we approach 2025, it is likely that stakeholders will echo these concerns, compelling manufacturers to evaluate the implications of industrial IoT technology on their data sharing and security practices. Some of the challenges are explained below:

- **High Costs**: The deployment of IIoT solutions can incur substantial expenses due to the necessity for specialized hardware, software, and supporting infrastructure.

- **Interoperability**: The absence of standardization and interoperability among different IIoT devices and systems can obstruct efficient data exchange and integration.

- **Data Volume and Complexity**: IIoT devices produce enormous quantities of data, which can pose challenges in terms of management, analysis, and storage.

- **Connectivity and Reliability**: Ensuring consistent connectivity in various industrial settings, particularly those with limited bandwidth or inadequate signal coverage, presents a significant challenge.

- **Scalability and Flexibility**: IIoT systems must be designed to be scalable and adaptable to meet future growth and evolving industrial needs.

Innovations and Research Trends

The past few years have witnessed significant advancements poised to greatly influence the application of IIoT technology within the manufacturing industry. Notably, edge computing has surfaced as an innovative approach for IIoT-enabled machinery to process data more swiftly and efficiently. Essentially, edge computing gathers, analyzes, and synchronizes data through on-site IIoT devices prior to transmitting it to the cloud. This method not only accelerates the analytical process but also ensures that only the most pertinent information is relayed to the cloud for sophisticated modeling or implementation in artificial intelligence algorithms. Furthermore, any discourse on technology in 2024 would be incomplete without addressing artificial intelligence and machine learning as distinct entities. These technologies have become increasingly embedded in various manufacturing processes, where they are deemed essential for predictive maintenance. By harnessing these advancements, manufacturers can more accurately anticipate when and where to direct their efforts to avert unforeseen equipment failures and the associated downtime.

Potential Trends in IIoT

The rapid evolution of the Industrial Internet of Things is transforming industrial environments by enabling intelligent connectivity between machines, sensors, and digital systems. Advances in sensing technologies, high-speed communication networks, data analytics, and artificial intelligence are driving the transition toward highly automated and data-driven manufacturing ecosystems. As industries move further toward the paradigm of Industry 4.0, emerging technologies such as edge computing, digital twins, advanced sensor networks, and predictive analytics are expected to redefine operational efficiency, reliability, and sustainability in industrial processes. These developments are paving the way for smart factories, enhanced human–machine collaboration, and improved decision-making through real-time data insights. The following sections highlight some of the key technological trends that are expected to shape the future landscape of IIoT in the coming years.

Condition Monitoring and Predictive Maintenance

Sensors play a pivotal role in the advancements associated with Industry 4.0, serving as a fundamental catalyst in this domain. A significant advantage of condition monitoring sensors is their ability to provide data and insights that are accessible from any location at any time. This capability facilitates remote monitoring and informed decision-making based on real-time Industrial Internet of Things (IIoT) data, regardless of personnel location. As technology progresses, condition monitoring and analytical solutions, such as Reliability 360°, will be essential in mitigating unplanned downtime. The implementation of machine learning across various operations aims to enhance the accuracy of these systems. In the coming year, it is anticipated that analytical tools will see increased adoption across the industry, alongside the integration of digital twin technology for thorough monitoring.

Advances and Innovations in Sensor Technology

The significant advancements in communication technologies, particularly the anticipated widespread rollout of 5G networks, will enable facilities to deploy a greater number of sensors for data collection, thereby enhancing the information available for decision-making. A particularly noteworthy development in IIoT sensor technology is the capability to derive more contextual information from data points through the use of multiple sensors. This approach provides a more comprehensive understanding of operations, facilitating insights into unforeseen events and enabling their prevention. As technology continues to evolve through 2025, sensors are expected to become increasingly compact and less obtrusive, with self-powered and energy-harvesting sensors gaining broader adoption.

Data-Driven Predictive Technologies

Unforeseen downtime remains one of the most significant resource drains for manufacturers, impacting profitability, jeopardizing deadlines, and negatively influencing both equipment longevity and product quality. The advancements in remote monitoring have brought us closer to real-time oversight than ever before, with cloud-based predictive technology achieving a significant milestone in 2024. Predictive maintenance stands out as the foremost application of these innovations, allowing manufacturers to detect potential issues early, plan downtime at convenient times, ensure readiness of parts and personnel, and maintain smooth operations. In the upcoming year, we can expect further progress in prescriptive analytics that will offer actionable insights. As these developments unfold, collaboration between humans and AI in the decision-making process will become increasingly prevalent.

5G and Edge Computing

Industrial edge computing signifies that not only do robots, motors, and other machinery communicate with the central server, but they also possess their own data processing capabilities. By relaying information such as operational conditions or cycle times back to the main server, this equipment located at the network's periphery can deliver valuable insights for performance enhancement. This trend is anticipated to gain momentum within the Industrial Internet of Things (IIoT) as 5G networks alleviate previous limitations on speed and bandwidth that hindered these connections. Many experts also foresee the integration of AI at the edge for more intelligent devices, while network slicing will provide enhanced customization for connectivity solutions.

Fog Computing

Cloud computing plays a vital role in facilitating the connections that underpin the Industrial Internet of Things (IIoT). Nevertheless, challenges arise due to the distance between cloud servers and IIoT networks, which can hinder transmission and propagation. Fog computing addresses these challenges by shifting intelligence closer to the network's edge, where the machinery operates. This approach allows for real-time control, improved security, and enhanced manageability. It is evident that fog computing should become a standard practice in the IIoT sector, particularly as we approach 2025, which may see greater standardization and interoperability among devices.

Digital Twins

Remote access has emerged as a key theme in recent IIoT developments, driven by the need for convenience, productivity, and health and safety considerations, which will be explored further below. A significant advancement in remote manufacturing is the advent of digital twin technology, which creates a virtual representation of a physical component or machine within a factory. By utilizing sensors and connectivity, the digital twin is continuously updated to mirror the actual condition, status, and performance of its physical counterpart. IIoT manufacturing technologies, including artificial intelligence, facilitate simulations that support planning and forecasting, all without requiring physical presence on the factory floor or at the site. The integration of virtual and augmented reality technologies by 2025 could enhance the realism and accuracy of these simulations, resulting in improved outcomes.

Health and Safety

The concept of worker health and safety evolved significantly during the pandemic, emphasizing the necessity of maintaining physical distance among employees and addressing health concerns for those sharing the same workspace. The foundational principles of monitoring technologies utilized for machinery can also be applied in this context, allowing for the tracking of employee locations on the production floor, monitoring close interactions, and efficiently measuring and recording employee temperatures. The innovative application of IoT manufacturing technology to promote worker health offers advantages for both employees and the facility. Some experts anticipate that artificial intelligence will be employed to create personalized risk profiles for each worker, facilitating tailored safety measures instead of a generic approach.

Flexibility and Agility

The early phases of the COVID-19 pandemic led to significant supply chain disruptions, placing additional strain on manufacturers striving to maintain their operations. The advancements in IIoT have enabled data analysis and communication that provide unparalleled flexibility in supply chain management, allowing manufacturers to adapt swiftly in areas such as supplier selection, ordering, procurement strategies, and inventory control. The experiences of recent years are likely to ensure that these aspects remain crucial by 2025. A prominent development in this regard may be the creation of improved collaboration platforms that foster enhanced communication between suppliers and manufacturers.

Cybersecurity

As the prevalence of wireless devices in manufacturing environments increases, so does the potential for cyber threats. Hackers now have more avenues for attack than ever before, making it imperative for manufacturers to prioritize cybersecurity to avoid severe repercussions. Fortunately, there are a variety of effective strategies available today to combat cyber threats, which can significantly enhance the protection of your systems. This issue is expected to remain a top priority for most operations in 2025, particularly with the advancement of quantum-resistant encryption technologies.

The Smart Factory

The integration and adoption of Industrial Internet of Things (IIoT) technology, coupled with the growing prevalence of 5G communications, signal the arrival of the smart factory era. By 2025, it is anticipated that smart factories will become increasingly standard. These developments highlight the continuous advancement of sensor technology and condition monitoring, while also addressing the emerging need for remote monitoring and access, along with new considerations for worker health and safety. The evolution of the smart factory has the potential to significantly empower manufacturers, enabling them to meet the demands of mass customization effectively.

AI and Machine Learning in IIoT

Artificial intelligence and machine learning have gained widespread acceptance, with numerous industries exploring ways to incorporate these technologies into their operations. The application of these innovations within IIoT systems is evident, particularly as many manufacturers leverage AI for predictive maintenance. A significant trend in IIoT this year is the ongoing expansion of AI across all aspects of the process. These technologies enhance predictive analytics, facilitate anomaly detection, and enable automated decision-making. By processing data almost in real-time and learning from historical events, AI can yield improved outcomes. Consequently, many experts foresee that artificial intelligence may pave the way for fully autonomous factories in the near future.

Sustainability and IIoT

A notable advantage of IIoT is its potential to bolster sustainability initiatives behind the scenes. Through inter-system communication, IIoT can effectively monitor and optimize energy management, minimize waste, and enhance resource utilization. As a result, IIoT is poised to play a crucial role in green manufacturing in the years ahead. With sustainability metrics increasingly gaining importance in the marketplace, it is expected that IIoT technology will be specifically tailored for environmental monitoring.

Integration with Legacy Systems

As the Industrial Internet of Things (IIoT) gains traction in the manufacturing industry, a significant challenge lies in the integration with pre-existing systems. Effectively combining these technologies is crucial for unlocking the full potential of a smart factory, necessitating specialized knowledge to achieve optimal results. This integration is poised to be a leading trend in IoT within manufacturing as the sector progresses towards Industry 4.0 and increased digitalization. The establishment of standardized protocols and interfaces will greatly facilitate this integration, resulting in scalable and modular IIoT platforms.

Human-Machine Collaborations

The connectivity provided by IIoT paves the way for innovative human-machine collaborations. For instance, the implementation of virtual reality in manufacturing and augmented reality for maintenance tasks is made feasible through the real-time data supplied by factory systems. As the interaction between humans and machines evolves into a more reciprocal relationship, the potential for increased productivity is expected to rise. By 2025, AI assistants are anticipated to become more prevalent, with virtual colleagues and advisors becoming standard in various roles within the manufacturing sector.

Conclusion

Photonic communication presents considerable potential for the future of IIoT, providing benefits such as rapid data transmission, lower latency, and enhanced bandwidth, all of which are essential for facilitating sophisticated applications like smart factories and autonomous systems. Nevertheless, obstacles persist, including the intricacy of photonic components and the necessity for smooth integration with current electronic systems.

CHAPTER 4

Photonics in Sensing and Imaging

Photonics is one of the burgeoning research fields showing its interdisciplinary relevance for industrial sectors. It broadly encompasses the study regarding the generation, manipulation, and detection of light and resulted in a multitude of fascinating applications in domains [1,2] including spectroscopy, sensing, environment, and imaging. This chapter reviews the potential developments in spectroscopy, specifically Raman spectroscopy, a non-destructive technique employed for examining materials in various forms, X-ray diffraction technique, and ultraviolet visible spectroscopy. This is followed by examining the role of photonics in sensing utilizing platforms like optical fiber, photonic crystal, and metamaterials, along with the Internet of Things (IoT). Further, advances in imaging are discussed at terahertz frequency, as well as employing meta-designs and confocal laser scanning microscopy. This can empower a new era of innovation for photonic and industrial sectors.

Overview: Spectroscopy, Sensing, and Imaging

Spectroscopy broadly refers to the investigation of the interaction between electromagnetic radiation and materials, resulting in their characteristic signatures. Raman spectroscopy is a popular non-destructive tool to obtain the details of the vibrations of molecules, utilizing the concept of the scattering of light. Various kinds of materials [3,4] such as polymers, carbon nanotubes, and superconductors are being characterized employing this technique. In this direction, Salahioglu et al. carried out the identification of traces of lipstick [5] on different substrate materials along with probing the effects of aging on their spectral features using Raman spectroscopy. Further, the structural analysis of crystals [6], along with finding spacing among atoms, is examined with X-ray diffraction (XRD) using the phenomenon of constructive interference among X-rays scattered from lattice planes in the targeted sample. This has blossomed its applications in key areas [7-9] like the glass industry, pharmaceuticals, and inspection of minerals. Liu and coworkers [10] studied different samples of coal, followed by identification of minerals utilizing XRD. Also, ultraviolet-visible (UV-Vis) spectroscopy, a potential analytical technique, has proved useful to comprehend the propagation of light through a medium via studying absorption or transmittance. This spans its applications [11-13], starting from treatment of wastewater and measurement of concentration of substances to impurity analysis. Chen et al. [14] discussed the role of ultraviolet-visible spectroscopy toward quality control of bolete mushrooms. Such spectroscopic investigations have helped us to gain profound knowledge of the materials [15]. This has further facilitated a new realm of possibilities to develop efficient photonic sensors for interdisciplinary applications in emerging fields [16,17] of security, defense, environment, etc. A photonic sensor uses light to enable the measurement of physical parameters, including temperature, refractive index, strain, etc. In this direction, Teng et al. carried out the measurement of refractive index [18] along with monitoring the level of liquid utilizing a surface plasmon resonance (SPR) sensor consisting of polymer optical fiber. This SPR is understood as a coherent oscillation of conducting electrons on the surface of metal excited via electromagnetic radiations. Further, Chen and coworkers [19] employed fiber optic sensors in integration with smartphone technology and artificial intelligence (AI) for the purpose of remote healthcare examination, which can pave the way for Internet of Things (IOT)-based applications in medical sectors. In fiber-inspired sensors, alterations in surroundings are monitored with the help of fiber. Also, Szendrei et al. showed the humidity sensor based on fluorescence [20] using nanosheets and nanospheres. Along with this, artificial subwavelength structures as metamaterials [21,22] have gained enormous attention recently due to their potential to show properties beyond natural materials. Their properties can be tuned via controlling the permittivity and permeability of their constituents, which can be designed in various shapes [23-25]. This has offered a landscape of opportunities in sensing using metamaterials owing to the strong localization of electric fields in the neighborhood of their building elements, resulting in improved interaction between matter and light. Sreekanth et al. studied stibnite and titanium nitride-based tunable hyperbolic metamaterial biosensor [26] operating at visible frequency. Also, Reinhard et al. [27] fabricated a metamaterial-based terahertz (THz) sensor for thickness as well as index of refraction measurements in reflection mode. These research endeavors guided us and opened a new paradigm via providing potential imaging solutions at a relatively less explored terahertz frequency region [28,29] lying between microwave and infrared domains. Hu et al. used [30] terahertz scattering-type scanning near-field optical microscopy (s-SNOM) to address the heterogeneity at the level of a single cell. Also, the developments [31-33] in the field of imaging are being made employing confocal laser scanning microscopy (CLSM) and metamaterials. Here, we will discuss the advancements in photonics in line with the above-mentioned ideas for the realization of novel sensing and imaging platforms to support the global market.

Spectroscopy Techniques for Materials

Herein, we explore the developments made in the identification of various materials employing Raman spectroscopy, X-ray diffraction technique, and ultraviolet-visible spectroscopy, proving their fundamental role in photonic and related applications.

Raman Spectroscopy

Raman spectroscopy is a powerful, non-destructive technique employed for examining materials in various forms, whether solid, liquid, or thin film [34]. Based on the concept of inelastic light scattering first observed by Raman and Krishnan [35], the method examines molecular vibrations (or phonons) occurring because of the interaction of light with materials. This interaction produces a slight shift in the wavelength of the scattered component of light, revealing molecular-level information that acts like a unique signature for each substance. One of the potential features of Raman spectroscopy is its minimal requirement for sample preparation. Unlike other analytical processes involving complex processes such as drying, dissolving, or creating thin films, Raman analysis can often be performed directly on samples in their natural state. This helps to reduce the level of risks toward altering or contaminating the material during preparation [36]. The technique is utilized for tasks such as identifying unknown materials, quality control, and studying the physical structure [37, 38]. It is exploited to study various materials to obtain information about defects and bonding [39-42]. We can gain details of the total number of layers by examining the shifts observed in peaks for two-dimensional systems. Also, knowledge about underlying interactions can be obtained with examination of Raman signals [43, 44]. Polarized Raman spectroscopy is playing a key role in exploring materials for interdisciplinary applications via analyzing the orientation details of crystals [45,46]. Further advancements in photo-induced enhanced Raman spectroscopy (PIERS) allow groundbreaking applications in various fields, including nanoelectronics, forensics, biomedicine, and environmental science [47,48]. Additionally, Raman spectroscopy, which depends on temperature and pressure, allows us to examine the response of materials when their temperature and pressure change [42,43,49,50]. A diagram illustrating the Raman spectrometer and its essential components is presented via Figure 4-1. Different lasers (e.g., argon ion, krypton ion, etc.) and detectors such as charge-coupled devices (CCDs) are used commonly [34]. A laser serves as a monochromatic source of light. The mirrors are employed to direct the laser beam toward a Raman probe followed by its focus on the sample using an objective lens. The scattered light due to interaction with the sample is made to pass through edge filters via the objective lens, facilitating the blocking of the Rayleigh component and allowing of the Raman signal. These Raman signals are directed toward the spectrometer, followed by collection at the CCD detector.

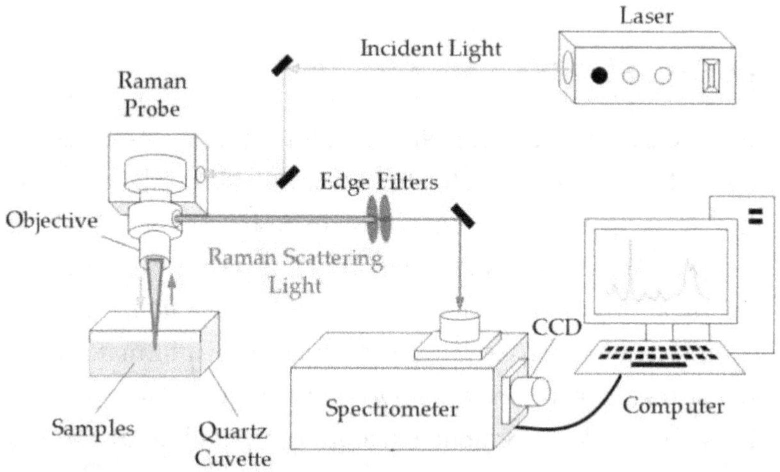

Figure 4-1. *Schematic Illustrating the Main Components of the Raman Instrument. "Reprinted from [51] © 2017 by the authors. Licensee MDPI, Basel, Switzerland, an open access article distributed under the terms and conditions of the Creative Commons Attribution (CC BY) license, http://creativecommons.org/ licenses/by/4.0/"*

Finally, the signal is processed and visualized on a computer as a Raman spectrum, displaying intensity versus Raman shift, thus providing detailed molecular and structural information regarding the sample [34,51]. The Raman effect explores the changes molecules undergo when exposed to an electric field, which then gives rise to a dipole moment. When a sample undergoes interaction with monochromatic light (having a wavelength of λ_0), the molecules within the sample find their electron cloud polarized, which leads to a dipole moment. This moment pushes the molecules to a virtual state, away from their ground state. As a result, the molecules give off energy, returning to their original state by emitting photons at various energy levels [34, 52]. These transitions primarily happen through two processes: elastic scattering and inelastic scattering. In elastic scattering, which is also called Rayleigh scattering, the wavelength (λ_s), or in other words, frequency (ν_s) of scattered light remains the same as the incident light (λ_0, ν_0). However, with inelastic scattering, the wavelength corresponding to scattered light is different from the incident light ($\lambda_s \neq \lambda_0$), which means there occurs an energy exchange between the light and the molecules, as for the case of Raman scattering. Specifically, when the incident radiations have a higher frequency than the scattered radiations ($\nu_0 > \nu_s$), it is referred to as Stokes scattering. Conversely, it is known as anti-Stokes scattering [52], as depicted in Figure 4-2, where $h\nu_0$ and $h\nu_s$ represent the energies corresponding to incident and scattered radiations, respectively. Further, details regarding the phase transitions along with structural information can be obtained via exploiting shifts in Raman modes as a function of temperature [43, 44, 53].

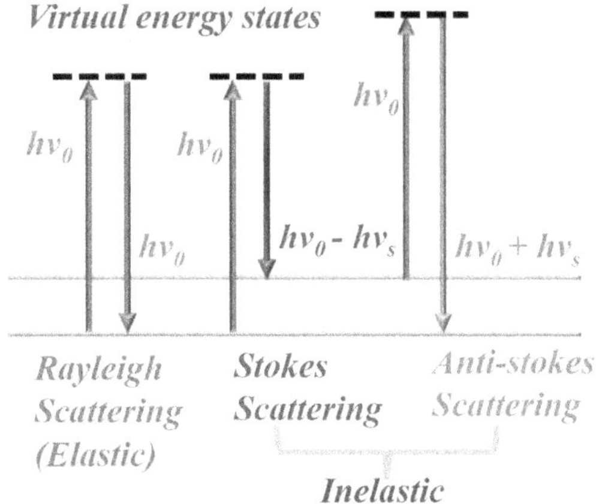

Figure 4-2. *Representation of Scattering Processes*

Also, Raman peak shifts can be utilized to examine the thermal expansion of materials and anharmonicity [43,44]. For instance, Rani et al. [43] performed temperature-dependent Raman spectroscopy on MoS_2 nanoflowers using 633 nm laser excitation across a temperature range of 173 to 498 K (Figure 4-3(a)). A red shift is observed in the E^1_{2g} and A_{1g} Raman modes of nanoflowers with increasing temperature as presented in Figure 4-3(b), while Figure 4-3(c) represents the field emission scanning electron microscopy (FESEM) image of MoS_2, which is grown as nanoflowers. This shift is primarily attributed to anharmonic effects, including phonon-phonon interactions and to thermal expansion of the crystal lattice, both of which alter the interatomic potential energy. Numerous studies show investigation of different materials, such as multiwalled carbon nanotubes and reduced graphene oxide, highlighting the role of temperature-dependent Raman spectroscopy in determining crystallite size, defects, and anharmonicity [39, 42].

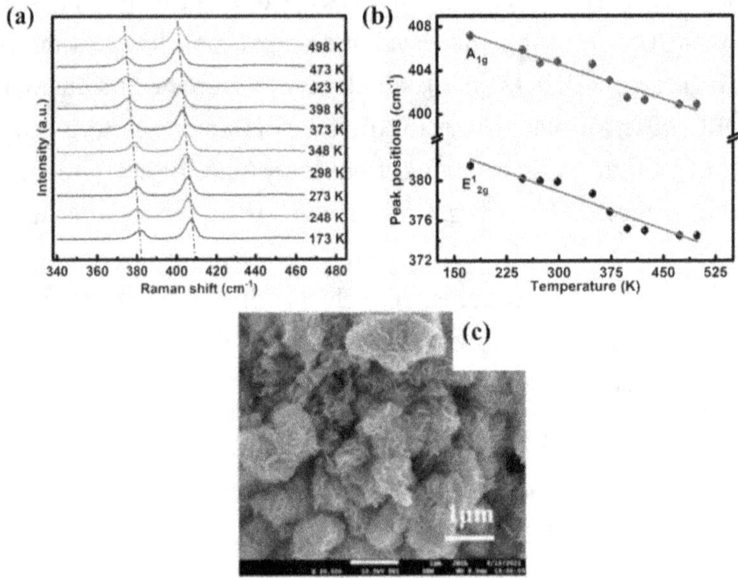

Figure 4-3. *(a) Raman Spectra of E^1_{2g} and A_{1g} Modes of MoS_2 Nanoflowers Within Temperature Range of 173-498 K. (b) Linear Fits of E^1_{2g} and A_{1g} Modes of MoS_2 Nanoflowers Using Voigtian Profile. (c) FESEM Image of MoS_2 Nanoflowers. "Reprinted (adapted) with permission from [43]. Copyright {2023} American Chemical Society"*

Further, Pawbake et al. examined the effect of pressure with magnitude up to 25 GPa corresponding to pristine as well as plasma-treated graphene [54] using Raman spectroscopy. Also, Li et al. investigated the structural aspects of molybdenum disulfide as a function of pressure employing this technique [55]. As we know, photo-treatment is a key area of research for transforming the structure and performance of materials. This has resulted in developments based on surface-enhanced Raman spectroscopy (SERS) in numerous disciplines [56-59], like environment and biomedical, further leading to techniques like photo-induced enhanced Raman scattering (PIERS) [60,61]. In 2016, research led by Ben-Jaber et al. [62] revealed that if an Ag (or Au) nanoparticle-TiO_2 substrate is treated with ultraviolet (UV) light prior to measurement, the Raman signals of target molecules become significantly enhanced.

Next, polarized Raman spectroscopy is worth noting because it delves into how light polarization affects Raman scattering. While traditional Raman spectroscopy looks at how intense the scattered light is, this approach takes a close look at the polarization features of both the light going in and the light coming out. By doing this, we get a lot of information about a substance's molecular structure, its symmetrical properties, etc. This technique also gives information on edge effects and the symmetry of vibrational modes. This detailed knowledge is key in developing novel materials [46]. It is also useful for studying how filler materials like carbon nanotubes line up in composite materials that use polymer matrices. In addition, we analyze that it helps figure out a material's crystallographic orientation using polarization data [63].

X-Ray Diffraction

X-ray diffraction (XRD) is a non-destructive, rapid, and versatile analytical technique. This method is used for analyzing crystalline materials. It requires easy sample preparation and can examine pure substances and multi-component mixtures. When an X-ray beam interacts with a crystalline material, it produces a unique diffraction pattern that shows the material's structural properties [64]. In practice, X-rays are produced using a sealed cathode ray tube, which are filtered through monochromators to ensure a single wavelength. The intensity of diffracted X-rays is recorded with different peak positions, revealing details regarding atomic arrangements in that material [65]. The underlying principle relies on the three-dimensional periodicity of the atoms inside crystalline materials. When a monochromatic beam of X-rays interacts with atomic planes (as shown in Figure 4-4), coherent scattering occurs, producing diffraction patterns governed by Bragg's Law, $n\lambda = 2d\sin\theta$, where λ is the X-ray wavelength, n shows an integer, d is interplanar spacing, and θ is the incident angle [66]. In XRD experiments, intense diffraction peaks are observed when scattering centers produce coherent, in-phase radiation.

This coherence condition means that incident and reflected beams must lie in the same plane and satisfy specific geometric constraints [67]. XRD is employed to find the crystal structure and atomic spacing as well as crystallite size. Researchers can study materials by matching diffraction patterns against the JCPDS (Joint Committee on Powder Diffraction Standards) database. This technique is widely applied in forensics, pharmaceuticals, and materials science [65]. XRD resolves crystal structures in solids and provides their structural determination [68]. Dahiya et al. [69] studied the XRD patterns of $NaNbO_3$ nanorods (NRs) and YBCO as well as YBCO: $NaNbO_3$ 2wt% composites fabricated employing the hydrothermal method and solid-state reaction.

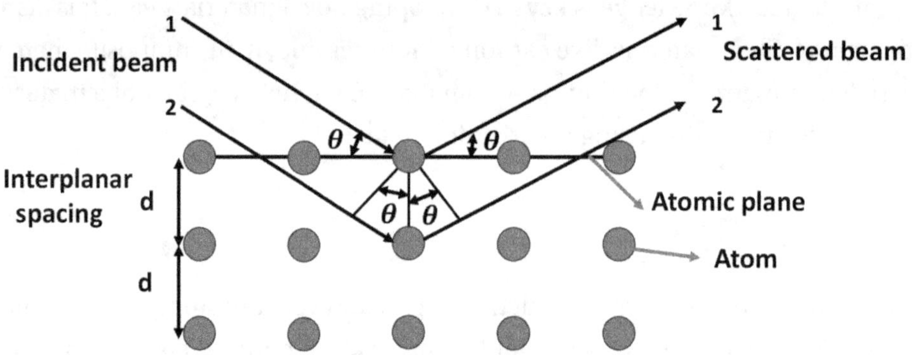

Figure 4-4. *Schematic Diagram for the Scattering of the X-Ray Beam*

It is observed that their X-ray diffraction data highlight the orthorhombic phase for YBCO and $NaNbO_3$. Also, Bindu et al. [70] employed X-ray diffraction to probe the structural features of ZnO nanoparticles. The XRD analysis confirmed the hexagonal wurtzite phase of ZnO, with distinct peak broadening highlighting the presence of nanocrystals.

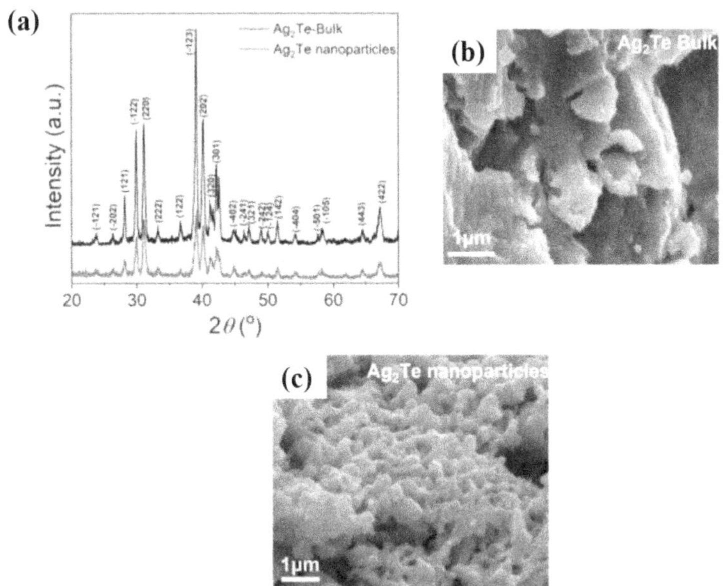

Figure 4-5. *(a) XRD Plots of Ag₂Te Nanoparticles and the Bulk Sample of Ag₂Te. (b) Morphology of Bulk Sample of Ag₂Te. (c) Morphology of Ag₂Te Nanoparticles. "Reprinted from [71], Copyright (2022), with permission from Elsevier"*

Further, Gautam et al. [71] synthesized Ag_2Te nanoparticles using the hydrothermal process and compared their crystallographic structure with the bulk sample of Ag_2Te using the X-ray diffraction (XRD) pattern (Figure 4-5(a)), showing their peaks and planes. A crystallite size of around 26 nm and 8 nm is obtained for the bulk sample of Ag_2Te and Ag_2Te nanoparticles, respectively. The details about their morphology are provided in Figure 4-5(b) for a bulk sample of Ag_2Te having features in micron size and in Figure 4-5(c) corresponding to Ag_2Te nanoparticles having the formation of a cluster.

Ultraviolet-Visible Spectroscopy

We discuss here potential technique like ultraviolet-visible (UV-Vis) spectroscopy, which is employed to evaluate the absorption of ultraviolet and visible light by the substances, hence providing details regarding their molecular structure & concentration [72]. This method is governed by the Beer-Lambert law, which states that the absorbance is directly proportional to analyte concentration and path length. Absorption spectra are plotted with respect to wavelength covering the ultraviolet and visible regions [73]. The ultraviolet-visible spectroscopy instrumentation consists of main components, which includes deuterium lamps (for emission of ultraviolet light) and tungsten-halogen lamps (for emission of light in the visible region). Monochromators are employed to isolate specific wavelengths, enabling accurate absorbance measurements. The chosen wavelength is directed through the sample. Detectors such as photomultiplier tubes and photodiodes convert the light as transmission into electrical signals impacting the sensitivity and accuracy of the analysis. For a double-beam system [74], the light is split into two paths passing through the sample cell and a reference cell. This setup improves accuracy as it helps compensate for fluctuations in light source intensity or detector sensitivity. Furthermore, the applications of UV-Vis spectroscopy can be found in analyzing the pharmaceuticals and the concentration levels of dyes, etc., thereby highlighting the technique's versatility [75,76]. Guo et al. [77] used UV-Vis spectroscopy for water quality assessment, enabling analysis of the contaminants. Also, this technique can be utilized to obtain the band gap of materials via Tauc's relation [78]. In this direction, Khosya et al. [79] studied hydrothermally grown zinc indium sulfide ($ZnIn_2S_4$) along with its coupling with polyaniline.

The band gap for $ZnIn_2S_4$ using the UV-Vis spectroscopy is found to be around 2.3 eV. Further, Hossain et al. [80] investigated the films of Cd-Zn sulfide to understand their optical response. Figure 4-6(a) displays their ultraviolet-visible spectra in terms of absorbance, where we observe that absorption increases with an increase in time of their deposition due to enhancement in the thickness of the films. Also, a blue shift in absorption edge is reported with different deposition times. These findings can be comprehended in terms of the quantum effects. The morphological details of the films, which are obtained employing a scanning electron microscope (SEM) for a deposition time of 1 hour, are given in Figure 4-6(b) with a grain size of around 150 nm, where the white and black grains represent cadmium and zinc, respectively. Overall, it can be analyzed that the advent of spectroscopy techniques has played a crucial role in accelerating the developments related to materials. We dedicate our further discussion to comprehend their utility for sensing and imaging applications.

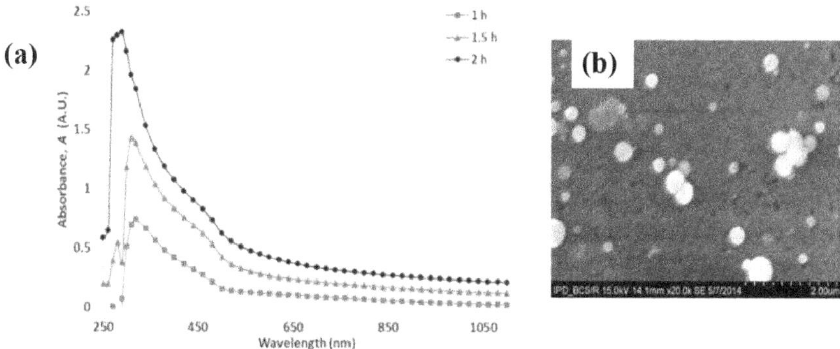

Figure 4-6. *(a) Absorbance for Cd-Zn Sulfide Films Measured Using Ultraviolet-Visible Spectroscopy Corresponding to Different Times of Deposition. (b) Scanning Electron Micrograph of the Films Corresponding to a Deposition Time of 1 Hour. "Reprinted from [80], Copyright (2016), with permission from Elsevier"*

Photonics for Sensing Applications

Sensing has emerged as a key research discipline, as we examine its direct relevance to activities of life. It has brought innovations in various sectors [81, 82] of science and engineering, where biomedical sensing utilizing photonics emerges as a pivotal research avenue for the scientific community. This integration, which sits at the nexus of cutting-edge science at its core, reveals the way light interacts with the biological world, enabling the detection and measurement of biochemicals with precision and specificity.

Sensing Employing Optical Fiber and Photonic Crystal

Biphotonic sensors are distinguished by their ability to deliver real-time, non-invasive, and accurate measurement. These sensors can monitor optical changes triggered by biological events [83] such as pathogen binding or the expression of disease biomarkers and have applications across various domains such as healthcare, environmental monitoring, etc. Biophotonic sensors leverage scientific principles to exploit optical phenomena such as fluorescence, surface plasmon resonance (SPR), Raman scattering, etc. for sensitive and specific detection. Fluorescence involves the emission of light by molecules that have absorbed electromagnetic radiation and is commonly used to tag and visualize biomolecules [84]. Pivovarenko et al. explored fluorescent probes [85], which are of great assistance in gaining biological information relevant to membranes.

Further, Raman scattering provides a molecular fingerprint of the analyte. Yang and coworkers [86] reported a sensor for glucose in integration with Raman spectroscopy and photonic crystal fiber. Surface plasmon resonance (SPR) detects changes in the index of refraction in the vicinity of a metal surface, making it ideal for real-time monitoring of molecular interactions [87]. Basically, optical sensor technology is a key tool for label-free and real-time detection of cancer biomarkers such as CD44 to allow early diagnosis. Paltusheva et al. used the ZnO-coated tip of a fiber-optic sensor capable of accurately quantifying as low as 0.8 fM CD44 concentrations [88]. The integration of these sensing modalities into portable lab-on-a-chip platforms has significantly advanced real-time and point-of-care diagnostics, enabling rapid, on-site testing [89]. In addition, Thawany et al. [90] showed a surface plasmon resonance-mediated optical fiber sensing element for carrying out sensing of multiple analytes, one of them being ferritin. This sensor is coated with gold metal along with the attachment of L-cysteine-conjugated MoS_2 in the form of nanosheets for its operation. Figure 4-7(a) represents the characteristics of the proposed sensor as transmittance for different concentrations of ferritin varied from 50 to 400, measured in ng/mL. The graph on the relevance of the PBS solution is also depicted. The spectra (Figure 4-7(a)) display a red shift in wavelength with an increase in concentration of analyte with a sensitivity of 0.024 nm per ng/mL, which can be attributed to the modulation in refractive index. Figure 4-7(b) provides details about the FESEM image of the sensor along with the interface formed due to the gold layer and nanosheets. Such study has paramount importance for medical sectors. Also, Chen et al. discussed the graphene biosensor [91] numerically, highlighting its broad significance across visible, ultraviolet, and infrared domains. In addition, photonic crystals [92] also attracted the attention of researchers and act as a testbed to control the propagation of light. These structures exhibit periodic variation of dielectric constant spatially. Rizk and coworkers [93] demonstrated a photonic crystal-based biosensor composed of silicon rods within a square lattice. The analyte, as a cancer cell, is placed in the cavity having the shape of an eye. The design has two line defects acting as output and input waveguides.

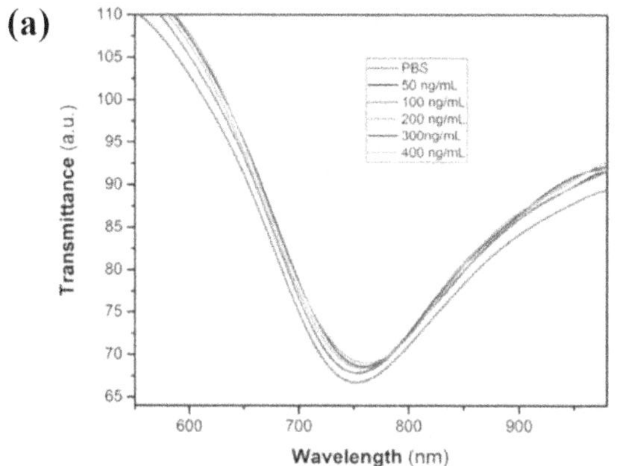
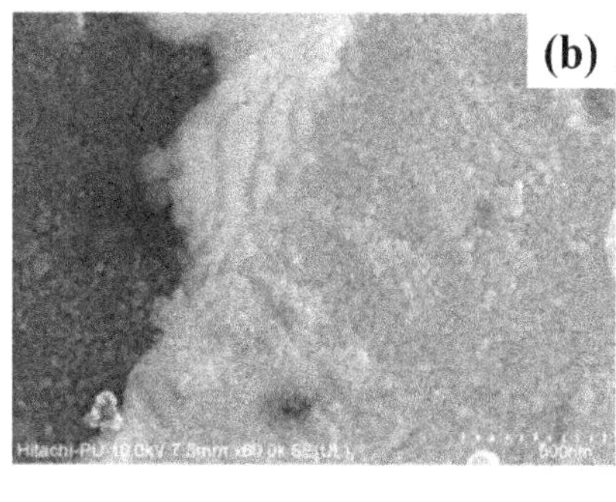

Figure 4-7. *(a) Transmittance Plots of the Optical Fiber Biosensor Corresponding to Various Concentrations of Ferritin. (b) FESEM Image of the Sensor. "Reprinted from [90], Copyright (2023), The Author(s), licensed under a Creative Commons Attribution 4.0 International License* http://creativecommons.org/licenses/by/4.0/*"*

The transmittance spectral information of the biosensor corresponding to normal and cancerous MCF-7 breast cells is given in Figure 4-8(a), representing sharp resonant characteristics.

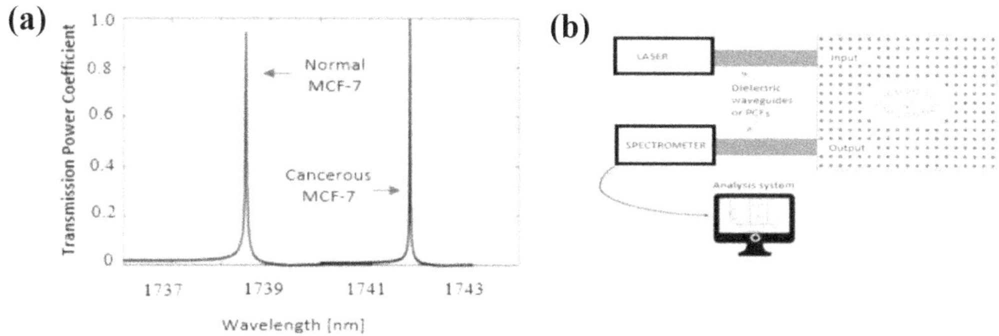

Figure 4-8. *(a) Transmittance Spectral Details of the Proposed Photonic Crystal Biosensor with Respect to Normal and Cancerous MCF-7 Cells. (b) Schematic Diagram of Entire Sensor System. "Reprinted from [93], Copyright (2025), The Author(s), licensed under a Creative Commons Attribution 4.0 International License* http://creativecommons.org/licenses/by/4.0/*"*

The schematic diagram for the used sensing system is depicted in Figure 4-8(b), where a laser is employed to excite the upper defect via a dielectric waveguide or photonic crystal fiber. Further, a spectrometer basically analyzes a signal obtained from a lower defect, followed by its further processing using a computer. This can pave the way for potential developments in next-generation sensors.

Sensing Employing Internet of Things and Metamaterials

Recently, sensors have been integrated with Industrial Internet of Things (IIoT) frameworks. Basically, the Internet of Things (IoT) is related to devices embedded with sensors and internet connectivity. This facilitates an exchange of information among them. IIoT is a specialized subset focused on industrial environments such as healthcare, energy, and logistics, aiming to optimize efficiency and safety. Farooq et al. [94] discussed ongoing trends in IIoT connecting multiple disciplines (Figure 4-9), including smart sensing elements measuring temperature, moisture, etc. Also, Bagha et al. [95] analyzed datasets from sensors employing the Internet of Things with an inclination toward precision agriculture.

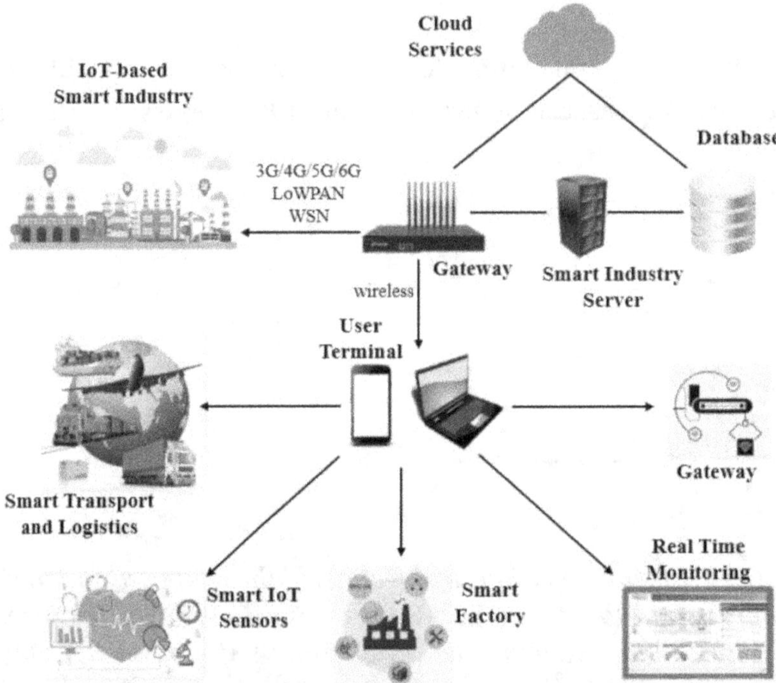

Figure 4-9. Industrial Internet of Things Frameworks Connecting Sensors with Cloud-Based Analytics. "Reprinted from [94] © 2023 by the authors. Licensee MDPI, Basel, Switzerland, an open access article distributed under the terms and conditions of the Creative Commons Attribution (CC BY) license, http:// creativecommons.org/licenses/by/4.0/"

This can help to monitor the real-time health of a crop. Next, Zha et al. [96] investigated the application of IoT in sectors of healthcare using optical fiber. The sensing element is designed with elastomer fiber sandwiched between polymethyl methacrylate fibers. The transmission of data is achieved via Bluetooth from sensor to computer along with connecting to the cloud for the next level of processing. Such efforts can open novel research avenues in remote analysis of health. Further, Souza et al. [97] emphasized the role of power over fiber technology in industrial IoT sensing applications toward modulating the energy efficiency. Also, Mishra et al. [98] discussed the progress in actualization of compact biosensors focusing on the market of digital healthcare. We infer that such developments can enable smart sensing platforms.

As we know, materials play a pivotal role in the proliferation of science and technology. With time, these are being examined to find their applications in diverse sectors [99-104], starting from medical, environment, energy harvesting, thermometry, topology, and optoelectronics. In recent times, controlling the properties of materials at subwavelength scales is a key focal point for the research community. This has driven the advances in metamaterials, which are artificially realized composites having subwavelength dimensions [105,106]. Their two-dimensional frameworks are known as metasurfaces [107,108], which can be realized using lithography processes. The idea of exploring the artificial structure has a long history, when Indian researcher Bose used the twisted jute [109] for analyzing the optical twist of the plane of polarization. With time, theoretical and experimental advancements [110-112] made by Veselago, Pendry, and Smith in the realization of metamaterials have opened new avenues of research. Further, metamaterials have shown numerous phenomena [113-117] so far, including bandwidth enhancement, beam shaping, extraordinary transmission, gain modulation, slow light, etc. Also, these have been designed in numerous passive as well as active tunable configurations [118-120], paving the way for building modulators, sensors, filters, flexible devices, etc. Out of these, metamaterials have enabled attractive possibilities in the interdisciplinary sector of sensing due to their sharp resonant features and are in great demand these days. In this direction, Hamdi et al. utilized a machine learning-based method [121] to detect cancer cells employing a graphene metamaterial sensor.

Further, Singh and coworkers employed a microwave metamaterial sensor [122] for the agriculture sector to measure moisture in almond kernels. Also, Barri et al. fabricated a concrete matrix with metamaterial for civil engineering applications [123]. A sensor converts the physical change happening in its vicinity into a measurable output signal. Plenty of strategies [124-127], like Fano, toroidal, bound state in continuum, and plasmonic metamaterials, are being examined across the electromagnetic spectrum for sensing. To utilize the potential of metastructures, Xin et al. investigated a biosensor [128] employing a terahertz metasurface. The design is made up of aluminum-based resonators with split gaps (Figure 4-10(a)), which are fabricated on polyimide as a substrate using ultraviolet lithography. Figure 4-10(b) shows the dual-band sensing performance of the device in terms of transmission corresponding to different concentrations of roxithromycin, which is an antibiotic, varying from 50-250 in units of ng/μL.

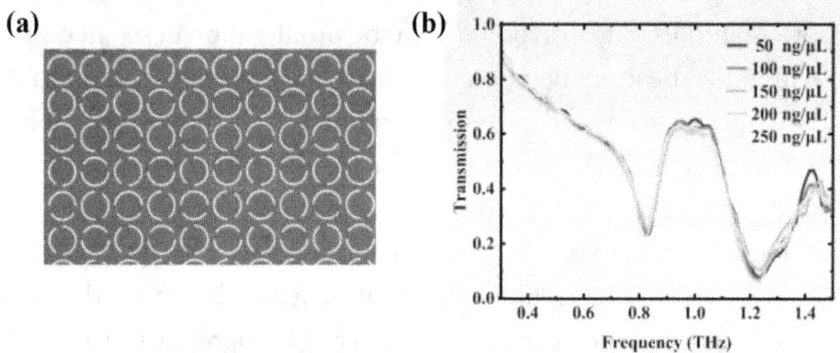

Figure 4-10. *(a) Array of Metamaterial Sensors with Dotted Lines Showing Single Unit Cell. (b) Transmission Plots as a Function of Frequency for Various Concentrations of Roxithromycin Molecules. "Reprinted from [128], Copyright (2025), with permission from Elsevier"*

The lower and higher resonances reveal a frequency shift from 0.829 to 0.820 THz and 1.232 to 1.215 THz, respectively because of modulation in dielectric constant due to the vicinity of the analyte. Further, we observe that transmission shows a decreasing trend with concentration due to enhancement in signal absorption. These findings can guide clinical sectors. Also, Bui and coworkers studied multilayered metamaterial design [129] based on silver and silicon, which is fabricated on sapphire as a substrate for the detection of protein molecules such as bovine serum albumin (Figure 4-11(a)). The transmittance behavior of the device is examined numerically with the CST Microwave Studio simulator. Figure 4-11(b) represents the tailoring of transmittance obtained via simulations with resonance frequency (ω_0) of the considered protein molecules. The spectrum shows an enhancement in magnitude of signal when resonance frequency is varied till 3.8×10^{13} rad/s. This number basically corresponds to a higher resonant frequency of the proposed metamaterial.

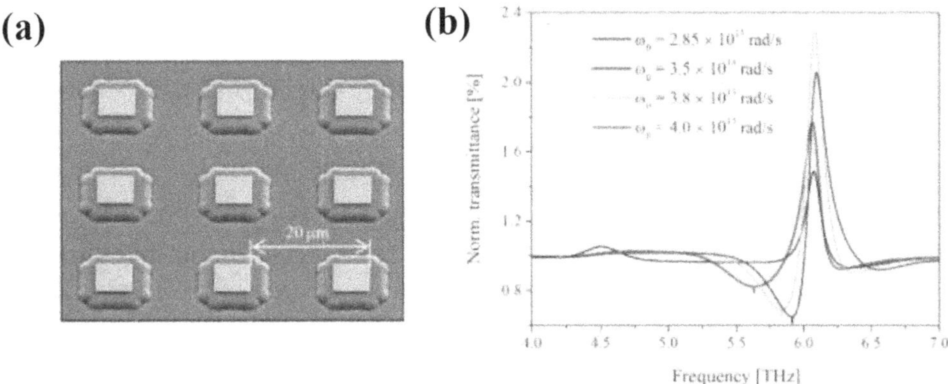

Figure 4-11. *(a) Fabricated Metamaterial Sample. (b) Variation in Transmittance with Resonance Frequency of Bovine Serum Albumin Molecules. "Reprinted from [129], Copyright (2016), The Author(s), licensed under a Creative Commons Attribution 4.0 International License* http://creativecommons.org/licenses/by/4.0/*"*

Thereafter, the transmittance starts decreasing on being frequency-tuned beyond this value. These results can be comprehended in terms of effective coupling between the resonance of the metamaterial and the vibration of the protein molecule and can pave the way for advancements in non-destructive testing of biomolecules. Along with this, we observe that metamaterials have shown appreciable innovations in other cross-disciplinary areas. Rahman et al. fabricated an antenna on Rogers RT-5880 as a substrate for IoT applications [130]. This antenna is loaded with a metasurface and metamaterials toward improving gain, efficiency, and isolation, respectively, and operates in microwave and millimeter wave frequency domains. Thus, it can be anticipated that metamaterials have potential to open new paradigms in sensing for multifaceted applications [131-134].

Photonics for Imaging Applications

The representation of the appearance of any specimen broadly refers to the imaging. Numerous compelling research outputs are being reported in the field of photonics with a focus on imaging applications [135, 136]. This is further elaborated with examples mentioned below.

Imaging at Terahertz Frequency

In the last few years, we see appreciable growth by utilizing THz radiations in the sectors [137-139] of spectroscopy, imaging, quality control, etc. This can be attributed to the fascinating aspects of THz radiation, like their non-ionizing nature and penetration through plastics. To mention, terahertz (THz) imaging-based systems have become potential tools to probe the chemical and material composition of samples, driving the evolution of THz science as a distinct and expanding discipline. Despite their transformative potential, THz imaging systems face significant engineering challenges, particularly in achieving a broad imaging area with fine spatial details. For instance, at 300 μm wavelength (equivalent to 1 THz frequency), the far-field spatial information is fundamentally limited by the Rayleigh diffraction principles, yielding a resolution limit of ~180 μm in vacuum [140]. This constraint inherently limits the space-bandwidth product of current THz imaging systems. In principle, image resolution depends on high-spatial frequency components in the scattered wavefront from a sample. However, during free-space propagation, these high-spatial frequency components diffract at larger angles than their low-spatial frequency counterparts, causing the diffraction pattern to extend beyond the field of view (FOV) of the detector [141]. The finite numerical aperture (NA) of an optical imaging system further compounds this issue by failing to capture the high-spatial frequency information, thereby restricting resolution [142]. To address the drawbacks inherent in standard THz imaging, a novel approach, scattering-type raster scanning of an imaging sample, integrated with near-field microscopy (also called s-SNOM), has been introduced [143]. This innovative methodology combines atomic force microscopy (AFM) with state-of-the-art THz time-domain spectroscopy, allowing hyperspectral imaging and sensing with nanoscale structural details in imaging samples. By exceeding the diffraction limit, this technique enables the investigation of low-energy molecular vibrational dynamics with remarkable sensitivity. Figure 4-12(a) shows the schematic of the THz s-SNOM experimental configuration designed for nanoscale-resolved, broadband spectroscopic imaging, containing a tungsten probe (tip diameter ~600 nm) employed for tapping-mode AFM and near-field detection. The region of interest (dashed black box) comprises a pressed pellet of crystalline lactose homogeneously mixed with high-density polyethylene (HDPE). The lactose component includes a mixture of two stereoisomeric forms: α-lactose (≥95% w/w) and β-lactose (≤4% w/w) anomers. As a compelling case study, the capabilities of such a platform are illustrated through the spectroscopic differentiation of a binary mixture consisting of two crystalline stereoisomers, the α- and β-anomers of lactose, a common disaccharide, as presented in Figure 4-12(b). The experiment successfully produces spatially resolved maps of the broadband complex dielectric function, facilitating the identification of localized intermolecular vibrational signatures unique to each anomer (Figure 4-12(c)). Such ability highlights the THz-SNOM potential for ultra-sensitive & broadband spectroscopic fingerprinting of biomolecules and organic crystals within heterogeneous mixtures.

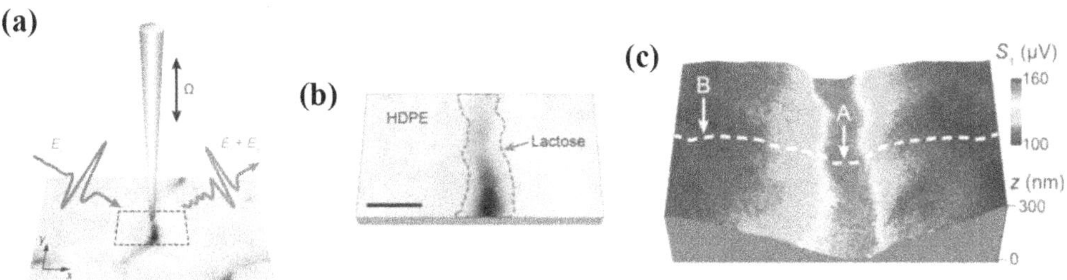

Figure 4-12. *Terahertz s-SNOM Imaging Platform for Spectroscopic Imaging of Biomolecular Fingerprints. "Reprinted from [143], Copyright (2019), The Author(s), licensed under a Creative Commons Attribution 4.0 International License http://creativecommons.org/licenses/by/4.0/"*

Moreover, the demonstrated method holds promise toward trace-level impurity analysis in organic crystalline systems, particularly in identifying isomeric and polymorphic variants that can significantly impact the performance metrics of organic electronic devices, such as thin-film transistors. Further, in THz near-field imaging direction, the **air-plasma dynamic aperture** technique has attracted great attention as a non-invasive, optically controlled approach [144]. A schematic of the experimental configuration for the air-plasma-based imaging system is shown in Figure 4-13(a), which employs a synthetic aperture where two ultrashort pulses are precisely focused along orthogonal optical paths to create intersecting air-plasma filaments, referred to as Plasma1 and Plasma2, adjacent to the sample surface. Two orthogonally intersecting femtosecond laser-induced air plasmas create a temporary cross-filament above the sample, which functions as a dynamic aperture that shapes the incoming THz beam, enabling precise, localized interaction with the surface. The THz signal reflected from the sample is then captured and analyzed. The inset shows how the plasma filaments, THz beam, and sample interface align in space. This technique offers quasi-subwavelength spatial resolution due to the proximity of the air plasma aperture to the sample interface. The non-contact setup protects fragile materials from physical damage while delivering high-resolution, near-field THz measurements. Additionally, the technique is inherently compatible with encapsulated samples as long as the encapsulation is transparent to both THz radiation and the control laser beams. Its capability to support both transmission and reflection modalities within a single framework further enhances its versatility, expanding its range of potential applications. Figure 4-13(b) illustrates the metallic resolution test target of three chromium (Cr) stripes deposited on a glass substrate as a relevant case example.

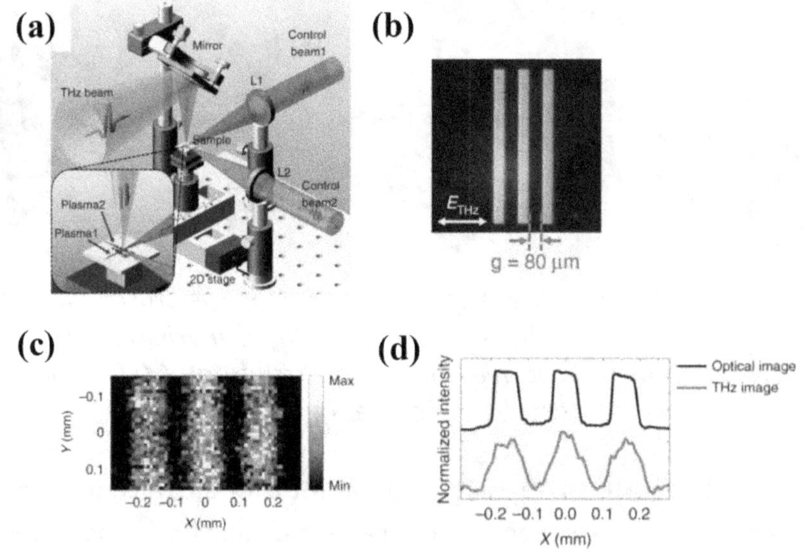

Figure 4-13. *Air-Plasma Dynamic Aperture-Based Terahertz Near-Field Microscopy. "Reprinted from [144], Copyright (2022), The Author(s), licensed under a Creative Commons Attribution 4.0 International License* http:// creativecommons.org/licenses/by/4.0/"

The separation between the two Cr stripes has been kept at 80 μm, serving as a benchmark for lateral resolution assessment. A near-field image of the test target at a frequency of 1.35 THz is shown in Figure 4-13(c), and its intensity profile along the X-direction is illustrated in Figure 4-13(d), demonstrating the subwavelength resolution obtained in THz images. Despite these merits, there remain scopes toward more refinement. For example, integrating advanced diffractive optical elements or programmable metasurfaces could offer enhanced control over the wavefront of the control beam, potentially allowing for the creation of fully three-dimensional micro-plasma apertures. Such improvements would enable further miniaturization of the plasma aperture, enhancing spatial resolution. Furthermore, the current imaging platform's low signal-to-noise ratio (SNR) impacts image reconstruction fidelity and contrast. Future advances could take advantage of high-efficiency THz emitters, such as organic nonlinear crystals, lithium niobate, or spintronic-based sources, promising improved spectral power and bandwidth.

By combining these hardware advancements with computational techniques, including advanced digital image reconstruction and denoising algorithms, it seems to be feasible to significantly boost the extraction and interpretation of near-field information scattered from the samples. As we know, the multiple scattering phenomenon of light is ubiquitous and can be found everywhere, such as in the opaqueness of fog, milk, and clouds. These media are structurally complex, composed of countless particles that scatter light in all directions and scramble electromagnetic waves, giving rise to complex light transport dynamics [145,146]. Achieving wave control in such scattering media represents a significant contemporary challenge in modern physics. Contrary to the conventional notion that multiple scattering leads to an irreversible loss of information, recent advancements have unveiled a more nuanced perspective [147]. As per its deterministic spatiotemporal dynamics, the scattering can be harnessed for wave manipulation, allowing the tailoring of desired transmitted field distributions by structuring the impinging wavefront on the scattering medium. This paradigm shift transforms the inherent complexity of scattering into an exploitable resource, enabling applications such as imaging through highly disordered media. To overcome the distortions induced by scattering, researchers have developed wavefront-shaping techniques facilitating the precise control of light propagation [148]. Feedback-based optimization of input probing wavefront has emerged as a potential strategy that uses spatial light modulator devices and iteratively refines the output [149]. As an alternative option, deterministic methods have been implemented to identify the scattering transfer matrix by decomposing it into an orthogonal set of wavefronts. While wavefront shaping has effectively gained control over wave propagation through the scattering media, simultaneously controlling the spatiotemporal behavior of ultrashort pulses through scattering media remains challenging [150].

In this context, an emerging technique that exploits the capability to detect the single-cycle oscillations in a THz ultrashort pulse opens the door for scattering-assisted analysis and provides unprecedented insights into how scattering affects the temporal and spectral characteristics of the wave. This could be achieved by identifying the optimal impinging spatiotemporal field distribution that produces a targeted output field transmitted through a scattering medium. However, the limited availability of spatial light modulator devices at the THz spectral range hinders the capability to modulate the probing field on the scattering samples. To address this limitation, a novel way is explored that leverages the shaping of an optical beam using a nonlinear crystal, a method introduced under the paradigm of time-domain nonlinear ghost imaging

[151]. Within this framework, any optical waveform shaped by a standard spatial light modulator device can be directly converted to spatiotemporal THz patterns. Therefore, exploiting the nonlinear quadratic process in a $\chi^{(2)}$ crystal, the relationship between the shaped optical intensity and THz field is established, allowing for precise THz field control by simply manipulating the spatial profile of the optical waveform. A key advantage of this method is the potential to achieve spatial resolutions for THz patterns well below the standard operative wavelength, as the resolution is determined by the diffraction limit of the optical beam rather than the THz wavelength. The deterministic space-time wave synthesis in random media fundamentally revolves around illuminating media with spatially orthogonal patterns and recording their corresponding transmitted and scattered wavefields. It means that a deterministic framework for sufficient complexity in media allows a unique association of the transmitted spatiotemporal field with each illumination pattern.

This association arises because the transformation between the input and output fields is linear and invertible. Thus, by recording the spatiotemporal output for a set of orthogonal input patterns, one can project an arbitrary observed scattered field onto this basis set. Such projections enable the reconstruction of the input field as a linear combination of the corresponding orthogonal input functions. Notably, this method does not rely on statistical models or specific portions of the scattered field (e.g., ballistic or diffusive components). Instead, it leverages the inherent capability of a scattering medium to act as a linear, invertible combinatory system [152]. Following this, the theoretical understanding was developed initially to demonstrate the nonlinear conversion of ultrafast, wavefront-shaped optical light into structured THz radiation [153]. Such structured THz radiation is then employed to probe complex media positioned in close proximity to the nonlinear crystal. As illustrated in Figure 4-14(a), the deterministic methodology involves projecting a series of Walsh-Hadamard patterns onto the media and capturing the transmitted spatiotemporal fields using a near-field THz imager. Through this, the complex-valued elements of the broadband transfer matrix are resolved and characterized by distinct spectral correlations. The optimal input wavefront can be calculated using constrained inversion techniques, which enable spatiotemporal localization of the waveform at the output of media and provide deterministic spatial and spectral control over the transmitted THz field. Figure 4-14(b) illustrates an example of single-focus generation, where the entire source spectrum is concentrated at a single output location.

Similarly, Figure 4-14(c) demonstrates the creation of multiple foci. Additionally, Figure 4-14(d) showcases multiple foci for two different spectrum pass filters. In the experimental scenarios, THz spatial light modulation has predominantly relied on indirect and cost-ineffective methods, including the use of metallic masks [154, 155], carrier-based masks [156-159], metamaterial-based modulation [160-162], electro-optic [163], nonlinear [164], and spintronic-based [165] modulation. However, available diffraction-limited patterns provided by these techniques cannot access a significant diversity of propagating modes in scattering samples [166]. To address this limitation, a knife-edge mechanism [167] has been implemented to generate various impinging patterns. As a proof of concept, transfer matrix retrieval and deterministic imaging through scattering media have been demonstrated experimentally, as shown via Figure 4-14(e, f). It is shown that THz wavefront modulation can be achieved by moving a one-dimensional knife-edge placed at the input facet of the random media, and corresponding spatiotemporal field measurements could be employed to retrieve the broadband transfer matrix of the scatterers. Since this method does not utilize any statistical characterization of the scatterer and instead relies on the principle of superposition, the benchmark experiment successfully demonstrated its full operation with broadband waveforms. Such capability allows us to obtain the full spectrum of the transmitted waveform, essentially revealing its spectral fingerprint. This particular technique is currently the focus of ongoing research, and we believe that such a THz microscopy approach opens up new possibilities for exploring complex media, especially scattering microstructures such as cells or microorganisms.

Metamaterials for Imaging and Confocal Laser Scanning Microscopy

Further, new research avenues such as metamaterials emerged as potential candidates recently for wavefront engineering in terms of amplitude, polarization, and phase, bringing advances in imaging. This has resulted in novel design strategies to overcome the diffraction limit. Li et al. studied the computational as well as non-computational aspects [168] of metamaterial-based imaging. A plenty of metadevices [169-171], such as polarizers, lens, filters, etc. have been shown via various research groups across the electromagnetic spectrum, which can spur new innovations in imaging.

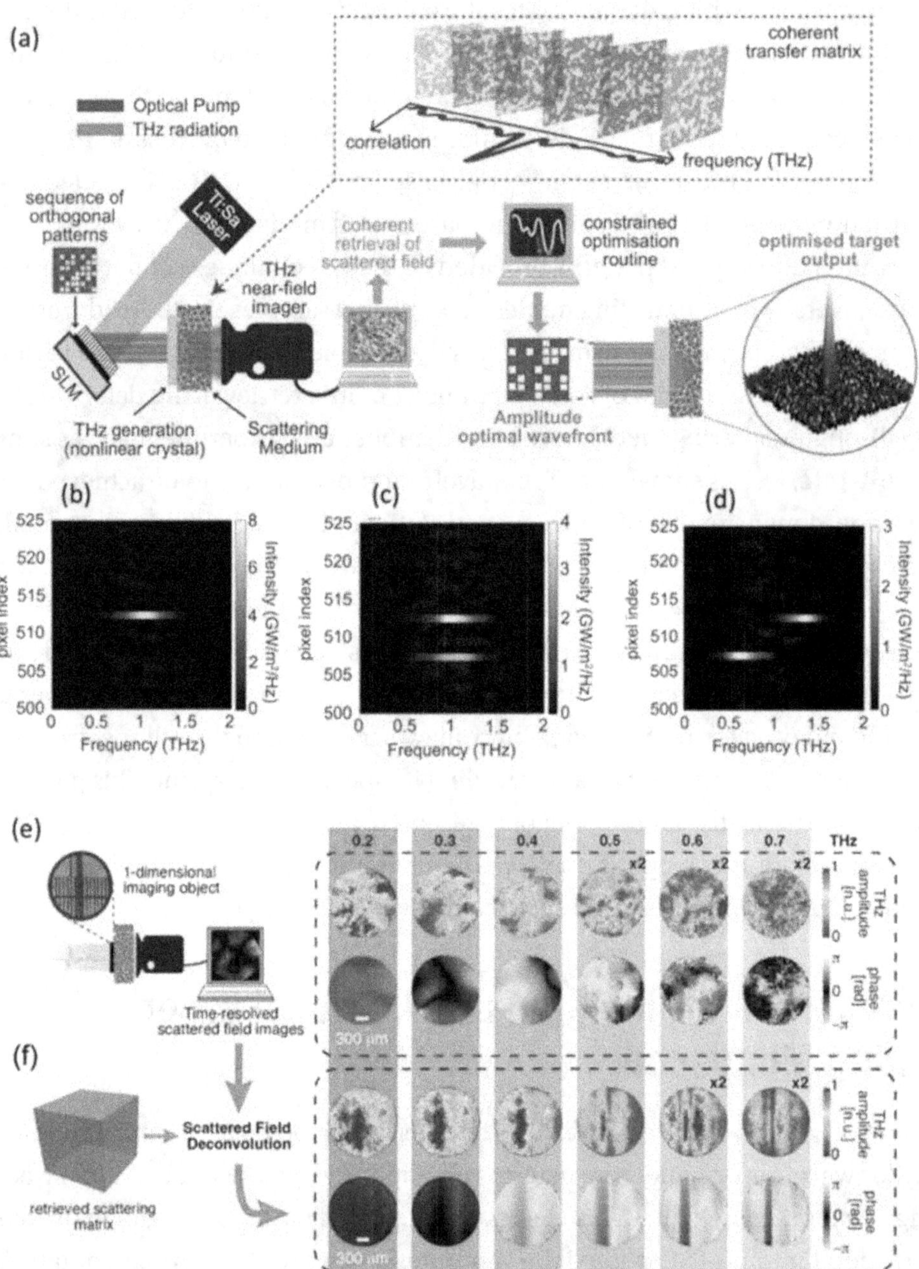

Figure 4-14. *Deterministic THz Focusing and Imaging Through Scattering Media. "Subfigures (a,b,c,d) are reprinted (adapted) with permission from [153]. Copyright © 2022 The Authors. Published by American Chemical Society, licensed under CC-BY 4.0" and "Subfigures (e,f) are reprinted from [167], Copyright (2025), The Author(s), licensed under a Creative Commons Attribution 4.0 International License* http://creativecommons.org/licenses/by/4.0/"

Hossain et al. fabricated an antenna in a three-dimensional configuration in integration with metamaterial (Figure 4-15(a)) to demonstrate the imaging of tumors [172] in the brain. The metamaterial is realized as a spider net shape and measured with a power network analyzer at GHz frequencies with the maximum value of efficiency of 94%. This can be of great help to bring developments in medical sectors. Further, Lio et al. [173] employed deep machine learning (Figure 4-15(b)) methodology to examine molybdenum disulfide-based metamaterial in combination with liquid crystal. The proposed design operates at 1550 nm and can be advantageous for light detection and ranging applications. The color combinations in Figure 4-15(b) represent the various orientations of liquid crystal molecules as a function of externally applied voltage.

In addition, Xie et al. [174] utilized labyrinthine unit cells for obtaining acoustic metamaterial-based holograms (Figure 4-15(c)). These are fabricated with the help of the 3D printing method. Such outcomes are of paramount significance in fields of trapping of particles and imaging for interdisciplinary applications.

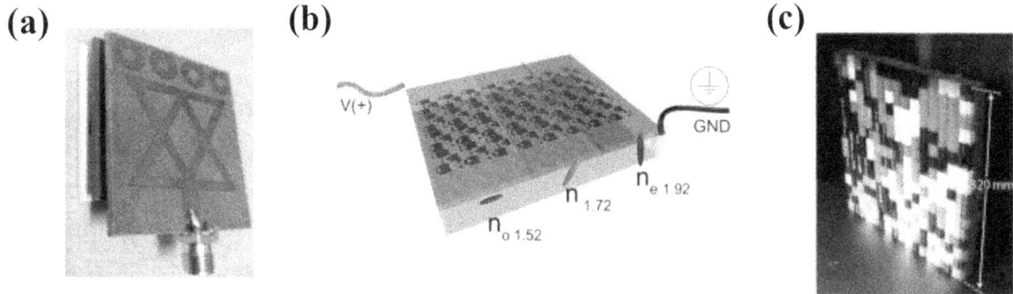

Figure 4-15. *Metadesign Strategies Helpful for Imaging. (a) Antenna in Combination with Metamaterial. (b) Metamaterial with Liquid Crystals. (c) Acoustic Metamaterial-Based Hologram. "Subfigure (a) is reprinted from [172], Copyright (2022), The Author(s), licensed under a Creative Commons Attribution 4.0 International License http://creativecommons.org/licenses/ by/4.0/." "Subfigure (b) is reprinted from [173], © 2021 by the authors. Licensee MDPI, Basel, Switzerland, an open access article distributed under the terms and conditions of the Creative Commons Attribution (CC BY) license, http:// creativecommons.org/licenses/by/4.0/" and "Subfigure (c) is reprinted from [174], Copyright (2016), The Author(s), licensed under a Creative Commons Attribution 4.0 International License http://creativecommons.org/licenses/by/4.0/"*

Further, microscopy techniques such as confocal laser scanning microscopy (CLSM) are widely employed for numerous applications because they can provide 3D images of the specimens under consideration. In this technique, at a time only one focal plane is analyzed, resulting in the image of that plane, while eliminating the light from other planes to get a good contrast image [175].

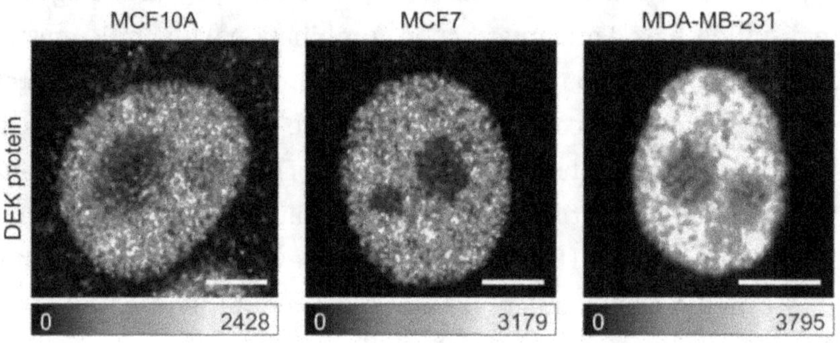

Figure 4-16. *Fluorescence Images Showing the Nuclear Distribution for the DEK Protein in Breast Cancer Cells such as MCF10A (Left Panel), MCF7 (Middle Panel), and MDA-MB-231 (Right Panel) Employing Confocal Microscopy. "Reprinted from [178], Copyright (2023), The Author(s), licensed under a Creative Commons Attribution 4.0 International License http://creativecommons.org/licenses/by/4.0/"*

Panchal et al. explored CLSM to carry out optical imaging in the context of graphene [176]. Also, Kumar and team members [177] investigated the morphological features of screen-printed film with this technique. In addition, Pierzynska-Mach et al. [178] utilized fluorescence confocal microscopy for the investigation of breast cancer cells. The nuclear distribution regarding DEK protein is being analyzed as shown in Figure 4-16, where the largest intensity of fluorescence signal is observed for MDA-MB-231 cells (right panel) in comparison to MCF7 (middle panel) and MCF10A (left panel) cells, highlighting the advanced phase of cancer evolution. Overall, we witness fascinating research developments in the key sectors of sensing and imaging serving as a guide for the photonic industry.

Future Perspectives

Despite the immense potential shown by photonic sensors, they might face several challenges, including issues with signal stability, biocompatibility, environmental interference, etc. The integration of wireless modules often requires precision fabrication and standardization, which can drive up costs. Additionally, ensuring accuracy and repeatability under real-world conditions remains a significant hurdle. Looking to the future, the advancement of sensors will likely focus on further miniaturization, measuring multiple parameters, integration with artificial intelligence-powered analysis, and monitoring phase shifts in signals along with shifts in frequency in metamaterial sensors and Internet of Things platforms. Innovations in nanophotonic and biocompatible materials along with cost-effective fabrication techniques will be critical in developing the next generation of biosensors enabling real-time, personalized, and decentralized diagnostics for both healthcare and industrial sectors. Further, the future of THz imaging is poised to be shaped by synergistic advancements in hardware innovation, computational algorithms, and novel physical principles.

Despite its great potential, the widespread adoption of THz imaging remains hindered by several persistent limitations. Low-power THz sources restrict the achievable signal strength, particularly in reflection mode and through-thickness measurements. At the same time, low-sensitivity detectors compromise the dynamic range and fidelity of the acquired images, especially in broadband or time-resolved configurations. Additionally, though beneficial for compressive imaging and cost reduction, single-pixel detection schemes suffer from slow acquisition times and poor scalability for high-throughput applications. Also, there is strong absorption of THz radiation by water, which limits penetration depth in biological samples and introduces spectral distortions that obscure material signatures.

To overcome these challenges, a growing emphasis is being placed on near-field imaging methodologies, such as s-SNOM and air-plasma dynamic aperture techniques, both of which provide subwavelength resolution and minimal sample perturbation. In highly scattering media, wavefront shaping and transfer matrix reconstruction, facilitated by nonlinear optical-to-THz conversion, offer new avenues for deterministic imaging through optically opaque structures. These advances will be further empowered by computational enhancements, including AI-driven reconstructions, digital denoising, and adaptive sampling strategies, all of which aim to mitigate signal-to-noise ratio (SNR) limitations and reduce data acquisition overhead. Emerging technologies such as spintronic THz emitters, organic nonlinear crystals, programmable metasurfaces, and fast electro-optic modulators hold promise for addressing core limitations in source power and wavefront control.

Also, advances in confocal microscopy in integration with a temperature-controlled platform can pave the way for interdisciplinary pursuits. As these capabilities mature, the imaging sector is expected to transition from proof-of-concept experiments to robust, high-resolution, and spectrally sensitive platforms suitable for real-world applications in biomedical diagnostics, chemical sensing, security screening, and non-destructive evaluation of materials.

Conclusion

Here, we have discussed significant advances in materials and photonics broadly in spectroscopy, sensing, and imaging. This will help in addressing the ongoing challenges leading to novel research possibilities for academicians and industrialists.

Acknowledgments

We sincerely acknowledge the valuable contributions of Sonam Rani (Department of Physics, Guru Jambheshwar University of Science and Technology, Hisar, Haryana, India), Mamta Dahiya (Department of Physics, Indian Institute of Technology Delhi, New Delhi, India), Vinita Sharma (Department of Environmental Science and Engineering, Guru Jambheshwar University of Science and Technology, Hisar, Haryana, India), Naveen Kumar Baskaran (Department of Computer Science and Engineering, Faculty of Engineering and Technology, JAIN (Deemed-to-be University), Bengaluru, India), Vivek Kumar (Laboratoire Kastler Brossel, ENS-Université PSL, CNRS, Sorbonne Université, Collège de France, Paris, France), and Sushil Kumar (Om Sterling Global University, Hisar, Haryana, India) to help in preparing the content.

CHAPTER 5

Photonics in Data Processing and Analytics

Bringing photonics into the Industrial Internet of Things (IIoT) is a real game-changer for how we handle data. Instead of relying on slower, energy-hungry electronics, industries can now tap into the speed, bandwidth, and parallel power of light itself. That means massive datasets can be processed and analyzed in real time, all while using less energy. In this chapter, we'll walk through how photonics reshapes IIoT, from the latest applications and the advantages it has over traditional systems to the key technologies driving it, real-world case studies, and where the future is headed.

Photonics and IIoT Primer

IIoT systems are exploding in scale, and with that comes a flood of data from countless sensors and machines. Traditional electronics are starting to hit their limits—they struggle with speed, bandwidth, and energy demands. That's where photonics steps in. By using light instead of electricity, photonics makes it possible to move and process data at incredible speeds while consuming far less power. In this chapter, we'll explore how photonics is changing the game for IIoT: from its advantages over electronics to the latest applications, breakthrough technologies, real-world case studies, and where the future is headed. Figure 5-1 gives us a glimpse of how light moves through a photonic crystal. It's a simple image, but it captures the essence of why photonics is so powerful. In today's industrial world, sensors are everywhere, and they're generating an overwhelming amount of data. Traditional electronics are starting to buckle under the sheer speed and scale of it all. Photonics, on the other hand, uses light to transmit and process information, making it faster, more efficient, and far less energy-hungry.

Dr. P. Sharan et al., *Photonics in Industrial IoT: Transforming Manufacturing and Beyond*,
https://doi.org/10.1007/979-8-8688-2694-8_5

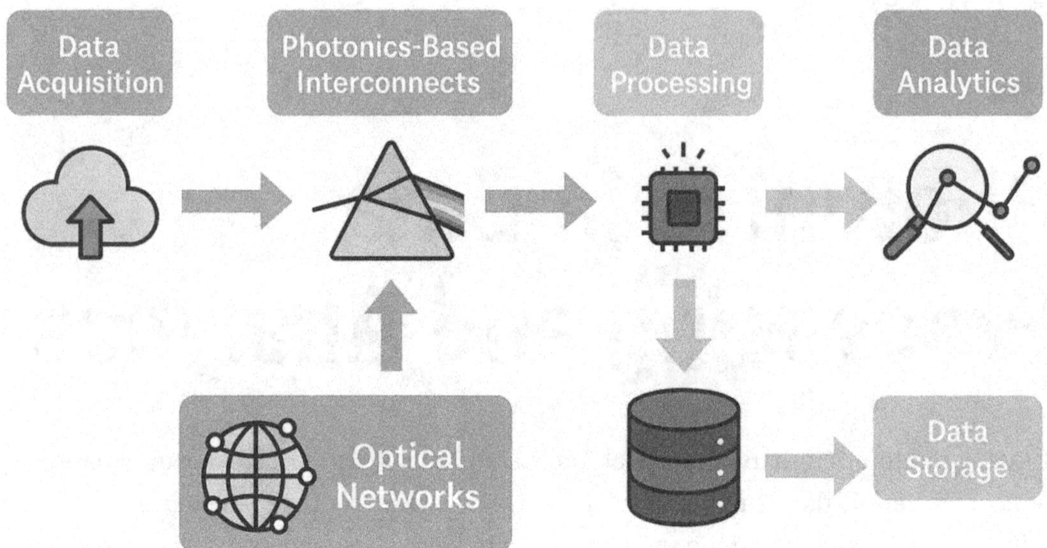

Figure 5-1. *Photonics in Data Processing and Analytics*

Using light (photons) rather than electricity (electrons), photonics transmits, processes, and analyzes data at ultra-high speeds and low power. As shown in Figure 5-1, it combines into the data workflow as follows.

Raw data is captured by sensors and IoT devices; this is usually sent optically over fiber networks. Use of lasers, modulators, and waveguides—photonics-based interconnects—rapidly move data between hardware components (CPUs, GPUs, memory).

Particularly beneficial in artificial intelligence and high-throughput analytics because of their parallelism and bandwidth, photonic processors or photonic-assisted computing units handle challenging operations. Optical interconnections allow high-speed access to storage systems, enabling faster read/write cycles and lower latency.

Data Analytics: High-performance systems, frequently aided by photonic interconnects that speed up data transfer between nodes, are used to analyze the processed data.

All layers are supported by optical networks, which allow cloud infrastructure, edge computing, and distributed systems to function with the least amount of latency and energy consumption.

Literature Review

As IIoT systems became more complex, electronics started showing cracks in their ability to keep up. Researchers began turning to photonics, and over the past decade, the field has taken off. Early work focused on optical interconnects and silicon photonics—laying the groundwork for faster, more efficient data pipelines. Then came neuromorphic networks and photonic AI accelerators, which opened the door to predictive maintenance and smarter industrial intelligence. More recently, quantum photonics and photonics-enabled edge computing have pushed the boundaries even further, promising secure communications and lightning-fast analytics right at the edge of industrial networks. Together, these advances show a clear trend: photonics isn't just a niche technology anymore—it's becoming essential for scaling IIoT.

The integration of photonic technologies with data systems has advanced significantly in the last ten years. Integrated optical circuits, photonic memory, and optical interconnects have become promising elements for high-throughput computing settings.

A slow but revolutionary change in computing and sensing technologies is reflected in the development of photonics in data processing and analytics. Using a carefully selected list of academic and commercial sources arranged by reference number, this review charts the evolution of photonics research and applications over time. Every contribution is examined contextually, highlighting its contribution to the development of a thorough knowledge of integrated, computational, and applied photonics.

Recent research shows how photonics is increasingly being used to speed up computation and optimize data processing. By lowering latency and energy consumption in industrial data analytics, photonic accelerators perform noticeably better than traditional electronics, as highlighted by Petit and Sieffermann (2021). In order to indirectly inform design strategies for human-photonics interaction systems, they used photonics in sensory analysis to investigate the contextual influence of the environment on consumer preferences [1]. The significance of photonic accelerators for data processing was emphasized by Kitayama et al. (2019), who demonstrated their benefits in parallelism and latency [2] computing frameworks, which use photonic processors to improve IIoT intelligence and predictive maintenance applications [3].

Fu et al. (2023) promoted co-design paradigms for optimal intelligent systems, highlighting the convergent evolution of photonics and AI. By facilitating real-time data processing and high-speed analytics, they illustrated how photonics is essential to smart manufacturing and industrial automation [4].

In order to improve processing capabilities, Shaker et al. (2023) investigated the integration of photonics with electronic systems [5]. Khan (2024) presented an industrial viewpoint on photonics in data centers, emphasizing efficiency and scalability. As mentioned, recent studies on photonic AI accelerators point to notable advancements in industrial intelligence, automation, and processing power [6]. Zhou et al. (2024) developed silicon photonics for high-speed communications [7]. Further, this article emphasized IIoT applications, demonstrating industry adoption [8].

Roy and Sharan (2018) covered photonic crystals in DNA-based cancer diagnostics [9]. Their 2016 study showed how to use photonic sensors and machine learning to evaluate salinity in real time [10]. Photonics-based sensors enhance monitoring and fault detection precision, which is advantageous for predictive maintenance in industrial settings. Furthermore, fiber-optic data transmission improves secure industrial communications, especially in cybersecurity applications, as shown by high-speed optical networks. Pathak et al. (2025) proposed a two-stage photonic system for the detection of thyroid cancer [11]. The study uses regression analysis to investigate the new field of photonic sensing and shows how well it can handle intricate computational models with little learning. Sharan et al. (2013) used finite element analysis to investigate strain measurement, showcasing advancements in photonic sensing. This analysis is heavily data-driven and uses optical capability to measure strain [12].

Willner et al. (2014) examined all-optical signal processing and its applicability to next-generation data systems [13]. Miller (2017) discussed attojoule optoelectronics for processing that uses less energy, while Bogaerts et al. (2012) created silicon microring resonators and showed scalable silicon photonics for data center applications [14]. They offered a thorough analysis of optical interconnects and how they are used in data processing [15]. Soref (2006) and Jalali first presented photonic integration for optical signal processing [16]. In addition to describing silicon photonics as a scalable platform for optics-based data systems, Fathpour (2006) provided fundamental insights into the feasibility of silicon photonics [17].

Shen et al. (2017) employed deep learning with nanophotonic circuits and explained further how photonics supports industries that need quick, low-power calculations for Internet of Things systems by accelerating real-time big data analytics [18]. In photonics, Tait et al. (2017) and Shastri et al. (2016) made contributions using weight banks and neuromorphic networks [19]. Thomson et al. (2016) provided a roadmap for silicon photonics [21], while Smit et al. (2012) highlighted the implications of Moore's Law in photonics [20]. Reed et al. (2010) created silicon modulators [22]. Sun et al. (2015) first presented a microprocessor that can communicate with light [23].

Xu et al. (2005) covered silicon modulators [24]. Photonics was extended to III-V-on-silicon devices by Roelkens et al. (2015) [25]. By processing large datasets without the heat dissipation problems associated with conventional electronic processors, photonic artificial intelligence (AI) accelerators improve industrial IoT data workflows [26]. Using photonic principles, Chatterjee et al. (2016) investigated theoretical extensions in electron correlation models [27].

Wang et al. (2020) introduced quantum photonics for secure communications. Investigating how quantum photonics might revolutionize encrypted communications and cybersecurity in IIoT ecosystems. The future of industrial IoT will be shaped by developments in quantum photonics, optical deep learning, and AI-integrated photonic systems [28]. Photonics was first used in edge computing by Bhargava et al. (2020). Photonics-based solutions have greatly enhanced the idea of edge computing, which decentralizes data processing. The authors of Optica analyze edge computing based on photonics, emphasizing the higher bandwidth and lower latency attained through optical processing techniques [29]. Pan et al. (2020) focused on the coordinated data distribution in diverse IoT environments [30].

Optical neural networks are becoming a game-changing technology as artificial intelligence in IIoT grows. Feldmann et al. (2021) used photonic tensor cores to demonstrate parallel convolutional processing. They investigate AI-driven photonic processing models that enable deep learning algorithms to be executed more quickly in industrial environments. Additionally, it explores the mutually beneficial development of photonics and AI, describing how photonics' ultrafast computations and adaptive learning mechanisms improve machine learning applications [31].

Photonic technologies are crucial for large-scale computing because industries demand effective data handling and real-time analytics. Jost (2006) established the mathematical underpinnings for photonic simulations using PDEs [32]. Popović et al. (2006) first presented microring filters for wavelength routing [33].

Photonics has developed from discrete experimental methods into integrated systems for practical applications, spanning consumer behavior, sensor systems, neuromorphic computing, and quantum optics. On-chip light communication, photonic accelerators, and photonic-AI convergence are important turning points. Scaling these innovations will require ongoing multidisciplinary research and fabrication advancements.

In data-driven industries, photonics has become a key technology that seamlessly integrates with edge computing, artificial intelligence, and medical diagnostics. This historical analysis demonstrates a distinct trend toward growing functionality, downsizing, and practical implementation.

The cutting-edge field of photonics, which makes use of light-based technologies, has revolutionized analytics and data processing in a number of industries, most notably in the Industrial Internet of Things (IIoT). The inability of traditional electronic computing to scale to handle large datasets has led to the incorporation of photonic technologies.

Review of Existing Methods

Optical Interconnects

Think of optical interconnects as the highways of data. Instead of copper wires, they use light to move information between CPUs, GPUs, memory, and storage. The result? Much higher bandwidth, lower energy use, and almost no signal loss. For industries that rely on real-time analytics like smart factories or AI-driven logistics, this speed and reliability make all the difference. Taubenblatt (2011) discussed high-performance computing optical interconnects [34]. Liu et al. (2021) provided information about silicon photonic modulators with high speed [35].

Optical interconnects are fast communication links that move data between parts of and between computer systems using light, usually from lasers and optical fibers or waveguides. Figure 5-2 shows the essential components. Here is a brief synopsis of their role in the data pipeline:

- **High-Bandwidth Data Transfer:** Compared to conventional electrical links, optical interconnects have a substantially higher bandwidth for moving massive amounts of data between CPUs, GPUs, memory, and storage units.

- **Low Latency Communication:** Optical interconnects allow for faster and more dependable communication by minimizing signal degradation and avoiding electrical resistance. This is essential for workloads involving real-time analytics and AI.

- **Energy Efficiency:** Photonic transmission is perfect for high-density, sustainable data centers because it uses a lot less energy per bit than copper interconnects.

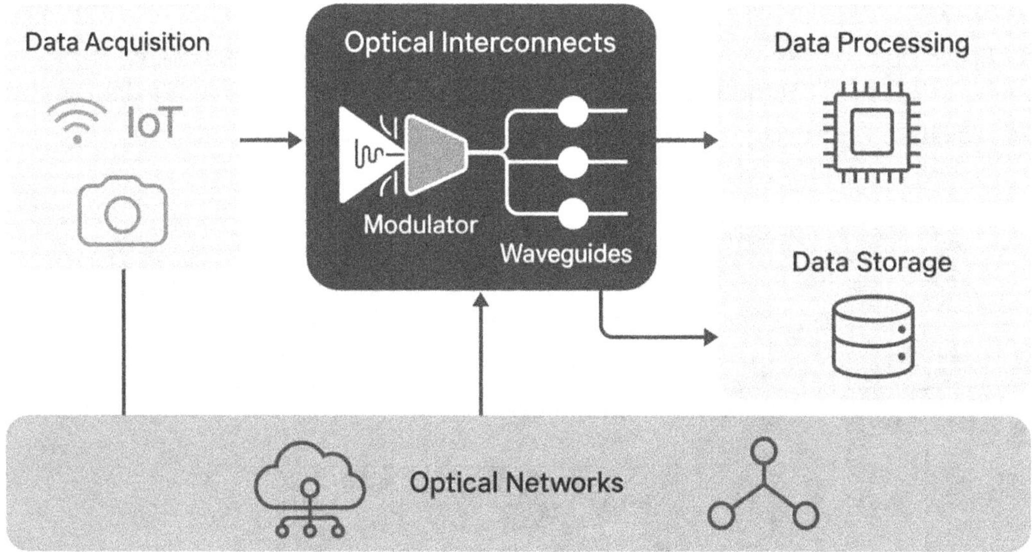

Figure 5-2. *Optical Interconnects in Data Processing and Analytics*

- **Scalability in Cloud and HPC Systems:** By preserving performance as systems expand, optical links in large-scale computing clusters enable scalable architectures.

- **Integration with Photonics:** Optical interconnects serve as the foundation for next-generation data infrastructure, which is light-based and incredibly fast. They complement photonic processors and memory.

- **Support for Disaggregated Architectures:** These allow modular systems (such as compute nodes, storage clusters, and memory pools) to operate as a single platform with few restrictions on physical proximity.

Photonic Integrated Circuits (PICs)

PICs are basically the optical version of electronic chips. They pack lasers, modulators, detectors, and waveguides onto a single chip, letting light do the heavy lifting. For IIoT, that means compact, energy-efficient devices that can process data in parallel and resist electromagnetic interference—perfect for noisy industrial environments. Figure 5-3 shows the essential components of PIC. They play a crucial role in enabling data centers and edge devices to become smaller, less expensive, and simpler.

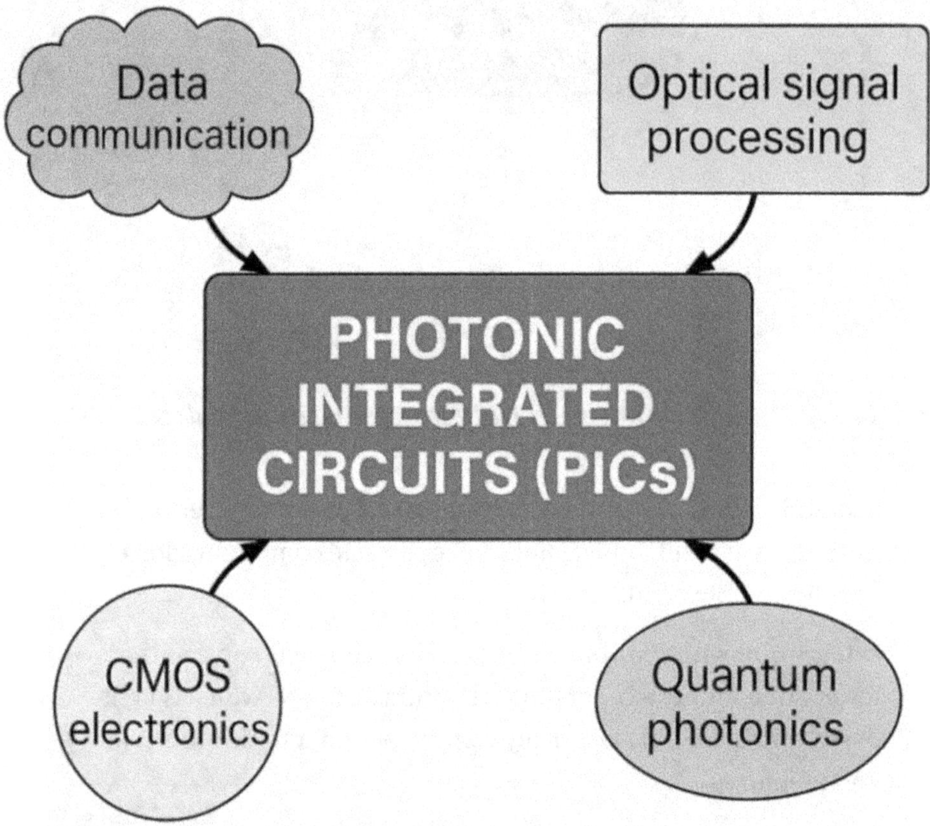

Figure 5-3. *PIC Components*

The optical equivalent of electronic integrated circuits (ICs), PICs are made to control photons rather than electrons. They combine several photonic functions onto a single chip, such as waveguides, detectors, modulators, and lasers. In data processing and analytics, they operate as follows:

- **Transmission of Signals Based on Light:** Instead of using copper wires to route light signals, PICs use waveguides. This makes it possible to move data at extremely high speeds while generating very little heat or energy loss.

- **Processing and Modulation:** Electro-optic modulators and other on-chip components are used to modulate (encode with data) light. These parts work at very high frequencies, which allows for quick processing and switching of signals.

- **Processing of Optical Signals:** PICs are capable of processing tasks like filtering with optical ring resonators and switching (for dynamic data routing). For AI and analytics tasks, Fourier transforms, convolution, and even matrix multiplication are used.

- **Integration with CMOS**: Photonic-electronic hybrid computing systems are made possible by the close coupling of optical speed with digital logic made possible by the frequent co-integration of CMOS PICs with CMOS electronics.

- **Specialized Uses:** Fiber-optic networks and high-speed optical interconnects for data transmission. Secure communication using on-chip quantum light sources and detectors. In lab-on-chip and biosensing platforms, sensing and spectroscopy

- **Principal Advantages**: Quicker than circuits that use electricity, unaffected by electromagnetic interference, large-scale energy efficiency, scalable using photonics foundries for silicon.

Photonic Memory and Storage

Storage is another area where photonics shines. Instead of relying on electrons, photonic memory uses light pulses to encode and retrieve data almost instantly. That means real-time analytics and in-memory computing become possible, with far less heat and energy waste compared to traditional DRAM or flash.

A schematic diagram of the use of photonic memory storage is shown in Figure 5-4.

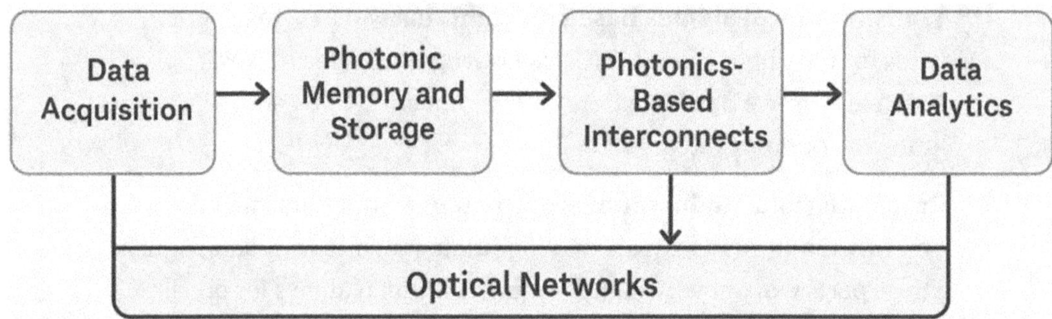

Figure 5-4. *Use of Photonic Memory Storage*

Photonic memory and storage systems store and retrieve data using light (photons) rather than electrical charge (electrons). High-bandwidth, ultra-fast, and energy-efficient memory systems are made possible by this new technology.

Photonics-based data processing relies on light-driven encoding, storage, and high-speed memory operations, offering a transformative alternative to conventional electronic systems. Data encoding using light is achieved through optical modulators, which embed digital information into signals by altering wavelength, phase, or intensity. This enables ultra-fast, energy-efficient data transmission across optical computing frameworks. Photonic storage utilizes specialized mechanisms such as resonant optical cavities, phase-change materials (PCM) that shift states under laser pulses, and temporary optical buffers or waveguide delay lines for holding light-based data. These methods facilitate nonvolatile and semi-volatile memory, ensuring rapid access and reliable data retention.

One of the major advantages of photonic memory is its fast read/write capability, surpassing traditional DRAM and flash memory. The near-instantaneous data retrieval enables real-time analytics and in-memory computing, making photonic storage ideal for high-performance applications requiring minimal latency. To build an all-optical data pipeline, photonic memory units are closely integrated with photonics-based interconnects and processors, minimizing electron-photon conversion bottlenecks and enabling seamless data flow from acquisition to analytics. This integration ensures efficient processing across advanced computational systems.

Scalability is another critical aspect, as photonic memory architectures support distributed data storage across edge, fog, and cloud infrastructures. Their smooth integration into optical networks allows high-speed data access and management, reinforcing their role in next-generation computing environments.

This technology represents a significant leap forward in computing performance, efficiency, and scalability, paving the way for advanced AI-driven analytics, real-time decision-making, and large-scale industrial applications. The following are the advantages:

- High speed (bandwidth on a terabit scale)

- Minimal latency and energy usage

- Unaffected by electromagnetic interference

- Compatible with quantum photonics and neuromorphic systems in the future

Data Analytics and Machine Learning

These technologies analyze data from multiple sensors to forecast yields and monitor crop health. They help farmers optimize their resources and manage crops more effectively. A recent study proposes a two-stage method for thyroid cancer detection using photonic crystals and AI techniques. The findings demonstrate how photonics and AI can be used in tandem to accurately and early detect cancer [36]. In a recent study, a novel multichannel biosensor that analyses different skin types using photonic crystals was introduced. The biosensor uses the unique optical properties of photonic crystals to detect variations in the skin's refractive indices, allowing it to differentiate between Asian, Dark, and Caucasian skin types. The study demonstrates that the biosensor can distinguish between these skin types by tracking various wavelength changes when the sensing hole size is altered. This innovative technique, which leverages data analytics and machine learning, shows the potential of photonic sensors in dermatology for applications such as personalized skincare and skin cancer detection [37].

By using light to detect physical, chemical, or biological signals, photonic sensors transform them into data that can be processed, examined, and utilized in predictive modeling. This is an explanation of how machine learning and data analytics function in this situation. Figure 5-5 shows a schematic of data analytics and machine learning.

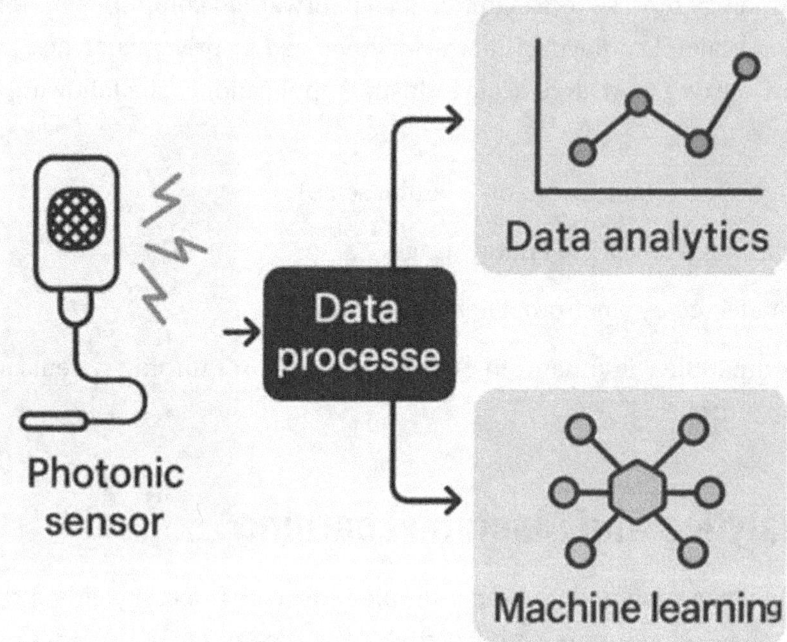

Figure 5-5. *Data Analytics and Machine Learning*

Photonics plays a crucial role in advanced sensing, information processing, and AI-driven analytics, enabling high-speed, high-resolution detection across multiple domains. Photonic sensing can detect variables such as vibration (using fiber Bragg gratings), temperature, strain, and chemical composition through optical spectroscopy. Additionally, biometric indicators like oxygen or glucose levels can be monitored with exceptional accuracy, benefiting healthcare and industrial applications. One of the key advantages of photonic sensors is their ability to provide rapid, high-resolution measurements with minimal electromagnetic interference and noise, making them highly reliable for precision monitoring.

Once collected, raw optical signals undergo information processing, where they are converted into digital form through normalization, signal conditioning, noise reduction, and feature extraction. These features may include amplitude shifts and spectral patterns, ensuring that the extracted data is refined for further analysis. Following this, statistical and analytical tools process the data to identify trends, detect irregularities, and generate insights via dashboards, enabling real-time monitoring and decision-making in industrial, environmental, and healthcare applications.

Machine learning further enhances data-driven intelligence, allowing algorithms to learn from sensor data to classify conditions (e.g., healthy vs. faulty, clean vs. contaminated), predict future states (such as climate trends or equipment failure), and automate responses like triggering alerts or system actuation. Techniques such as neural networks, decision trees, clustering, and regression are commonly employed to refine AI-driven decision models, ensuring adaptability to dynamic environments. As photonics continues to integrate with AI, it enables smarter, more responsive systems, revolutionizing applications across industries. Common techniques include regression, clustering, decision trees, and neural networks.

Case Studies

The real impact of photonics shows up in industry. In smart manufacturing, optical sensors catch defects at the micrometer level, preventing costly downtime. In logistics, fiber-optic networks and scanners keep track of assets in real time. And in healthcare, photonic sensors enable precise patient monitoring. These examples highlight how photonics and IIoT together create systems that are faster, smarter, and more reliable.

Logistics and Supply Chain

Smart manufacturing increases production efficiency, reduces waste, and enhances product quality by utilizing state-of-the-art technologies. Photonics is revolutionizing the field of smart manufacturing in conjunction with the following essential techniques shown in Figure 5-6.

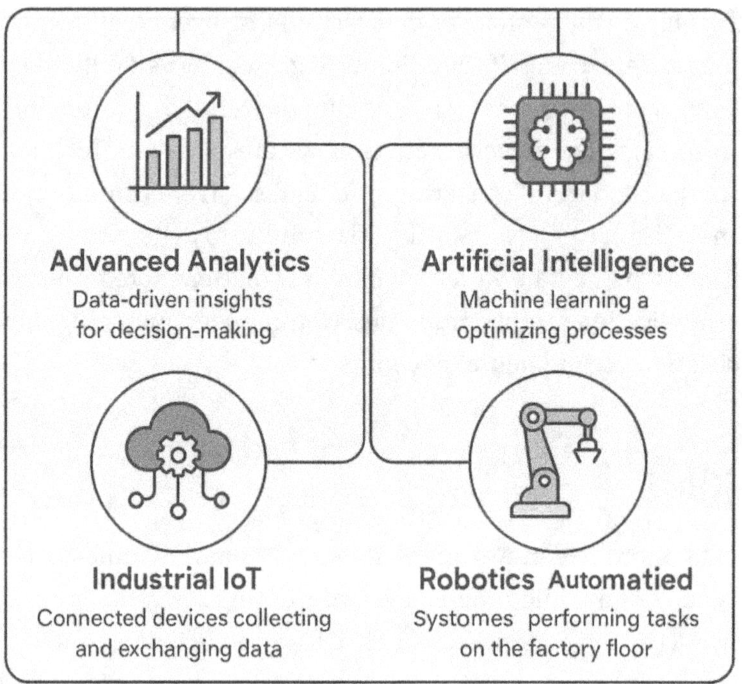

Figure 5-6. *Smart Manufacturing Components*

Photonics serves as the backbone of Industry 4.0, enabling ultra-precise, high-speed sensing, communication, and automation across various domains. In precision sensing and quality control, laser-based sensors and optical inspection systems detect defects at the micrometer level, ensuring consistent product quality in fast-paced production lines. For smart inventory and asset tracking, optical scanners and RFID systems utilize light-based signals to monitor goods in real-time, enabling accurate stock management, precise location tracking, and effective loss prevention. Machine vision and automation benefit from photonic sensors that allow robots to visually interpret their environment, improving accuracy in pick-and-place operations, packaging, and sorting tasks. Figure 5-7 describes the role of photonics in smart manufacturing.

Precision Sensing & Quality Control
Laser-based sensors and optical inspection systems cotect defects at micrometer levievels. Ensures consistent product quality in high-speed production lines

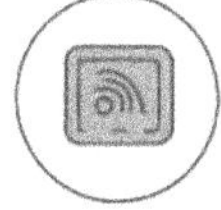
Smart Inventory & Asset Tracking
Optical scanners and RFID systems use light-based signals to track goods in real time. Enables accurate stock monitoring, location tracking, and loss prevention

MACHINE VISION & AUTOMATION
Cameras with photonic sensors enable robots to "see" and respond to dynamic environments. Improves pick-and-place accuracy, packaging, and sorting efficiency

High-Speed Communication
Fiber optics ensures fast and secure data transfer between machines (M2M). Critical for real-time decision-making and remote manufacturing control

Sustainable Operations
Photonics enables non-contact, energy-efficient processes like laser cutting and additive manufacturing

Figure 5-7. *Role of Photonics in Smart Manufacturing*

Additionally, fiber optics-driven high-speed communication ensures seamless, secure data transfer between interconnected machines, playing a crucial role in real-time decision-making and remote manufacturing control. Lastly, sustainable operations leverage photonics for energy-efficient, non-contact processes like laser cutting and additive manufacturing, significantly reducing material waste and overall energy consumption.

Aerospace and Defense

Photonics empowers aerospace and defense systems with unmatched speed, accuracy, and security. As threats evolve and digital warfare intensifies, photonics will be central to next-gen platforms, enabling smarter, faster, and more resilient operations as shown in Figure 5-8.

Figure 5-8. *Role of Photonics in Aerospace and Defense*

It powers systems that require extreme precision, speed, and security, transforming how nations communicate, navigate, detect threats, and engage in tactical operations.

Laser-Based Communication

- Uses laser beams to create optical links between aircraft, satellites, drones, or ground stations.

- Delivers high-bandwidth, line-of-sight data transmission, and far surpassing traditional radio frequency (RF) systems in both speed and security.

- Enables encrypted, jam-resistant communication. Reduces electromagnetic interference (EMI), crucial in combat zones.

- Supports inter-satellite links (ISLs) and airborne relays in military networks (e.g., NASA's Laser Communications Relay Demonstration (LCRD) Military UAV-to-satellite laser communications).

Precision Navigation

Photonics-based gyroscopes (e.g., fiber-optic gyroscopes, ring laser gyroscopes) and accelerometers provide inertial navigation without GPS.

- Delivers ultra-accurate location and movement data, essential in GPS-denied environments (e.g., deep space, enemy territory).

- Enhances targeting precision for guided missiles and drones.

- Provides low-drift, high-reliability positioning for aircraft and naval systems.

- Inertial measurement units (IMUs) are used in fighter jets and submarines.

Remote Sensing

Electro-optical (EO) and infrared (IR) sensors use light to detect, classify, and monitor terrain, atmospheric conditions, and objects. Figure 5-9 shows the schematic of remote sensing in action.

Figure 5-9. *Schematic of Remote Sensing*

Primary uses are:

- Facilitates surveillance, reconnaissance, and intelligence (ISR) missions.

- Capable of day/night and all-weather operations using multispectral/ hyperspectral imaging.

- Critical for disaster monitoring, environmental mapping, and tactical planning.

- Satellite-based EO systems provide early warning for missile detection.

- Drone-mounted LiDAR supports topographic analysis with high accuracy.

Directed Energy Weapons (DEWs)

High-energy lasers (HELs), microwaves, or particle beams are used to disable or destroy enemy assets.

- Enable speed-of-light engagement with minimal collateral damage.

- Highly cost-effective for intercepting drones, missiles, and aircraft, offering an advantage over traditional kinetic interceptors.

- Also applicable in non-lethal roles such as crowd control and asset denial operations.

- Examples:

  - HELIOS (High Energy Laser and Integrated Optical-dazzler with Surveillance) deployed on U.S. Navy ships.

  - Airborne laser platforms for real-time missile defense and neutralization.

Sensor Fusion and Situational Awareness

Photonics enables the fusion of multiple sensor inputs (EO, radar, LiDAR) to create a real-time operational picture.

- Enhances decision-making and targeting accuracy.

- Supports autonomous UAV navigation, battlefield awareness, and force coordination.

- Ensures secure sharing of fused sensor data across allied platforms.

- F-35's Distributed Aperture System (DAS) using photonic sensors to provide 360° situational awareness.

High-Speed Optical Networks in IIoT

High-speed optical networks, as shown in Figure 5-10, particularly those leveraging fiber-optic technology, are fundamentally transforming the IIoT by enabling rapid, secure, and scalable communication across interconnected industrial systems. These networks provide the foundation for real-time data exchange, ensuring synchronized operations in smart factories, autonomous industrial processes, and large-scale automated environments.

HIGH-SPEED OPTICAL NETWORKS IN IIoT

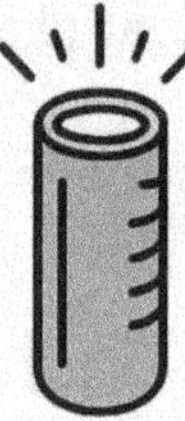

Figure 5-10. *Schematic of High-Speed Optical Networks in IIoT*

One of the most significant advantages of optical networks is their ultra-fast data transmission capability. Fiber optics can transmit data at near-light speed, facilitating seamless machine-to-machine (M2M) communication. This is crucial for high-speed manufacturing lines, where robots, sensors, and control units must coordinate efficiently to maintain precision in industrial workflows. By supporting instantaneous feedback loops, fiber-optic networks enhance automation, reducing delays in quality control, predictive maintenance, and real-time monitoring. Security is another critical benefit of optical networks in IIoT.

Unlike conventional copper-based communication systems, fiber-optic transmission is immune to electromagnetic interference (EMI) and radio frequency interference (RFI), ensuring signal integrity in heavy industrial environments. Additionally, fiber-optic cables are harder to tap or intercept, making them ideal for securing proprietary data and sensitive industrial operations. This enhanced security plays a pivotal role in protecting IIoT systems from cyber threats and unauthorized access.

Scalability and low-latency communication further amplify the effectiveness of optical networks in industrial settings. Fiber-optic infrastructure can support large-scale IIoT deployments, accommodating hundreds of sensors, actuators, programmable logic controllers (PLCs), and robotic units within expansive plants. The low latency characteristic of optical transmission enables edge computing, allowing smart sensors to process and react to data locally before sending relevant insights to centralized platforms. This supports AI-driven predictive maintenance, smart monitoring systems, and instant operational adjustments.

Integration with smart systems is another crucial aspect of fiber-optic networks in IIoT. These networks enable cloud connectivity, digital twins, and real-time control platforms, making them essential for industrial AI applications. As factories evolve into intelligent production hubs, fiber optics facilitate seamless data exchange between AI-powered diagnostics, machine learning models, and industrial automation frameworks, ensuring optimized decision-making and resource efficiency.

In terms of practical applications, high-speed optical networks support real-time quality control using machine vision and photonic sensors, enabling precise defect detection and automated adjustments in manufacturing workflows. Additionally, optical backhaul infrastructure allows remote asset monitoring across distributed industrial facilities, ensuring uninterrupted performance tracking and resource optimization. Fiber-optic links also contribute to deterministic high-speed synchronization in precision robotics, guaranteeing accurate coordination between autonomous machines.

A prominent example of fiber-optic network deployment is Industry 4.0 factory floors, where high-speed fiber connectivity links sensor networks to centralized control platforms, ensuring efficient data distribution and streamlined industrial processes.

Another emerging use case is smart grids, which leverage fiber-optic transmission for real-time energy distribution coordination across cities, supporting sustainable power management and intelligent grid balancing.

By enabling secure, rapid, and highly scalable industrial communication, fiber-optic networks remain at the heart of IIoT advancements, driving efficiency, precision, and automation across a wide range of industrial sectors. Let me know if you'd like further refinements or additional examples!

AI-Driven Photonic Processing

AI-driven photonic processing, as shown in Figure 5-11, merges the speed of light-based data handling with the intelligence of machine learning algorithms, unlocking new possibilities in computing and sensing systems. This integration enhances data throughput, decision-making, and real-time responsiveness, making it a foundational technology for advanced industries. Ultrafast data processing is a key advantage, as photonics enables near-instantaneous signal manipulation, far surpassing traditional electronic processors in speed and bandwidth. Embedded AI models within photonic chips allow real-time filtering, feature extraction, and classification at terabit-per-second rates, ensuring high-speed performance in applications requiring rapid inference.

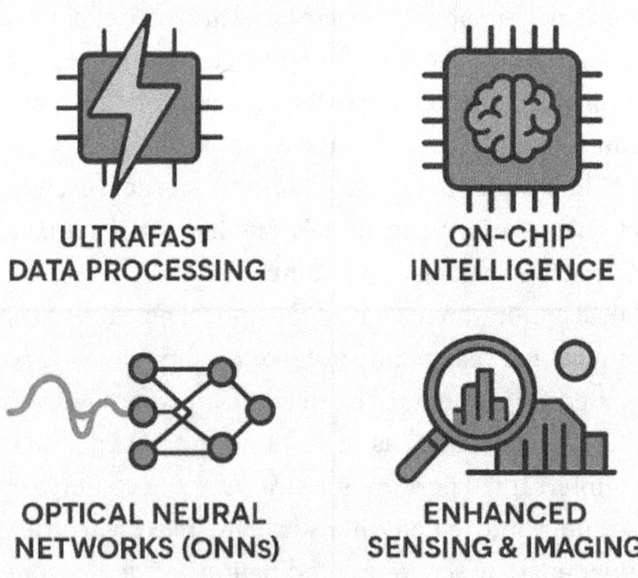

Figure 5-11. *AI-Driven Photonic Processing*

Beyond processing speed, on-chip intelligence is revolutionizing computational capabilities. Neural network algorithms embedded in photonic integrated circuits (PICs) facilitate edge-level analytics, reducing dependence on cloud computing and making autonomous systems, industrial robotics, and remote AI decision-making more efficient. In parallel, optical neural networks (ONNs) replace electrons with light beams to simulate neural layers, enabling massive parallelism and superior energy efficiency, which is particularly advantageous in image recognition, signal interpretation, and complex pattern detection.

AI-driven photonics also enhances sensing and imaging technologies, improving adaptive optics, hyperspectral imaging, and lidar signal interpretation. This leads to higher resolution, noise reduction, and faster object classification, making photonics indispensable in aerospace, defense, biomedical imaging, and industrial automation. The technology's impact extends to industrial applications, where smart factories utilize predictive fault detection and adaptive control via real-time photonic AI processors, optimizing production efficiency. In telecom, photonics enables high-speed routing and signal optimization through AI-driven photonic switches, ensuring seamless data flow across vast networks. Meanwhile, autonomous systems leverage optical edge inference to enhance real-time situational awareness, improving decision-making in dynamic environments.

By combining the unparalleled speed of photonic processing with the adaptability of AI algorithms, this technology is shaping the future of high-speed computing, industrial automation, and intelligent sensing applications across diverse domains.

Further Research

Looking ahead, the possibilities are huge. Quantum photonics could make IIoT communications virtually unhackable. Neuromorphic photonics—think brain-inspired optical processors—could deliver low-power, real-time analytics. And with sustainability in mind, eco-friendly optical systems will help industries cut energy use and carbon emissions. Photonics isn't just improving IIoT, it's redefining what's possible. Meanwhile, AI-powered photonic chips are being tailored to support AI inference and training at the edge, allowing faster real-time processing in autonomous systems and intelligent monitoring. Quantum photonics, with its ability to manipulate quantum light states, is proving crucial for next-generation secure communications and complex industrial data processing. Furthermore, advancements in photonic networking seek to replace conventional electronic switches in IIoT infrastructures, establishing high-speed, energy-efficient networks that enhance industrial connectivity and automation. These developments collectively signify a shift toward highly optimized, ultra-fast, and secure IIoT environments powered by photonic technology.

Conclusion

Photonics is emerging as a transformative force in the IIoT, enabling highly efficient computational and communication systems. Photonics is reshaping IIoT by enabling ultra-fast, scalable, and intelligent data workflows. As industries demand low-latency analytics and secure transmission, photonics forms the bedrock of next-gen automation, AI, and cyber-physical systems. Quantum photonic computing has the potential to revolutionize IIoT applications by leveraging quantum states of light for advanced data analytics and ultra-secure encryption. As photonics continues to evolve, its integration with AI and machine learning will redefine AI-driven IIoT analytics, enabling real-time pattern recognition and adaptive decision-making in industrial automation. Additionally, ONNs are gaining traction, with ongoing research focused on developing photonic deep learning models that enhance parallel computing capabilities while reducing energy consumption.

CHAPTER 6

Case Studies: Photonics in Action

Photonics is one of the driving forces behind Industry 4.0—it brings intelligence, scalability, and precision to modern industrial systems. In this chapter, we'll look at how photonics is reshaping areas like precision agriculture, smart manufacturing, and sustainable energy management through real case studies and cutting-edge technologies.

It's not just about faster data or sharper sensors. Photonics enables real-time data collection, predictive analytics, and seamless automation, going well beyond the obvious advantages. Think LiDAR for mapping, hyperspectral imaging for crop health, optical sensors for monitoring, and even quantum photonics for secure communications. Together, these tools help tackle persistent challenges such as decentralized energy systems, waste reduction, resource optimization, and soil health restoration.

Within Industrial IoT ecosystems, photonics plays a crucial role—bridging the gap between theory and practice. And looking forward, this chapter also explores how combining photonic solutions with AI frameworks could unlock even greater sustainability and efficiency across industries.

Photonics in Action Primer

Photonics is right at the forefront of IIoT innovation. At its core, it's the science of creating, controlling, and detecting light—but in practice, it's becoming a powerful driver of intelligence, efficiency, and adaptability across industries. The basics of photonics are well understood, yet its full potential is still unfolding. By enabling real-time monitoring, predictive insights, and precision automation, photonic technologies are helping industries meet the growing demands for sustainability and operational excellence.

Dr. P. Sharan et al., *Photonics in Industrial IoT: Transforming Manufacturing and Beyond*,
https://doi.org/10.1007/979-8-8688-2694-8_6

In smart manufacturing, tools like high-speed imaging, LiDAR, laser systems, and hyperspectral sensing are streamlining production, cutting waste, and improving quality control. In agriculture, photonics gives farmers data-driven insights into crop health, soil conditions, and environmental factors, supporting sustainable practices and boosting yields. And in energy management, innovations such as photovoltaic cells and fiber-optic sensors are making smart grids more efficient and paving the way for cleaner, more resilient energy solutions.

Rather than staying at the level of theory, this chapter focuses on real-world applications where photonics delivers unique value, whether it's improving performance, reducing inefficiencies, or solving long-standing challenges. We'll look at what's already been achieved, as well as the research directions that will shape the next generation of IIoT solutions. Photonics is lighting the path toward a smarter, more sustainable world, and the future looks bright. Figure 6-1 shows how light propagates through a photonic crystal, a simple but powerful illustration of the science at work.

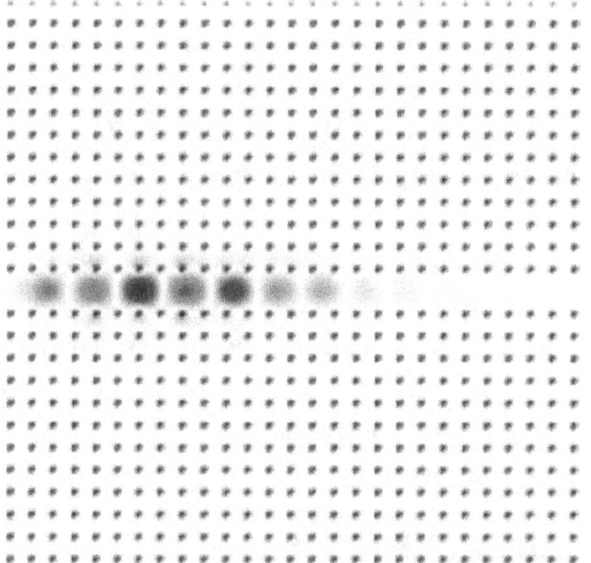

Figure 6-1. *Light Propagation in Photonic Crystal*

Literature Review

Photonics has completely changed the way smart manufacturing works, bringing more speed, accuracy, and productivity across industries. High-resolution cameras and advanced imaging tools are now central to metrology, inspection, and quality control. Picture a conveyor belt with products flying past—high-speed imaging systems can spot defects instantly, ensuring only top-quality goods make it to the market.

Another exciting frontier is quantum machine learning. It's still a young field, but it holds huge promise for intelligent manufacturing. Researchers are exploring how quantum computing can supercharge machine learning models, making them faster and more powerful for tasks like predictive analytics and process optimization. In fact, a recent review looked at 45 studies published between 1995 and 2021, mapping out how this area has evolved. Interest is growing quickly, with countries like the U.S. and China leading the way in applying quantum machine learning to smart manufacturing. The takeaway? Quantum and photonics together could redefine what's possible in industrial automation [1].

In the agricultural sector, photonics technologies such as spectroscopy, imaging, and spectrum imaging have demonstrated promise in enhancing crop cultivation and harvesting. These technologies enable accurate crop health, irrigation control, and soil condition monitoring. For example, hyperspectral imaging can detect nutritional deficiencies and crop diseases, allowing for timely treatment [2]. Resource optimization and a reduction in greenhouse gas emissions are two benefits of precision farming technologies for the environment. Another synthesis study analyses prior research to look at many aspects of evaluating the impact of using such technologies. The results of the analysis demonstrated that the study of the effects of applying precision technology was centered on three significant microeconomic factors: the agronomic, environmental, and economic aspects. The majority of earlier research on the benefits of precision technology focused on quantitative analytical techniques and experimental analysis to gauge the effects on agronomic, environmental, and economic factors. The study's findings illustrated the benefits and enhanced sustainability of agricultural production systems resulting from the use of precision farming technologies. In particular, reducing greenhouse gas emissions and the environmental impact by over 80% [3].

Energy conversion and conservation depend on photonics. Fuel production, chemical energy conversion, and the generation of thermal and electrical power are the primary applications of solar light harvesting. Energy-related applications of photonic sensors include optical communications, solid-state lighting, and flat-panel displays [4]. Recent advancements in artificial photonic structures, such as plasmonic and photonic crystals, have opened up new possibilities for energy harvesting and management. These structures' remarkable optical properties enable efficient energy use in a number of ways. The internal absorption mechanisms, influencing factors, and solar energy absorption performance are all investigated using the finite difference time domain (FDTD) technique. The majority of solar energy will be captured by the suggested absorber, which achieves nearly total absorption in the wavelength range of 300–2400 nm with an average absorptance of over 98%. Furthermore, cross nanostructures and multi-material nanocylinders interact to produce the magnetic polariton and plasmon resonances of cross resonators, which are responsible for the high absorptance in the solar spectrum. Our absorbers are also sensitive to the angle of incidence of the light, but not to its polarization, due to the symmetry of the structures [5].

Future research will primarily concentrate on designing and developing a plantar pressure measuring device based on optical sensors. A photonic micro-electromechanical systems (MEMS) sensor based on silicon nanostructures is being developed for biosensing applications, the study highlights how well the sensor can identify biological substances due to its great sensitivity and specificity, and the results demonstrate how photonic MEMS sensors can be used for biochemical analysis, environmental monitoring, and medical diagnostics in robotic process implementation [6]. The device aims to provide accurate and up-to-date pressure distribution data to diagnose and treat foot-related conditions, as well as highlighting the optical sensor's potential applications in robotic process automation-based footwear design and medical diagnostics [7]. A simple study discusses the development of an ultra-highly sensitive biosensor for the detection of *E. coli* bacteria in water. According to the study, the sensor's exceptional accuracy in identifying trace amounts of *E. coli* makes it a valuable automated tool for ensuring water safety and preventing waterborne illnesses. The study demonstrates the potential applications of photonic biosensors for environmental and public health monitoring [8].

A plasmonic biosensor method uses metal-dielectric interactions to detect malignant tumors. The study found that the sensor's high sensitivity and specificity in identifying malignant tissues make it a promising tool for early cancer detection and diagnosis. The study highlights the advantages of plasmonic biosensors in medical diagnostics due to their rapid response and high accuracy [9]. The use of photonic crystal-based sensors for DNA analysis in cancer detection. The study shows how the sensor can identify specific DNA sequences associated with cancer, providing a non-invasive and extremely accurate diagnostic technique. The findings show how photonic crystal sensors can be used for early cancer detection and individualized treatment. Applications based on robotic process automation may result from this [10]. The development of a photonic crystal-based micro-interferometer biochip (PC-IMRR) for the early detection of melanoma is an interesting method. The study found that the biochip's high sensitivity and specificity in detecting melanoma cells make it a useful tool for early detection and treatment. The study emphasizes the potential for photonic crystal biochips to enhance cancer diagnosis [11]. Future research will primarily concentrate on developing an optical biosensor for the detection of Mycobacterium tuberculosis bacteria. According to the study, the sensor is a useful tool for early tuberculosis diagnosis because of its high sensitivity and quick response time. The results demonstrate how optical biosensors can enhance automated early infectious disease detection [12]. The sensor is a promising tool for law enforcement and healthcare providers because of its high sensitivity and quick response in identifying different drug substances, according to another study. The study emphasizes the benefits of plasmonic sensors for rapid and precise drug detection [13].

These summaries, which provide a broad overview of the numerous applications of photonics in robotic processes for public health, environmental monitoring, medical diagnostics, and structural health monitoring areas, demonstrate the transformative potential of photonic technology.

Review of Existing Methods for Photonics in Action

Machine Learning (ML) and Internet of Things (IoT)

Process control, security improvements, and predictive maintenance are made possible by these technologies. To forecast equipment breakdowns and enhance production procedures, machine learning algorithms examine data from IoT devices. One of the earliest efforts was the use of machine learning to assess the salinity (or TDS) of drinking water in real time using photonic sensors. This work investigates the assessment of drinking water's salinity and TDS using machine learning algorithms in conjunction with photonic sensors. The technique shows how photonics and artificial intelligence may improve environmental monitoring and is successful in ensuring water quality through real-time monitoring and data processing [14].

Figure 6-2. *(a) Integrated Device Display with Raspberry Pi (Red Circle). (b) The 2000 ppm Salinity Result (Yellow Circle). (c) The 1000 ppm Salinity Water Result (Blue Circle)*
(Image Credit: `https://doi.org/10.5194/dwes-9-37-2016`*)*

Using the AdaBoost algorithm and machine learning techniques, spectrum analysis of photonic crystal-based biosensors provides an additional method. This method demonstrates how to apply the AdaBoost algorithm to spectral analysis for a photonic crystal-based biosensor. The technique demonstrates the promise of integrating photonics with machine learning for medical diagnostics by concentrating on the highly accurate and sensitive detection and categorization of biological molecules [15]. A deep learning and thermal imaging approach to breast cancer detection. The study shows how AI (via deep learning) and photonics (through thermal imaging) might collaborate to enhance early cancer diagnosis and detection, potentially saving lives through more efficient medical screening [16]. Another study uses a combination of artificial intelligence and photonics to compare the hormonal abnormalities in hypothyroidism.

It demonstrates how hormonal behavior may be analyzed and predicted by AI algorithms, which aids in the diagnosis and treatment of thyroid conditions [17]. Deep learning and infrared thermography are commonly used techniques for nodule detection. A recent study emphasizes how well photonics (infrared imaging) and artificial intelligence (deep learning) work together in medical diagnostics, especially when it comes to identifying anomalies that could point to dangerous medical disorders [18]. Additionally, YOLACT++, a dual attention network-based program that integrates a photonics-based imaging system, is used to segment brain tumors for MRI image processing. This method shows how powerful AI algorithms and advanced photonic imaging techniques can increase the precision and effectiveness of medical picture analysis [19].

Additive Manufacturing (3D Printing)

Complex pieces can be created with this technique with little material waste. It is frequently employed in the production of customized components and prototypes. In manufacturing, measuring dimensions is essential. Finite elements are used in an analysis for dynamic strain measurement with greater sensitivity. It highlights how photonics can improve measuring methods, which is essential for structural analysis applications in 3D printing. Sensitive patient data is protected when 3D printed medical devices are used with sophisticated server cryptography that is appropriate for quantum implementation for safe communication and data protection in medical technology. Figure 6-3 shows a 3D-printed robotic hand.

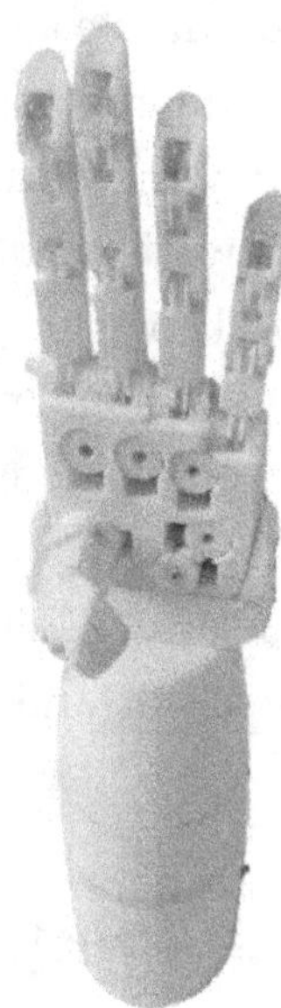

Figure 6-3. *3D-Printed Robotic Hand*

Robotics and Automation

In manufacturing operations, automated technologies and robotic arms increase accuracy and lower human error. For jobs like welding, inspection, and assembly, they are indispensable. For structural health monitoring, a recent study compares strain gauge and fiber Bragg grating (FBG) devices. The study assesses the accuracy, sensitivity, and dependability of both systems, emphasizing the benefits of FBG sensors' high sensitivity, multiplexing capabilities, and immunity to electromagnetic interference. According to the results, FBG sensors are more suited for applications involving long-term structural health monitoring for robot-based agents [20]. A 3D-printed robotic hand is seen in Figure 6-4.

Figure 6-4. *Robotics and Automation in Manufacturing (Image Credit: https://www.jrautomation.com)*

Precision Agriculture

Advanced technologies are used in precision agriculture to maximize crop management and boost yields. Important techniques consist of:

GIS and remote sensing are two technologies that offer comprehensive data on environmental variables, crop health, and soil conditions. They support farmers in making well-informed choices about pest management, fertilization, and irrigation. The first study focuses on mapping different water constituents using photonic crystals. It investigates how well photonic crystals recognize and measure various water constituents, highlighting their potential for environmental monitoring and water quality evaluation [21]. The integration of remote sensing technologies with photonic sensors and geospatial science is the main focus. It showcases cutting-edge studies that use or integrate remote sensing with modeling, geospatial analytics, and sophisticated computational techniques. Using photonic sensors to record and examine dynamic geospatial phenomena at various scales is part of the methodology. This covers the fundamentals of GNSS, GIS, and remote sensing, including digital image processing methods, earth observation sensors and platforms, and remote sensing principles. Additionally, it talks about how photonic sensors might improve the collecting and interpretation of geographical data in remote sensing and GIS applications. With an emphasis on the use of photonic sensors for precise data collection and analysis, current approaches investigate the uses of remote sensing data in GIS, such as land cover classification and environmental impact assessment.

Data Analytics and Machine Learning

To track crop health and forecast yields, these technologies evaluate data from several sensors. They assist farmers with better crop management and resource optimization. Using photonic crystals and artificial intelligence (AI) methods like logistic regression and artificial neural networks, a recent study offers a two-stage approach for thyroid cancer detection. The results show how photonics and AI can be combined to detect cancer early and accurately [22]. A new multichannel biosensor that uses photonic crystals to analyze various skin types has been presented in a recent study. The biosensor distinguishes between Asian, Dark, and Caucasian skin types by using the special optical characteristics of photonic crystals to identify changes in the refractive indices of the skin. By monitoring different wavelength changes when the sensing hole size is changed, the study shows that the biosensor can differentiate between these skin types. This novel method, which makes use of machine learning and data analytics, demonstrates the promise of photonic sensors in dermatology for uses including skin cancer detection and customized skincare [23].

Case Studies

As photonics continues to transform the landscape of the Industrial IIoT, its practical implementation is becoming both more sophisticated and more essential. Theoretical knowledge and foundational technologies are only part of the story; it is in real-world applications that photonics demonstrates its full potential to revolutionize industrial systems. This chapter presents a curated selection of case studies that showcase how photonics-based technologies are being deployed across a range of IIoT environments—from smart manufacturing and predictive maintenance to high-speed data communication and environmental sensing. Each case highlights the integration of optical sensors, fiber-optic networks, and advanced imaging systems into existing industrial frameworks, illustrating both the challenges faced and the breakthroughs achieved. Through these examples, readers gain insight into the tangible impact of photonics on operational efficiency, data accuracy, and system resilience. These stories are not just success narratives—they are blueprints for innovation, offering lessons and inspiration for engineers, researchers, and decision-makers seeking to harness light for a smarter, more connected industrial future.

Smart Manufacturing: Case-Driven Insights

Smart manufacturing increases production efficiency, reduces waste, and enhances product quality by utilizing state-of-the-art technologies. Photonics is revolutionizing the field of smart manufacturing in conjunction with the following essential techniques.

Use Case 1: Defect Detection Using High-Speed Imaging

In a high-throughput production environment, traditional visual inspection is inadequate. A photonic imaging system from Hamamatsu enabled the detection of subsurface defects in perishable goods, reducing spoilage and increasing throughput.

By increasing productivity, accuracy, and speed in a variety of industries, photonics technology has completely transformed smart manufacturing. High-resolution cameras and sophisticated imaging methods are used for metrology, inspection, and quality control. To guarantee that only superior products make it to market, high-speed imaging equipment, for example, can identify flaws in goods travelling along conveyor belts. LiDAR technology, which maps environments and measures distances using laser light, is essential for automating quality control and security procedures. An imaging system based on photonics is depicted in Figure 6-5 to identify flaws that are hidden from view beneath the fruit's skin.

Figure 6-5. *Detect Defects Forming Beneath the Fruit's Skin, Invisible to the Human Eye [24]*
(Image Credit: Hamamatsu Photonics Europe)

Use Case 2: Secure Med-Tech Manufacturing

This technique makes it possible to create complex parts with very little material waste, which is why it's often used for customized components and prototypes. In manufacturing, accurate measurement is everything—getting dimensions right ensures quality and reliability. To push precision even further, engineers use finite element analysis for dynamic strain measurement, giving them greater sensitivity and deeper insight into how materials behave under stress. It highlights how photonics can improve measuring methods, which is essential for structural analysis applications in 3D printing [25]. Sensitive patient data is protected when 3D printed medical devices are used with sophisticated server cryptography that is appropriate for quantum implementation for safe communication and data protection in medical technology [26].

Secure, scalable medical technology fabrication with low material waste was demonstrated by a hybrid framework that combined 3D-printed devices with photonic cryptography. These summaries provide a broad overview of the various applications of photonics and AI across various fields, showing how they could revolutionize environmental monitoring, medical diagnostics, structural health, and more.

The device's design is displayed in Figure 6-6. The 3D printed gadget is depicted in Figure 6-7.

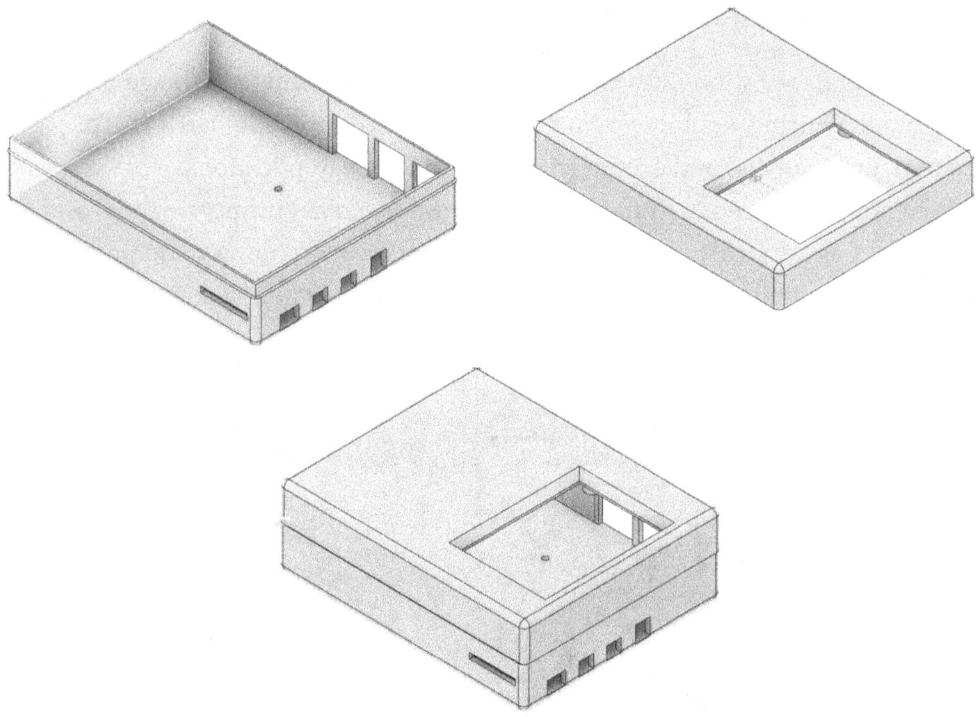

Figure 6-6. *3D Device Design [29]*

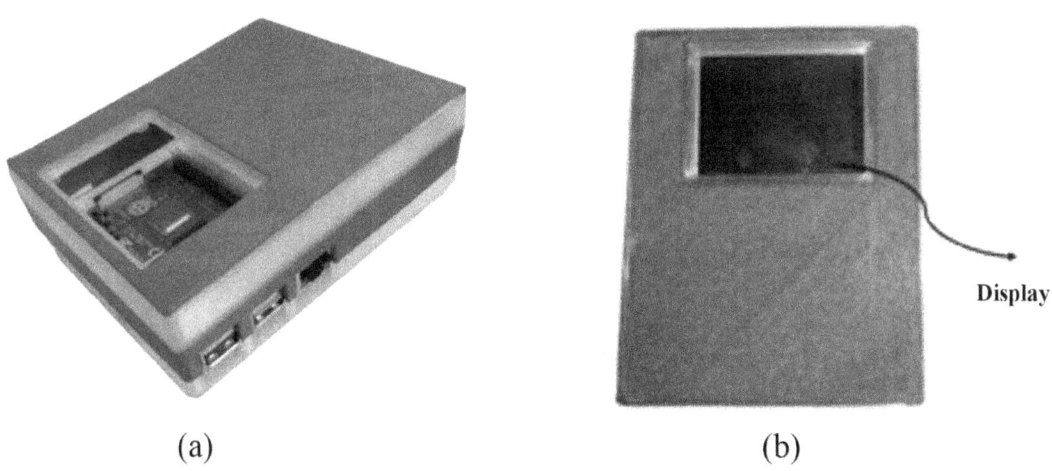

(a)   (b)

Figure 6-7. *3D-Printed Device (a) Without Display View and (b) Top View with Display*

Use Case 3: Robotics and Automation in Manufacturing

Figure 6-8 illustrates how photonics has become a crucial element in the growth of smart manufacturing, enabling industries to achieve unprecedented levels of automation, productivity, and accuracy. Among the main applications of photonics in this field are laser-based manufacturing processes such as cutting, welding, and additive manufacturing (3D printing). By creating incredibly complex and precise components with minimal waste, these techniques reduce material costs and their environmental impact.

Figure 6-8. *Robots Are Working in a Factory with a Machine (Courtesy: https://www.pexels.com)*

Moreover, quality control and inspection processes depend on photonic sensors. Technologies such as optical coherence tomography (OCT) and laser scanning, for example, enable real-time, high-resolution imaging of manufactured parts, ensuring that any defects are discovered early and that products meet stringent quality standards.

Furthermore, machine vision systems—which are essential for automated assembly lines and robotics—rely on photonics. These systems use state-of-the-art optics and imaging technologies to guide robotic arms and ensure precise component alignment and positioning.

Precision Agriculture: Case-Driven Insights

Use Case 1: Monitoring Soil Health with Photonic Sensors

In modern agriculture, robots and autonomous systems are taking on tasks like planting, weeding, and harvesting. By automating these processes, they help reduce labor costs while boosting efficiency, allowing farmers to focus on strategy rather than repetitive manual work. These systems are part of a broader shift toward precision farming, where technology ensures that every resource—whether water, fertilizer, or time—is used in the smartest way possible.

Photonics adds another layer of intelligence to this picture. For example, researchers have used photonic sensors to study how different water conditions—saline versus non-saline–affect tomato yields. By capturing subtle changes in plant response, these sensors provide farmers with real-time insights that can guide irrigation strategies and improve crop outcomes. It's a clear example of how light-based technologies are helping agriculture become more data-driven, sustainable, and productive. The researchers' assessment of the effects of water salinity on tomato growth and productivity underscored the importance of water quality in agriculture and the potential of photonic sensors in monitoring and regulating irrigation operations [27]. Another study presents a new platform that uses a photonic crystal-based ring resonator to detect magnesium in seawater. By showcasing the platform's sensitivity and specificity in measuring magnesium concentrations, the study draws attention to its possible applications in automation in environmental sciences and agriculture [28]. The development of an optical sensor to measure the brininess (salt content) of water represents a major breakthrough for automated tools [29]. The sensor's proven ability to accurately measure salt levels emphasizes its significance for applications in water quality monitoring and management.

Figure 6-9 shows an overhead photo of a milling truck harvesting crops in a field in Austin, Minnesota. The use of photonics in precision agriculture has revolutionized the way farmers monitor and care for their crops and livestock. Remote sensing technologies, such as multispectral and hyperspectral imaging, allow farmers to assess the condition and health of their crops from a distance. These imaging tools capture data at various wavelengths, providing accurate information about plant physiology, soil moisture content, and nutrient levels. With this knowledge, farmers can make informed choices about irrigation, fertilization, and pest control, ultimately increasing crop yields and reducing resource waste.

Figure 6-9. *Aerial Photo of Milling Truck on Field Harvesting Crops, Austin, MN, USA (Courtesy: https://www.pexels.com)*

LiDAR is another widely used photonic technology in precision agriculture. It assists farmers in evaluating the topography, identifying erosion hotspots, and creating more efficient planting schedules by creating detailed 3D maps of fields. Additionally, automated systems that monitor the health and behavior of cattle use photonic sensors. These sensors' capacity to identify variations in temperature, heart rate, and movement allows farmers to promptly identify and address potential health concerns.

Use Case 2: Disease Detection with Hyperspectral Imaging

Early detection of hibiscus crop diseases has been made possible by hyperspectral photonic systems combined with deep learning, allowing for proactive treatment and yield optimization. By highlighting the precision and effectiveness of deep learning models in identifying plant diseases, the study illustrates how they can enhance agricultural productivity and plant health management [30].

The integration of remote sensing technologies with photonic sensors and geospatial science is the main focus. It features state-of-the-art research that combines remote sensing with advanced computational methods, modeling, and geospatial analytics. The methodology includes the use of photonic sensors to capture and analyze dynamic geospatial phenomena at different scales. The foundations of GNSS, GIS, and remote sensing are covered here, along with digital image processing techniques, earth observation platforms and sensors, and remote sensing concepts. It also discusses how photonic sensors could enhance the gathering and analysis of geographic data for GIS and remote sensing applications. Current methods explore the applications of remote sensing data in GIS, including environmental impact assessment and land cover classification, with a focus on the use of photonic sensors for accurate data collection and analysis.

Energy Management: Case-Driven Insights

Use Case 1: Advanced Solar Absorption

Using photonic crystals and plasmonic structures, researchers have achieved near-total solar absorptance across a wide spectrum, significantly improving PV efficiency.

In Figure 6-10, a solar specialist inspects a solar glass. Photonics is revolutionizing energy management systems to make them more efficient and sustainable. Photonics has contributed significantly to energy management in the field of solar energy. Advances in photovoltaic (PV) technologies have been driven by photonics research, leading to the development of highly efficient solar panels that more efficiently transform sunlight into electrical power. Innovations like bifacial solar cells, which absorb light from both sides, and tandem solar cells, which use multiple layers to absorb different wavelengths, are pushing the efficiency of solar energy conversion.

Figure 6-10. *Solar Technician Inspecting Solar Panel (Courtesy: https://www.pexels.com)*

In addition to solar electricity, photonics is being used to develop energy-efficient lighting solutions. Light-emitting diodes (LEDs) have become the industry standard for energy-efficient lighting because of their longer lifespans and lower power consumption compared to traditional incandescent and fluorescent bulbs. Photonic sensors and communication technology are also essential components of smart grids and energy management systems. These systems use optical fibers and photonic sensors to monitor and control energy distribution in order to guarantee optimal performance and reduce energy loss.

In conclusion, the use of photonics in industrial IoT applications is driving significant advancements in several fields. At the forefront of technological advancement, photonics is transforming agriculture, enhancing energy management, and boosting manufacturing operations' precision and efficiency to pave the way for a smarter, more sustainable future.

Conclusion

Photonics has moved from being a quiet background enabler to a strategic pillar of industrial digital transformation. Its impact is visible in energy management, smart manufacturing, and precision agriculture, where it delivers measurable gains in intelligence, sustainability, and efficiency. But to unlock its full value, photonics needs to work hand-in-hand with cloud platforms, data systems, and AI. That means businesses must invest not just in photonic hardware, but also in systems integration and interdisciplinary talent. When used strategically, photonics can cut energy consumption, streamline supply chains, and uncover insights that drive smarter decisions.

Across industries, photonics is already reshaping the way things are done. In smart manufacturing, LiDAR, high-speed imaging, and laser systems have transformed production processes, improving quality control and enabling real-time monitoring. In agriculture, LiDAR and hyperspectral imaging give farmers powerful tools to maximize crop health and resource efficiency. And in energy management, technologies like photovoltaic cells and fiber-optic sensors are boosting renewable energy performance and enabling smarter grids. The case studies in this chapter show just how significant photonics has become in IIoT applications. As the technology continues to evolve, its role will only expand—driving efficiency, sustainability, and opening doors to new innovations.

Further Research

The goal of future developments should be to increase the accessibility, interoperability, and industry adaptability of photonic systems.

Advances in photonics are predicted to bring about radical change in a number of industries and facets of daily life, setting the field up for an exciting and revolutionary future. Photonics will be crucial to developing faster and more efficient communication networks as the demand for high-speed internet and data transmission increases. Improvements in fiber optics and photonic integrated circuits (PICs) will enable faster data rates and lower latency, facilitating the growth of 5G networks and the Internet of Things.

With features like low noise and fast speed, photonic quantum bits (qubits) are opening the door to more potent and effective quantum computers. Photonics will continue to advance medical imaging, diagnosis, and treatment. Examples of more accurate and accessible techniques that can improve patient outcomes and lower medical costs include laser surgery, photodynamic therapy, and OCT. Photonics is also helping to develop renewable energy sources, particularly in the areas of solar energy and energy-efficient lighting. Developments in photovoltaic materials and photonic devices will increase the efficiency and cost of solar panels, while LED technology will continue to advance and reduce energy consumption and greenhouse gas emissions.

The use of photonics in manufacturing processes will increase accuracy, speed, and efficiency. Because they enable the production of complex and customized parts with minimal waste, laser-based technologies like additive manufacturing (3D printing) and laser cutting will become more widely used.

Photonics will play a key role in defense and security applications such as communication, navigation, and surveillance. LiDAR (light detection and ranging) devices, for example, will increase the precision and situational awareness of autonomous vehicles.

CHAPTER 7

Challenges and Future Directions

Photonics—the science and technology of generating, controlling, and detecting photons—is becoming increasingly central to the evolution of IIoT systems. Its inherent advantages, such as high bandwidth, immunity to electromagnetic interference, and precision sensing capabilities, make it suitable for the stringent requirements of industrial environments.

This chapter provides a comprehensive overview of the key challenges hindering the large-scale deployment of photonics in the Industrial Internet of Things (IIoT) and explores the potential advancements and future trends that can transform photonic systems into mainstream IIoT enablers.

Scalability and Integration Issues

Heterogeneous integration in photonic systems involves combining dissimilar materials such as silicon with indium phosphide, lithium niobate, or polymers onto a single chip. While this enables diverse functionalities, it presents significant challenges due to differences in thermal expansion coefficients, lattice constants, and fabrication techniques among the materials. These mismatches can lead to thermal stress, resulting in cracking or delamination, fabrication yield losses, and difficulty in maintaining precise optical alignment across materials. Another critical challenge is precision optical alignment. Photonic components like waveguides, lasers, and photodetectors must be aligned with micrometer-level accuracy. Coupling light between fibers and chips or between chips demands high-precision packaging and alignment techniques.

© Dr. Preeta Sharan, Dr. Sandip Kumar Roy, Harshada J. Patil, Aryan Chaudhary, and Dr. Deepak Kumar 2026
Dr. P. Sharan et al., *Photonics in Industrial IoT: Transforming Manufacturing and Beyond*,
https://doi.org/10.1007/979-8-8688-2694-8_7

Any misalignment leads to insertion losses, thereby reducing the sensitivity
and efficiency of the system. These requirements not only increase manufacturing
complexity but also drive up cost and reduce yield. Thermal management is also a
major concern, as photonic devices such as fiber bragg gratings (FBGs), resonators, and
interferometers are highly sensitive to temperature fluctuations. Heat generated from
cointegrated electronic components can shift the refractive index of photonic elements,
altering their performance. Although thermoelectric coolers (TECs) and thermal design
approaches can mitigate these effects, they come at the expense of increased power
consumption, cost, and design complexity. Furthermore, photonic components like
modulators and tunable lasers require analog bias voltages, precise current control, and
thermal tuning, whereas traditional electronic integrated circuits (ICs) operate using
standardized digital power supplies.

This discrepancy poses a challenge in developing effective mixed-signal interfaces
and on-chip drivers that can support both domains efficiently. Lastly, standardization
remains a persistent issue in the field of photonic integration. The lack of unified
platforms and fabrication standards hinders interoperability and scalability. While
silicon photonics is gaining traction as a standard platform, many applications
still depend on custom fabrication processes. This results in higher customization
costs, limited compatibility between systems, and prolonged development cycles.
The difficulties in incorporating photonic elements into IIoT systems are illustrated
graphically in Figure 7-1.

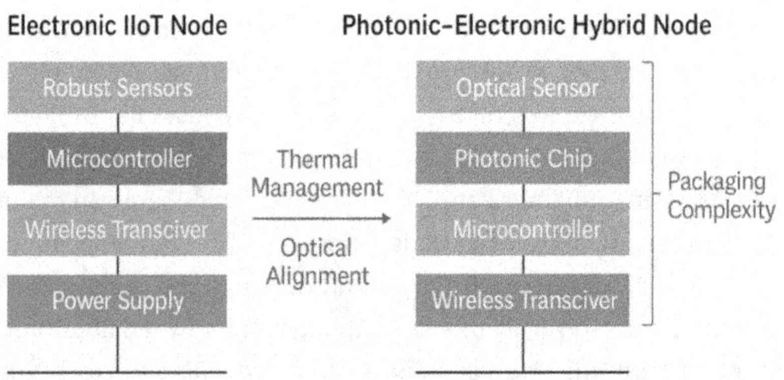

Figure 7-1. *Challenges in Integrating Photonic Components into IIoT Systems*

Scalability Issues in Photonic Systems

Scalability in photonic systems faces significant hurdles that limit their widespread adoption and integration, particularly when compared to electronic systems. One of the key limitations lies in wafer-scale fabrication. While electronic devices benefit from highly mature CMOS technology—allowing billions of transistors to be packed onto a single chip—photonic devices remain limited in scale due to their inherently larger dimensions (micron-scale rather than nanometer-scale), greater process variability, and the absence of a universal foundry ecosystem akin to TSMC or Intel. This makes consistent, high-volume photonic manufacturing difficult to achieve. Testing and packaging further compound scalability issues. Unlike electronic devices, which can be electrically tested with high-speed, automated systems, photonic components require optical probing that is slower, often manual or semi-automated, and significantly more expensive.

In fact, packaging alone can account for 50–80% of the total cost of photonic components, making this a critical bottleneck in scaling production. Another scalability challenge is interconnect density. Electronics have advanced by using dense electrical interconnects and multi-layered PCBs, but optical interconnects rely on waveguides or fibers, which require a minimum bend radius and cannot easily cross layers. This limits the ability to build compact, multilayered optical circuits, constraining the design flexibility and scalability that electronics enjoy. Yield and repeatability also pose significant barriers. Photonic devices are highly sensitive to fabrication variations such as etch depth and doping concentrations. As a result, complex circuits like on-chip spectrometers or optical processors suffer from low yields, with inconsistent device characteristics that make mass production unreliable and costly. Finally, cost and supply chain limitations restrict the scalability of photonic systems. There are only a few commercial foundries offering photonic fabrication services, and prototyping remains both expensive and time-consuming. The lack of standardized, off-the-shelf solutions adds further delays, making it difficult to rapidly scale photonic technologies for industrial applications like the Industrial Internet of Things (IIoT). Emerging research and development efforts are actively addressing the scalability and integration challenges in photonic systems through a variety of promising solutions. Silicon photonics foundries—such as those operated by Intel, IMEC, and AIM Photonics—are pioneering scalable, CMOS-compatible photonic manufacturing processes that leverage existing semiconductor infrastructure.

This approach holds the potential to bring photonic integration closer to the mass production capabilities of electronics. Another key advancement is 3D integration, where photonic and electronic components are stacked vertically using through-silicon vias (TSVs), enabling compact, high-density integration without sacrificing performance. To streamline the complex design processes inherent in photonics, photonic design automation (PDA) tools are being developed, analogous to the electronic design automation (EDA) tools long used in the semiconductor industry. PDA enables automated layout generation, simulation, and verification, significantly reducing development time and errors. Additionally, additive manufacturing techniques are emerging as a novel solution, allowing for the direct printing of waveguides and optical circuits. This approach can reduce the need for high-precision alignment and potentially lower the overall cost and complexity of photonic packaging and assembly. Collectively, these innovations are paving the way for more scalable, efficient, and commercially viable photonic systems.

Making photonic devices compact and robust for field deployment, especially in Industrial Internet of Things (IIoT) environments, is a significant engineering challenge. Table 7-1 is handy for key takeaways for IIoT.

Table 7-1. *Key Takeaway for IIoT*

Factor	Impact on Scalability
Material incompatibility	Hinders heterogeneous photonic circuit fabrication
Alignment & packaging	Major cost driver; slows manufacturing and increases footprint
Testing complexity	Reduces throughput and increases time to market
Yield variability	Impacts device reliability and batch consistency
Lack of standards	Prevents a plug-and-play ecosystem, delaying industrial adoption

Physical Size vs. Photonic Constraints

Photonic systems are inherently constrained by diffraction-limited design, as the size of photonic components is fundamentally governed by the wavelength of light—typically around 1 to 1.5μm. This limitation makes photonic elements such as waveguides, resonators, and interferometers significantly larger than their electronic counterparts, like transistors. Attempts to miniaturize these components often lead to increased signal loss due to sharp bends in waveguides and unwanted crosstalk between adjacent structures, compromising performance and efficiency. In addition to size constraints, coupling space presents another critical design limitation. Efficient input and output coupling—such as interfacing photonic circuits with optical fibers or photodetectors—requires highly precise physical alignment. This necessity for accurate alignment not only consumes valuable chip real estate but also imposes significant constraints on circuit layout and integration flexibility, further complicating the design and scalability of photonic systems.

Environmental Robustness

Photonic devices such as fiber Bragg gratings (FBGs) and microring resonators are highly sensitive to temperature changes, as their operation relies on the refractive index of materials, which varies with temperature. In real-world field environments—like factories or outdoor installations—temperature fluctuations can be substantial, leading to challenges such as wavelength drift and loss of calibration. To counter these effects, solutions like thermo-electric coolers (TECs) and athermal design strategies are employed; however, these approaches come with trade-offs, including increased system size, added power consumption, and greater complexity. Mechanical stability is another critical concern, especially in Industrial Internet of Things (IIoT) environments where shocks, vibrations, and mechanical disturbances are common. Precise optical alignment is essential for maintaining signal integrity, and even minor disruptions can impair optical coupling or cause cracks and misalignments in fiber interfaces. To ensure reliable performance under such conditions, photonic packaging must be ruggedized, which often results in bulkier and more complex systems. These mechanical and thermal sensitivities pose significant barriers to the deployment of photonic technologies in harsh or dynamic environments.

Packaging Complexity

Hybrid integration is a common approach in photonic systems, involving the combination of various materials such as silicon, indium phosphide, and lithium niobate to leverage their distinct optical properties. However, each material brings unique characteristics, including differing coefficients of thermal expansion and bonding requirements. These differences make it difficult to achieve seamless integration, often resulting in complex, multi-layer packaging architectures. Such packaging not only adds to the design and fabrication challenges but also limits the potential for miniaturization, which is critical for compact, scalable systems. Optical isolation adds another layer of complexity. To maintain signal integrity and prevent issues like light leakage, back-reflection, and interference from ambient light, photonic systems require shielding layers, optical filters, and meticulously planned layouts. While these measures are essential for reliable performance, they inevitably increase the physical footprint of the device, making it more difficult to achieve the compactness and integration density commonly seen in electronic systems.

Power and Interface Overhead

Even compact photonic devices require various supporting functionalities that complicate efforts toward full miniaturization. For instance, modulators often need biasing voltages, while many photonic components demand precise temperature control to maintain performance stability. Additionally, photodetector outputs typically require signal conditioning through amplification and filtering. To enable these functions, support electronics such as amplifiers, drivers, and controllers must be integrated alongside the photonic components. This necessity for additional circuitry increases the overall system complexity and size, making it challenging to achieve truly miniaturized and self-contained photonic solutions.

Field Calibration and Maintenance

Unlike electronic systems, many photonic devices require regular calibration to maintain accurate and reliable performance. For example, fiber Bragg gratings (FBGs) depend on precise wavelength references, while interferometric sensors are particularly sensitive to environmental drift. These calibration needs present significant challenges, especially in field deployments where recalibration can be complex, time-consuming, and often impractical. Moreover, ensuring long-term stability typically necessitates active compensation techniques, which not only increase the system's size and power requirements but also add to its overall cost and design complexity. Following Table 7-2 is a ready reference for key difficulties in IIoT.

Table 7-2. *Summary of Key Difficulties in IIoT*

Challenge Area	Details
Size constraints	Wavelength-scale optics resist extreme miniaturization
Thermal effects	Cause wavelength shifts; require active or passive thermal control
Mechanical robustness	Sensitive to vibration/shock; alignment can degrade
Material integration	Multimaterial systems are hard to scale and package tightly
Environmental exposure	Dust, moisture, and electromagnetic interference can degrade performance
Interface electronics	The need for signal conditioning and control systems limits compactness

Ongoing solutions and research in photonic technologies are focused on addressing integration, stability, and scalability challenges. Photonic Integrated Circuits (PICs) are advancing the monolithic integration of photonic elements, significantly reducing device size and improving reliability. Athermal device design is also gaining traction, using specialized materials or geometries to counteract thermal shifts and enhance performance stability across varying temperatures. Meanwhile, flexible photonics is emerging as a novel approach, utilizing polymer waveguides and two-dimensional materials on bendable substrates to enable lightweight, adaptable systems. In the realm of manufacturing, passive optical packaging techniques—such as align-once, glue-and-cure processes—are simplifying volume production by eliminating the need for repeated precision alignment. Additionally, machine learning-based calibration methods are being developed to automatically compensate for performance drift, reducing or eliminating the need for manual recalibration and paving the way for more autonomous, long-term deployment of photonic systems.

Integration with Electronic Systems

Combining electrical and photonic systems on a single chip presents significant challenges due to the fundamentally different physical and operational characteristics of these technologies. Photonic components, which manipulate light signals, often require materials and device structures that differ greatly from those used in traditional electronics. For example, photonics may involve materials like silicon, indium phosphide, or lithium niobate, each with distinct thermal expansion rates and fabrication requirements. Integrating these with electronic circuits, which typically rely on silicon CMOS technology, can lead to issues such as thermal stress, cracking, and misalignment due to incompatible material properties. Additionally, photonic devices often need analog bias voltages, precise current control, and temperature stabilization, while electronic circuits generally operate digitally with standardized power supplies. This disparity necessitates complex mixed-signal interfaces and driver circuits to bridge the two domains, complicating design and fabrication. Furthermore, packaging and alignment of optical components must achieve micron-level precision, which is more demanding than typical electronic packaging. Managing heat dissipation is also critical, as temperature fluctuations affect photonic device performance and can degrade overall system reliability. These combined factors make the co-integration of electrical and photonic systems on a single chip a complex, multidisciplinary challenge requiring advanced materials engineering, precise fabrication, and sophisticated circuit design.

Network Scalability and Interoperability

Managing high-throughput photonic data across large Industrial Internet of Things (IIoT) networks involves several complex challenges. First, the sheer volume of data generated by photonic sensors and devices—such as fiber optic sensors, spectrometers, or optical communication links—can be immense, requiring robust data handling, transmission, and processing infrastructure. Ensuring reliable, low-latency transfer of this high-bandwidth data across extensive IIoT networks demands highly efficient optical interconnects and network architectures designed to minimize bottlenecks. Another major issue is signal integrity and noise management. Optical signals traveling over long distances or through numerous network nodes can suffer from attenuation, dispersion, and interference, leading to data degradation. Maintaining high signal quality requires advanced error correction, signal amplification, and repeaters, which add complexity and cost. Scalability also poses a significant challenge. As IIoT networks grow, integrating and managing numerous photonic devices across distributed sites becomes more complicated. Network management must handle dynamic routing, device calibration, and synchronization without overwhelming system resources. Additionally, the diversity of devices and lack of standardization in photonic components can lead to interoperability issues, complicating seamless data integration. Finally, energy efficiency and thermal management are critical in large-scale deployments, as photonic systems and their electronic counterparts consume considerable power and generate heat, impacting overall system stability and operational costs. Addressing these challenges requires coordinated advances in photonic hardware, network protocols, data analytics, and system design to fully leverage the benefits of high-throughput photonic data in IIoT environments.

Advancements in Photonic Materials

Different types of photonic materials are used to fabricate optical waveguides, photodetectors, laser diodes, modulators, and so on. The material list with their various properties such as refractive index, bandgap value, transparency range, nonlinear optical properties, and their integration compatibility is provided in Table 7-3.

Table 7-3. *Material Properties Comparison for Photonic Applications in IIoT*

Comparative Chart of Photonic Materials

Material	Refractive (Index)	Bandgap(eV)	Transparancy Range	Nonlinear Optical Properties	Integration Compatibility
Silicon	≈ 3.47 (at 1.55µm)	1.1	1.1 - 8	Moderate	Optical Waveguides, Modulators, Photodetectors
Silica (SiO_2)	≈ 1.44 (at 1.55µm)	9	0.2 - 3.5	Very Low	Low loss Waveguides
Silicon Nitride (Si_2N_4)	≈ 2 (at 1.55µm)	5	0.4 - 2.5	Low	Low loss Waveguides
Galium Arsenide (GaAs)	≈ 3.3 (at 1.55µm)	1.42	0.9 - 1.7	Moderate	Laser Diodes, Modulators, Photodetectors
Graphene	Variable	0 Semi Metal	Broad THz - UV	Very High	High Speed Telecom Devices, Quantum Photonics
Lithium Neobate ($LiNbO_3$)	≈ 2.2	0.4	Extremely High Pockels Effect	Under delelp	Electro optic modulators, non linear optics
Chalcogenide Glasses	2.0 - 2.8	0.35 - 5.5	Very High	Moderate	Modulators, Detectors, THz devices
Chalongee	2.0 - 3.15	0.5 - 10	Difficult to integrate	Moderate	Modulators, Detectors, THz devices

Silicon Photonics

CMOS compatibility is a major advantage of silicon photonics, as it allows photonic components to be fabricated using the same manufacturing infrastructure as conventional electronic integrated circuits. This compatibility promises reduced cost, higher integration density, and the potential for mass production using mature CMOS processes. However, despite these advantages, a key limitation of silicon photonics lies in silicon's poor efficiency as a light emitter. Silicon is an indirect bandgap material, meaning it does not efficiently emit light when electrically excited. In contrast to direct bandgap materials like indium phosphide (InP) or gallium arsenide (GaAs), silicon cannot support efficient spontaneous or stimulated emission of photons. This makes it extremely difficult to fabricate silicon-based lasers or optical amplifiers, which are essential for fully integrated optical systems. As a result, many silicon photonics platforms rely on hybrid integration—bonding or coupling III-V materials onto silicon substrates—to provide light sources. This introduces additional complexity, alignment challenges, and potential yield issues during fabrication. Moreover, integrating these non-CMOS-compatible materials undermines some of the cost and scalability benefits of a purely silicon-based approach. Researchers are exploring workarounds such as silicon-based light sources using Raman lasers, germanium-based emitters, and 2D materials, but none have yet matched the performance and efficiency of traditional III-V lasers. Until a CMOS-compatible, high-efficiency light source is fully realized; this limitation will remain a critical bottleneck in the evolution of silicon photonics for large-scale applications.

Polymer and Organic Photonic Materials

In the context of photonic devices, polymer and organic materials offer a promising path toward flexibility, but this comes at the expense of environmental stability. Polymers and organic compounds can be fabricated on lightweight, bendable substrates, making them ideal for applications requiring conformability—such as wearable sensors, flexible IIoT devices, or integration onto non-planar surfaces. Their low processing temperatures, cost-effectiveness, and tunable optical properties further enhance their appeal for scalable, low-cost photonic integration. However, the key trade-off is environmental stability. Unlike inorganic materials such as silicon or indium phosphide, polymers and organics are inherently more susceptible to degradation under environmental stressors. Exposure to moisture, oxygen, UV radiation, and temperature fluctuations can cause these materials to oxidize, deform, or lose their optical performance over time. This leads to drift in sensor readings, loss of signal fidelity, or complete device failure—especially in harsh or outdoor industrial environments common in IIoT deployments. Efforts to mitigate these issues include encapsulation techniques, UV-blocking coatings, and the development of more robust polymer formulations. Still, these add layers of complexity and cost and often compromise the very flexibility these materials are valued for. Thus, while polymers and organic materials are excellent for enabling mechanical flexibility, ensuring long-term environmental stability remains a central challenge in making them viable for reliable, large-scale photonic applications.

Two-Dimensional Materials

Two-dimensional (2D) materials such as graphene and molybdenum disulfide (MoS_2) have generated significant interest in photonics due to their exceptional optical and electronic properties. These atomically thin materials offer advantages such as high carrier mobility, strong light-matter interaction, and mechanical flexibility, making them suitable for a wide range of photonic and optoelectronic applications.

Graphene, for instance, is prized for its broadband optical absorption and ultrafast carrier dynamics. It has been explored for use in photodetectors, modulators, and saturable absorbers. Its ability to operate across a wide spectral range (from visible to mid-IR) and support high-speed modulation makes it especially attractive for integrated photonic circuits and optical communications. However, one of graphene's challenges is its lack of a bandgap, which limits its ability to achieve high on/off contrast in photodetectors and modulators. This makes it less ideal for applications requiring high signal discrimination or switching.

MoS_2, a transition metal dichalcogenide (TMD), does possess a direct bandgap when in monolayer form, making it suitable for light emission and photodetection in the visible spectrum. MoS_2 and related TMDs are being developed for ultra-thin photodetectors, LEDs, and even flexible laser components. Their atomically thin nature also allows for strong light absorption in a compact footprint, useful in miniaturized IIoT devices. Despite these advantages, integrating 2D materials into practical photonic systems remains challenging. Issues include material uniformity over large areas, interface quality with other materials (especially silicon), and environmental stability—many 2D materials degrade upon exposure to air, moisture, or light. Additionally, scalable fabrication techniques like chemical vapor deposition (CVD) often introduce defects or grain boundaries that impair performance. In summary, while 2D materials such as graphene and MoS_2 offer exciting potential in next-generation photonic devices due to their flexibility, speed, and spectral versatility, they still face significant challenges in large-scale manufacturing, device integration, and long-term reliability.

Photonic Crystals and Metamaterials

Photonic crystals and metamaterials represent cutting-edge approaches for manipulating light in ways not possible with conventional materials. These structures are engineered to have periodic variations in refractive index (photonic crystals) or subwavelength features (metamaterials), enabling precise control over light propagation, including bandgap filtering, negative refraction, slow-light effects, and enhanced light confinement. Photonic crystals use periodic dielectric structures to create photonic bandgaps—frequency ranges where light cannot propagate—allowing for highly selective optical filters, waveguides, and resonators. These are particularly useful in applications such as optical communications, biosensing, and on-chip routing of light. Meanwhile, metamaterials are designed to exhibit electromagnetic properties not found in nature, such as negative permittivity or permeability, enabling exotic effects like superlensing and cloaking. Despite their advanced capabilities, scalability remains a major hurdle. Fabricating photonic crystals and metamaterials with nanoscale precision over large areas is technically demanding and cost-intensive. Traditional techniques such as electron-beam lithography offer high resolution but are too slow and expensive for mass production. Furthermore, even small deviations in the structure—such as variations in hole size or placement—can lead to significant performance degradation, making high-yield manufacturing challenging. Additionally, integrating these structures with existing photonic or electronic platforms is non-trivial. For example, aligning photonic crystal waveguides with other on-chip components requires precise placement and often results in coupling losses. Thermal and mechanical stability can also be concerns, especially for metamaterials composed of fragile or exotic materials. In summary, while photonic crystals and metamaterials unlock powerful capabilities for controlling light in photonic systems, their adoption in practical, large-scale applications is limited by fabrication complexity, integration challenges, and sensitivity to imperfections. Overcoming these barriers will require innovations in materials science, nanofabrication, and hybrid integration techniques.

Emerging Trends in IIoT Enabled by Photonics

Nowadays there is a need to transform existing IIoT devices using photonic technologies in order to avail the advantages of light technology such as fast response and reliability. Figure 7-2 illustrates different photonic technologies that will transform IIoT.

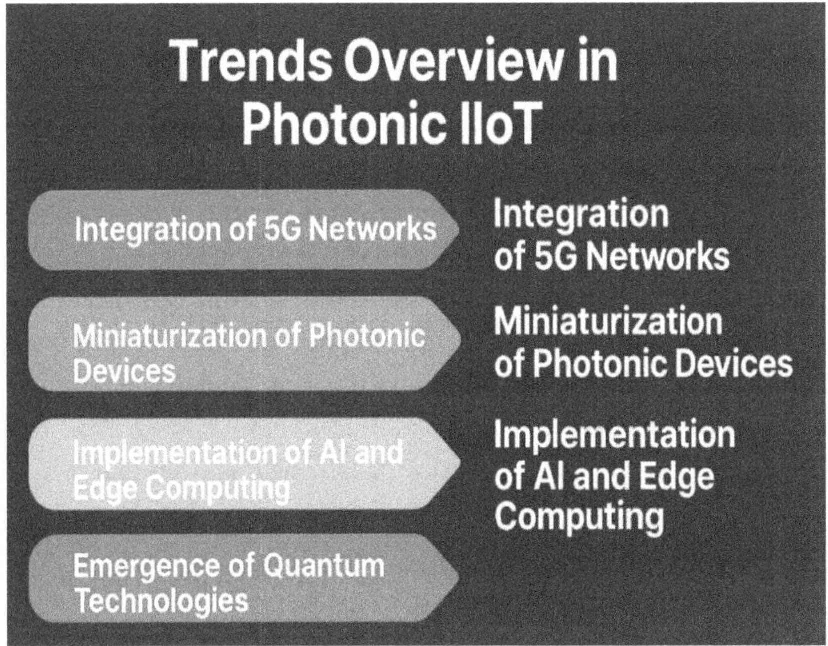

Figure 7-2. *Emerging Photonic Technologies Transforming IIoT*

Edge and Fog Computing with Integrated Photonics

Integrated photonics is increasingly being explored as a key enabler for edge and fog computing, especially in latency-sensitive Industrial Internet of Things (IIoT) applications. These computing paradigms push data processing closer to the source—whether it's a sensor, actuator, or local gateway—to minimize the time and energy involved in transmitting data to centralized cloud servers. Integrated photonics offers a compelling advantage in this context by leveraging the speed of light for high-bandwidth, low-latency data transmission and processing. Optical interconnects within or between edge nodes can dramatically reduce the bottlenecks associated with traditional electronic data movement, which becomes especially critical as the volume and velocity of sensor data continue to grow. Photonic systems can perform certain computational tasks—such as signal filtering, matrix multiplication, and Fourier transforms—directly in the optical domain, significantly accelerating processing speed while reducing power consumption. In fog computing architectures, where multiple edge devices coordinate and preprocess data collaboratively, photonic links can enable high-throughput inter-device communication without the need for bulky optical-to-electrical conversions at every node. This capability enhances real-time decision-making in environments like smart manufacturing, autonomous vehicles, and predictive maintenance systems. However, several challenges remain. Photonic processing components must be compact, cost-effective, and CMOS-compatible to be viable at the edge. Additionally, the need for optical-electrical conversion for tasks that can't be handled purely in the photonic domain still introduces complexity. Thermal management is another consideration, as even modest heating can affect the precision of photonic components. In summary, integrated photonics holds strong promise for enabling ultra-fast, efficient edge and fog computing by reducing latency and bandwidth constraints. Continued research in hybrid photonic-electronic integration and low-power optical computing architectures is key to realizing this potential.

Quantum Photonics for Secure Communication

Quantum photonics is emerging as a powerful tool for enhancing security in communication systems, particularly through Quantum Key Distribution (QKD). In QKD, encryption keys are generated and shared using quantum states of light—typically single photons—which are inherently secure due to the laws of quantum mechanics. Any attempt to intercept or measure the quantum signals disturbs them, alerting the parties to a potential breach. In industrial settings, where the security of sensitive data (e.g., operational parameters, control commands, or proprietary process information) is critical, QKD provides a robust defense against both current and future threats—including those posed by quantum computers. For Industrial Internet of Things (IIoT) networks that span across factories, substations, or remote infrastructure, QKD can secure communication links between edge devices, control centers, and cloud platforms. Quantum photonics plays a central role in enabling QKD systems, as it involves the generation, manipulation, and detection of individual photons with high precision. Integrated photonic chips can miniaturize these systems, making them more practical for deployment in harsh or space-constrained industrial environments. On-chip quantum sources, beam splitters, and detectors are being developed to create portable, scalable QKD devices. However, there are implementation challenges. Quantum systems are sensitive to environmental noise, require precise alignment, and often need cryogenic or low-noise detectors for optimal performance. Fiber loss over long distances can limit the range of QKD, although newer protocols like device-independent QKD and quantum repeaters aim to overcome this. Additionally, industrial adoption is slowed by the cost and complexity of quantum hardware, as well as the need to integrate QKD with existing security infrastructure. Despite these hurdles, pilot projects and early deployments of QKD in sectors like energy, manufacturing, and defense show strong promise. As quantum photonic technologies mature, they are expected to become a cornerstone of ultra-secure communication in future IIoT ecosystems.

AI-Driven Photonic Sensor Networks

AI-driven photonic sensor networks represent a convergence of two powerful technologies: optical sensing for high-resolution, real-time monitoring and machine learning (ML) for intelligent data interpretation. In Industrial Internet of Things (IIoT) environments—where vast amounts of data are generated by distributed sensors— this integration enables smarter, faster, and more adaptive systems. Photonic sensors, such as Fiber Bragg Gratings (FBGs), interferometers, and photonic crystal-based sensors, are widely used for measuring parameters like strain, temperature, pressure, and gas concentrations. They offer advantages such as immunity to electromagnetic interference, high sensitivity, and the ability to multiplex many sensors along a single fiber. However, the complexity and volume of data they produce—often in the form of spectral shifts or intensity changes—require sophisticated analytics to extract actionable insights. Machine learning enhances these photonic systems by enabling real-time calibration, anomaly detection, and predictive maintenance. For example:

- **Neural networks** can be trained to decode complex spectral data into accurate environmental parameters.

- **Support Vector Machines (SVMs)** or **decision trees** can detect patterns indicating system degradation or faults.

- **Reinforcement learning** can be used for adaptive control in dynamic environments.

Integration of ML algorithms directly into edge computing nodes or photonic chips themselves (where feasible) reduces latency and enables localized decision-making—critical in scenarios like structural health monitoring, smart manufacturing, and chemical leak detection. Despite the benefits, there are challenges. Photonic data is often high-dimensional and nonlinear, requiring well-curated training sets and significant computational resources. Sensor drift, environmental noise, and fabrication variability can complicate model accuracy. Additionally, deploying AI in critical systems requires strong robustness and explainability, particularly in safety-sensitive industrial contexts. In summary, the synergy between machine learning and photonic sensor networks is unlocking a new level of intelligence and autonomy in IIoT systems. With continued advances in edge AI and integrated photonics, these networks are poised to become central to next-generation smart infrastructure.

Hybrid Wireless-Photonic Systems

Hybrid wireless-photonic systems are a promising architecture for the future of the Industrial Internet of Things (IIoT), offering the flexibility of wireless communication alongside the ultra-high bandwidth and low latency of photonics. This hybrid approach addresses the limitations of each technology when used alone—wireless systems often struggle with interference and limited capacity, while photonic systems, though fast and secure, are typically constrained by physical fiber links.

In these systems, wireless modules (e.g., Wi-Fi, 5G, LoRa) are used for last-mile or mobile connectivity, while photonic backhaul networks handle heavy data transfer between edge nodes, gateways, and cloud or fog computing centers. This is especially beneficial in industrial settings with mobile sensors, robotics, or vehicles that require untethered communication but still generate large volumes of high-speed data. For example, real-time video feeds from machine vision systems or high-frequency sensor arrays can be transmitted wirelessly to a local access point, where data is then routed over a fiber-optic photonic network for fast analysis and storage. Photonic interconnects—due to their immunity to electromagnetic interference and low propagation delay—ensure high reliability in noisy factory environments. On the hardware side, Radio-over-Fiber (RoF) technologies and Millimeter-Wave-over-Fiber (mmWave-RoF) systems enable seamless integration between RF and optical domains. These platforms can transmit wireless signals directly over optical links, minimizing conversion losses and supporting centralized signal processing.

However, deploying hybrid systems presents several challenges:

- **Synchronization** between wireless and photonic domains can be complex, especially in time-sensitive applications.

- **Cost and infrastructure** for laying fiber and integrating photonic components remain high.

- **Thermal and environmental management** of photonic components must be carefully designed to operate reliably in harsh or mobile industrial settings.

In summary, hybrid wireless-photonic systems offer a compelling model for IIoT by combining mobility with high-speed optical transport. As integration technologies mature and costs decrease, such architectures will become increasingly vital for supporting advanced applications like real-time analytics, autonomous systems, and distributed control networks.

Green Photonics

Green photonics refers to the development and deployment of photonic technologies that reduce energy consumption, lower environmental impact, and promote sustainability—an increasingly critical concern in the Industrial Internet of Things (IIoT) era. As industries scale their use of connected devices and data-intensive applications, energy-efficient communication and sensing systems are vital to meeting both economic and environmental goals.

Photonic systems inherently offer energy advantages in data transmission. Optical fibers transmit signals over long distances with negligible loss and no electromagnetic interference, reducing the need for repeaters and shielding. Additionally, passive photonic components—such as multiplexers, filters, and splitters—operate without external power, contributing to a lower overall energy footprint compared to active electronic counterparts.

Key developments in green photonics include:

- **Low-Power Modulators and Detectors**: Advances in silicon photonics and nanophotonics have enabled modulators that operate with sub-volt control and photodetectors with high efficiency, reducing electrical overhead.

- **Athermal Designs**: These designs use materials or geometries that are stable over a wide temperature range, minimizing the need for active thermal management (e.g., TECs), which typically consume significant power.

- **Photonic Energy Harvesting**: Integration of photovoltaic elements with photonic circuits opens avenues for self-powered sensor nodes, especially in outdoor or remote IIoT deployments.

- **Eco-Friendly Materials**: Research is expanding into biodegradable polymers, lead-free materials, and low-temperature fabrication processes to lessen environmental impact during manufacturing and disposal.

Despite these advances, several challenges remain. High-precision fabrication of photonic components still requires energy-intensive processes. Some photonic systems depend on rare or non-renewable materials, and integrating green designs often leads to trade-offs in performance, size, or cost. Moreover, ensuring long-term reliability and recyclability of photonic components in industrial environments adds complexity to lifecycle management. In conclusion, green photonics is a vital pillar for sustainable IIoT growth, combining technological innovation with environmental responsibility. Continued investment in materials science, fabrication techniques, and eco-conscious design will be essential to realizing the full potential of low-energy photonic systems.

Case Study: FBG Sensors for Gas Detection

A schematic of an FBG sensor detecting changes in reflected wavelength due to strain or temperature changes caused by gas presence. Include interrogation unit and data acquisition system. Fiber Bragg Grating (FBG) sensors are emerging as powerful tools for gas leak detection in Industrial Internet of Things (IIoT) applications, owing to their compactness, sensitivity, and immunity to electromagnetic interference. Their operation is based on detecting wavelength shifts in reflected light due to strain or temperature changes—phenomena that can be induced by gas expansion, pressure variation, or thermal effects during leaks. When functionalized with chemical coatings, FBGs can even detect specific gases through refractive index modulation or localized heating. Figure 7-3 shows how FBG is used to detect gas leakage and can be called an FBG gas sensor.

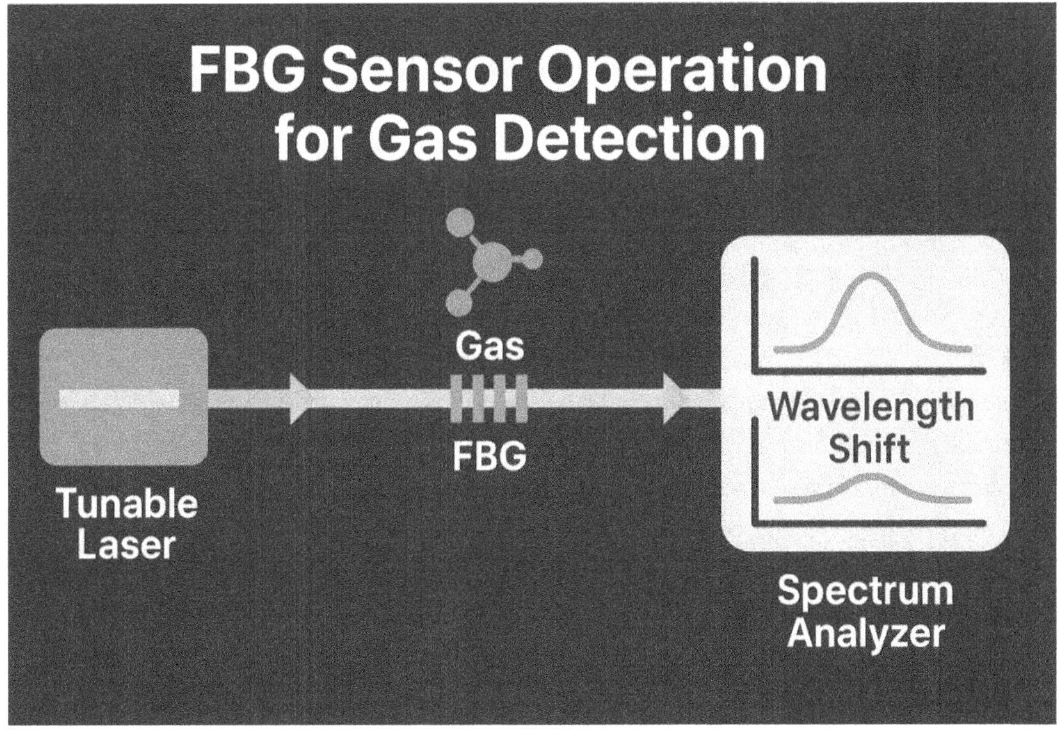

Figure 7-3. *Principle of Fiber Bragg Grating (FBG) Sensing for Gas Leak Detection*

Sensor Multiplexing

A key advantage of FBG technology is its multiplexing capability. Multiple FBGs can be inscribed along a single optical fiber at different grating wavelengths, enabling dozens of sensors to be deployed over long distances using a single interrogation unit. This reduces cabling complexity and cost, which is particularly valuable in large-scale industrial sites like oil refineries, pipelines, or chemical plants. It also allows distributed detection of leaks across wide or difficult-to-access areas with minimal infrastructure.

Benefits in Hazardous Environments

FBGs are inherently safe in explosive or hazardous environments, as they do not carry electrical current and are immune to electromagnetic interference. This makes them ideal for zones classified under ATEX or IECEx safety standards, where traditional electronic sensors might pose ignition risks. Additionally, FBGs are immune to

177

corrosion, can operate in high-temperature conditions, and are resistant to harsh chemicals—further enhancing their suitability for gas leak detection in demanding industrial settings.

Challenges in Rugged Packaging and Signal Processing

Despite their advantages, FBGs face several engineering challenges. One is the development of robust packaging that can protect the fragile fiber and grating structure from mechanical shock, vibration, and environmental wear while still allowing it to remain responsive to gas-induced changes. Encapsulation must balance sensitivity with durability, which is a non-trivial design constraint. Signal processing is another hurdle. FBG sensors require precise interrogation systems that can detect minute wavelength shifts (on the order of picometers), which often necessitates high-resolution optical spectrum analyzers or tunable lasers. In dynamic field conditions, temperature cross-sensitivity must be decoupled from gas-induced strain or refractive index changes—necessitating compensation algorithms or reference FBGs to isolate gas leak signals from background variations. These requirements can increase the cost and complexity of deployment compared to more traditional gas sensors. In summary, FBG-based gas leak detection systems offer a compelling solution for distributed, real-time monitoring in hazardous industrial environments. Their success depends on innovations in rugged packaging, interrogation technology, and smart signal processing to deliver reliable, scalable sensing networks.

Outlook and Recommendations

A clear timeline helps visualize the progressive milestones and goals for integrating photonics into IIoT, guiding research, development, and deployment efforts from near-term improvements to long-term transformative technologies.

Short-Term Goals (2025–2027): Improved Packaging and Early Standardization

In the immediate future, the focus will be on refining **robust, rugged packaging** techniques to protect photonic components in harsh industrial environments while maintaining sensitivity and miniaturization. Efforts will also target **early standardization** of photonic device interfaces, fabrication processes, and communication protocols to enable interoperability and reduce customization costs. Foundries will begin to offer more accessible fabrication runs, and early versions of photonic integrated circuits (PICs) will enter pilot applications.

Mid-Term Goals (2027–2030): AI-Driven Smart Sensors and Early Commercial Photonic ICs

By the late 2020s, integration of **machine learning and AI** with photonic sensor networks will become widespread, enabling smart, adaptive sensing and real-time data analytics at the edge. **Commercially viable photonic integrated circuits** with standardized form factors and improved performance will be available for IIoT applications, supported by advances in scalable manufacturing and automated testing. Hybrid architectures combining wireless and photonic connectivity will mature, improving system flexibility.

Long-Term Goals (2030+): Quantum Photonics and Fully Photonic IIoT Systems

Looking beyond 2030, the roadmap envisions **quantum photonic technologies** being integrated into IIoT systems for ultra-secure communication and sensing. Entire IIoT infrastructures may shift towards **fully photonic architectures** with optical processing, communication, and sensing seamlessly integrated. These systems will be highly scalable, energy-efficient, and capable of intelligent self-optimization.

Recommendations to Support This Roadmap

This roadmap and recommendations provide a strategic framework to accelerate the adoption and impact of photonics within the Industrial IoT landscape, as is given in Figure 7-4 and highlighted here:

1. **Standardization**: Develop and adopt industry-wide standards for photonic components, interfaces, and communication protocols to ensure interoperability and drive down costs.

2. **Open-Source Design Tools**: Promote open-source photonic design automation (PDA) tools and simulation frameworks to accelerate innovation and lower barriers for new entrants.

3. **Pilot Deployments**: Implement pilot projects across diverse industrial sectors to validate photonic technologies in real-world conditions, providing feedback to guide development.

4. **Interdisciplinary R&D**: Encourage collaboration across materials science, photonics, electronics, computer science, and industrial engineering to solve complex integration and application challenges.

5. **Training Programs**: Establish specialized educational and training programs to develop a skilled workforce proficient in photonics, AI integration, and IIoT systems.

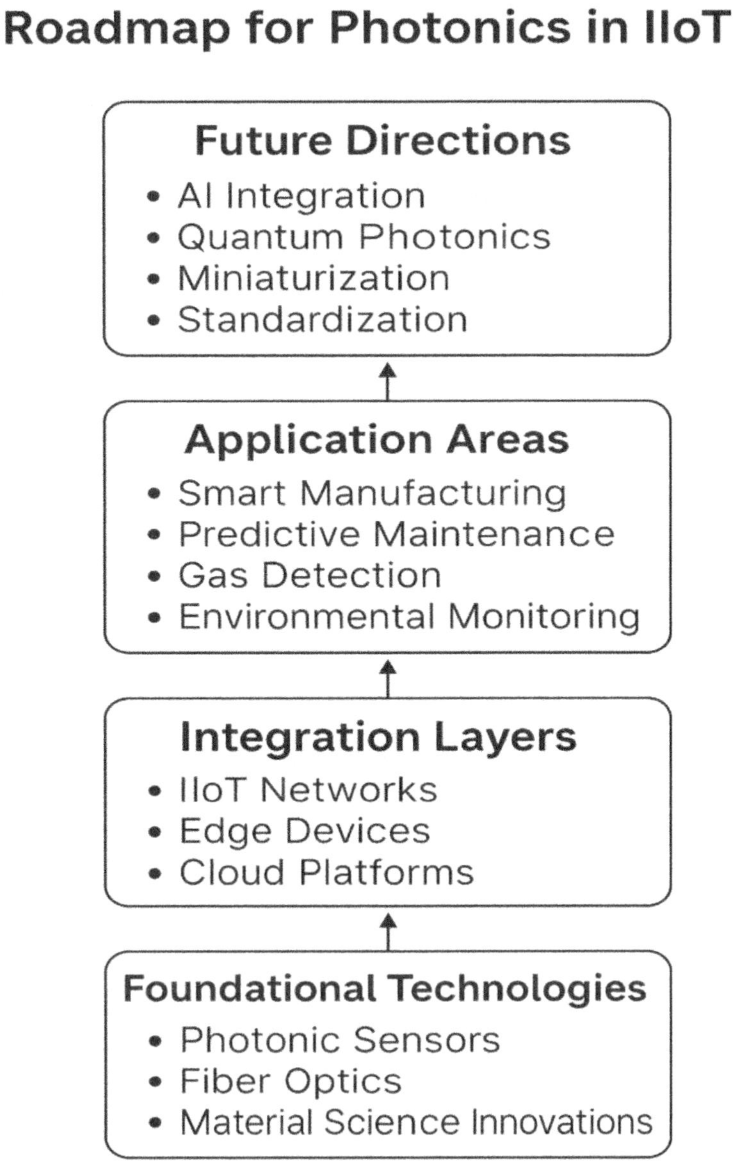

Roadmap for Photonics in IIoT

Future Directions
- AI Integration
- Quantum Photonics
- Miniaturization
- Standardization

Application Areas
- Smart Manufacturing
- Predictive Maintenance
- Gas Detection
- Environmental Monitoring

Integration Layers
- IIoT Networks
- Edge Devices
- Cloud Platforms

Foundational Technologies
- Photonic Sensors
- Fiber Optics
- Material Science Innovations

Figure 7-4. *Roadmap for Photonics in IIoT*

Conclusion

Photonics presents a transformative opportunity for IIoT systems, offering unprecedented capabilities in sensing, communication, and data processing. However, realizing this vision requires overcoming substantial technical and systemic challenges related to scalability, material development, and system integration.

References

Chapter 4

[1] Cui, X., Lengignon, C., Tao, W., Zhao, W., Wysocki, G., Fertein, E., Coeur, C., Cassez, A., Croize, L., Chen, W. and Wang, Y., 2012. Photonic sensing of the atmosphere by absorption spectroscopy. Journal of Quantitative Spectroscopy and Radiative Transfer, 113(11), pp.1300-1316.

[2] Svanberg, S., 2004. Environmental and medical applications of photonic interactions. Physica Scripta, 2004(T110), p.39.

[3] Zhao, Q. and Wagner, H.D., 2004. Raman spectroscopy of carbon-nanotube–based composites. Philosophical Transactions of the Royal Society of London. Series A: Mathematical, Physical and Engineering Sciences, 362(1824), pp.2407-2424.

[4] Kakihana, M., Osada, M. and Petrykin, V., 2000. Raman spectroscopy as a unique tool for characterizing high-Tc superconducting oxides. Physica C: Superconductivity, 338(1-2), pp.144-150.

[5] Salahioglu, F., Went, M.J. and Gibson, S.J., 2013. Application of Raman spectroscopy for the differentiation of lipstick traces. Analytical Methods, 5(20), pp.5392-5401.

[6] Bragg, W.H., 1914. X-rays and crystalline structure. Science, 40(1040), pp.795-802.

[7] Ward, C.R. and French, D., 2006. Determination of glass content and estimation of glass composition in fly ash using quantitative X-ray diffractometry. Fuel, 85(16), pp.2268-2277.

[8] Thakral, S., Terban, M.W., Thakral, N.K. and Suryanarayanan, R., 2016. Recent advances in the characterization of amorphous pharmaceuticals by X-ray diffractometry. Advanced Drug Delivery Reviews, 100, pp.183-193.

[9] Halvorsen, J.Ø., Stacey, P., Graff, P., Folven Gjengedal, E.L. and Ervik, T.K., 2025. Application of X-ray diffraction with Rietveld refinement to quantify mineral composition including crystalline silica in respirable dust. Journal of Occupational and Environmental Hygiene, 22(4), pp.248-258.

[10] Liu, S., Yang, H., Zhu, K., Liu, F., Zhao, L., Zhao, H., Zeng, M. and Ma, Z., 2025. Effect of heavy medium separation on the chemical structure and pyrolysis characteristics of Shenfu coal: Insights from FT-IR, XRD, and TG-DTG analysis. Journal of Analytical and Applied Pyrolysis, 186, p.106975.

[11] Brito, R.S., Pinheiro, H.M., Ferreira, F., Matos, J.S. and Lourenço, N.D., 2014. In situ UV-Vis spectroscopy to estimate COD and TSS in wastewater drainage systems. Urban Water Journal, 11(4), pp.261-273.

[12] Nkansah, K., Adedipe, O., Dawson-Andoh, B., Atta-Obeng, E., Slahor, J. and Osborn, L., 2015. Determination of concentration of ACQ wood preservative components by UV-Visible spectroscopy coupled with multivariate data analysis. Chemometrics and Intelligent Laboratory Systems, 147, pp.157-166.

[13] Antony, A. and Mitra, J., 2021. Refractive index-assisted UV/ Vis spectrophotometry to overcome spectral interference by impurities. Analytica Chimica Acta, 1149, p.238186.

[14] Chen, J., Li, J.Q., Li, T., Liu, H.G. and Wang, Y.Z., 2023. Application of UV-Vis and infrared spectroscopy on wild edible bolete mushrooms discrimination and evaluation: a review. Critical Reviews in Analytical Chemistry, 53(4), pp.852-868.

[15] Kumar, D. and Chaudhary, S., 2024. Database of critical materials applied as VOC sensors. In Complex and Composite Metal Oxides for Gas, VOC and Humidity Sensors (pp. 683-690). Elsevier.

[16]   Leheny, R.F. and McCants, C.E., 2009. Technologies for photonic sensor systems. Proceedings of the IEEE, 97(6), pp.957-970.

[17]   Hasan, M.G., Islam, M.A., Ferdous, A.I., Noor, K.S., Islam, M.S., Sadeque, M.G. and Rashed, A.N.Z., 2025. Environmental monitoring with sensitive photonic fiber sensors for hazardous chemicals. International Communications in Heat and Mass Transfer, 162, p.108631.

[18]   Teng, C., Yang, R., Min, R., Lu, J., Deng, S., Xue, M., Chen, M., Yuan, L. and Hu, X., 2025. Simultaneous Measurement of Liquid Level and Refractive Index Employing a Side-Polished Spiral Polymer Optical Fiber Based SPR Sensor. Photonic Sensors, 15(3), p.250318.

[19]   Chen, J., Wang, Z., Xiao, K., Ferraro, M., Ushakov, N., Kumar, S., Ge, F., Li, X. and Min, R., 2024. AI-enabled scalable smartphone photonic sensing system for remote healthcare monitoring. IEEE Internet of Things Journal.

[20]   Szendrei, K., Jiménez-Solano, A., Lozano, G., Lotsch, B.V. and Míguez, H., 2017. Fluorescent humidity sensors based on photonic resonators. Advanced Optical Materials, 5(23), p.1700663.

[21]   Karmakar, S., Kumar, D., Varshney, R.K. and Roy Chowdhury, D., 2020. Lattice-induced plasmon hybridization in metamaterials. Optics Letters, 45(13), pp.3386-3389.

[22]   Landy, N.I., Sajuyigbe, S., Mock, J.J., Smith, D.R. and Padilla, W.J., 2008. Perfect metamaterial absorber. Physical review letters, 100(20), p.207402.

[23]   Karmakar, S., Kumar, D., Pal, B.P., Varshney, R.K. and Roy Chowdhury, D., 2021. Magnetic wire: transverse magnetism in a one-dimensional plasmonic system. Optics Letters, 46(6), pp.1365-1368.

[24] Ben-Abu, E., Zigelman, A., Veksler, Y., Givli, S., Filipov, E., Lipson, H. and Gat, A.D., 2025. Reprogrammable 3D Shapes from 1D Metamaterial. Advanced Materials Technologies, 10(4), p.2401113.

[25] Rao, S.J.M., Kumar, D., Kumar, G. and Chowdhury, D.R., 2016. Probing the near-field inductive coupling in broadside coupled terahertz metamaterials. IEEE Journal of Selected Topics in Quantum Electronics, 23(4), pp.1-7.

[26] Sreekanth, K.V., Ouyang, Q., Sreejith, S., Zeng, S., Lishu, W., Ilker, E., Dong, W., ElKabbash, M., Ting, Y., Lim, C.T. and Hinczewski, M., 2019. Phase-change-material-based low-loss visible-frequency hyperbolic metamaterials for ultrasensitive label-free biosensing. Advanced Optical Materials, 7(12), p.1900081.

[27] Reinhard, B., Schmitt, K.M., Wollrab, V., Neu, J., Beigang, R. and Rahm, M., 2012. Metamaterial near-field sensor for deep-subwavelength thickness measurements and sensitive refractometry in the terahertz frequency range. Applied Physics Letters, 100(22).

[28] Ukirade, N.A., 2025. A review on advancement of materials for terahertz applications. Next Materials, 6, p.100479.

[29] Hu, B.B. and Nuss, M.C., 1995. Imaging with terahertz waves. Optics letters, 20(16), pp.1716-1718.

[30] Hu, X., Zhang, G., Qian, J., Lu, J., Zhu, Y. and Peng, Y., 2024. Terahertz s-SNOM imaging of a single cell with nanoscale resolution. Nano Letters, 24(25), pp.7757-7763.

[31] Amos, W.B. and White, J.G., 2003. How the confocal laser scanning microscope entered biological research. Biology of the Cell, 95(6), pp.335-342.

[32] Davidovits, P. and Egger, M.D., 1969. Scanning laser microscope. Nature, 223(5208), pp.831-831.

[33] Herrmann, T., Liebig, T., Mallow, J., Bruns, C., Stadler, J., Mylius, J., Brosch, M., Svedja, J.T., Chen, Z., Rennings, A. and Scheich, H., 2018. Metamaterial-based transmit and receive system for whole-body magnetic resonance imaging at ultra-high magnetic fields. PloS one, 13(1), p.e0191719.

[34] Pitt, G.D., Batchelder, D.N., Bennett, R., Bormett, R.W., Hayward, I.P., Smith, B.J.E., Williams, K.P.J., Yang, Y.Y., Baldwin, K.J. and Webster, S., 2005. Engineering aspects and applications of the new Raman instrumentation. IEE Proceedings-Science, Measurement and Technology, 152(6), pp.241-318.

[35] Raman, C.V. and Krishnan, K.S., 1928. A new type of secondary radiation. Nature, 121(3048), pp.501-502.

[36] Bertrand, L., Schöder, S., Joosten, I., Webb, S.M., Thoury, M., Calligaro, T., Anheim, É. and Simon, A., 2023. Practical advances towards safer analysis of heritage samples and objects. TrAC Trends in Analytical Chemistry, 164, p.117078.

[37] Sekar, S.K.V., Mosca, S., Farina, A., Martelli, F., Taroni, P., Valentini, G., Cubeddu, R. and Pifferi, A., 2017. Frequency offset Raman spectroscopy (FORS) for depth probing of diffusive media. Optics Express, 25(5), pp.4585-4597.

[38] Gerasimova, Y., Laptash, N., Krylov, A., Vonog, V. and Vtyurin, A., 2021. Structural Phase Transition in (NH4) 3GeF7–Raman Spectroscopy Data. Crystals, 11(5), p.506.

[39] Sharma, M., Rani, S., Pathak, D.K., Bhatia, R., Kumar, R. and Sameera, I., 2021. Temperature dependent Raman modes of reduced graphene oxide: Effect of anharmonicity, crystallite size and defects. Carbon, 184, pp.437-444.

[40] Krylov, A.S., Kolesnikova, E.M., Isaenko, L.I., Krylova, S.N. and Vtyurin, A.N., 2014. Measurement of Raman-scattering spectra of Rb2KMoO3F3 crystal: Evidence for controllable disorder in the lattice structure. Crystal growth & design, 14(3), pp.923-927.

[41]   Krylov, A.S., Vtyurin, A.N., Oreshonkov, A.S., Voronov, V.N. and Krylova, S.N., 2013. Structural transformations in a single-crystal Rb2NaYF6: Raman scattering study. Journal of Raman Spectroscopy, 44(5), pp.763-769.

[42]   Sharma, M., Rani, S., Pathak, D.K., Bhatia, R., Kumar, R. and Sameera, I., 2021. Manifestation of anharmonicities in terms of phonon modes' energy and lifetime in multiwall carbon nanotubes. Carbon, 171, pp.568-574.

[43]   Rani, S., Tanwar, M., Rani, C., Bhatia, R., Kumar, R. and Sameera, I., 2023. Interplay between anharmonic and lattice effects in mos2 nanoflowers: Probing through temperature-dependent raman spectroscopy. The Journal of Physical Chemistry C, 127(36), pp.17843-17850.

[44]   Ghanghass, A., Rani, C., Sameera, I., Kumar, R. and Bhatia, R., 2024. Interlayer Vibronic Interactions and Phonon Anharmonic Decay in Few-Layer WS2 Nanoflakes. The Journal of Physical Chemistry C, 128(22), pp.9202-9208.

[45]   Das, R.S. and Agrawal, Y.K., 2011. Raman spectroscopy: Recent advancements, techniques and applications. Vibrational spectroscopy, 57(2), pp.163-176.

[46]   Xu, B., Mao, N., Zhao, Y., Tong, L. and Zhang, J., 2021. Polarized Raman spectroscopy for determining crystallographic orientation of low-dimensional materials. The Journal of Physical Chemistry Letters, 12(31), pp.7442-7452.

[47]   Orlando, A., Franceschini, F., Muscas, C., Pidkova, S., Bartoli, M., Rovere, M. and Tagliaferro, A., 2021. A comprehensive review on Raman spectroscopy applications. Chemosensors, 9(9), p.262.

[48]   Zhao, J., Wang, Z., Lan, J., Khan, I., Ye, X., Wan, J., Fei, Y., Huang, S., Li, S. and Kang, J., 2021. Recent advances and perspectives in photo-induced enhanced Raman spectroscopy. Nanoscale, 13(19), pp.8707-8721.

[49]   Gim, D.H., Sur, Y., Lee, Y.H., Lee, J.H., Moon, S., Oh, Y.S. and Kim, K.H., 2022. Pressure-Dependent Structure of BaZrO3 Crystals as Determined by Raman Spectroscopy. Materials, 15(12), p.4286.

[50]   Jaykhedkar, N., Tripathy, N., Shah, V., Pujari, B. and Premkumar, S., 2020. A comprehensive study of pressure dependent phase transitions in ferroelectric PbTiO3, PbZrO3 and BaTiO3. Materials Chemistry and Physics, 254, p.123545.

[51]   Wan, F., Du, L., Chen, W., Wang, P., Wang, J. and Shi, H., 2017. A novel method to directly analyze dissolved acetic acid in transformer oil without extraction using Raman spectroscopy. Energies, 10(7), p.967.

[52]   Smith, E. and Dent, G., 2019. Modern Raman spectroscopy: a practical approach. John Wiley & Sons.

[53]   Paul, S., Karak, S., Mathew, A., Ram, A. and Saha, S., 2021. Electron-phonon and phonon-phonon anharmonic interactions in 2 H-Mo X 2 (X= S, Te): A comprehensive resonant Raman study. Physical Review B, 104(7), p.075418.

[54]   Pawbake, A.S., Mishra, K.K., Machuno, L.G., Gelamo, R.V., Ravindran, T.R., Rout, C.S. and Late, D.J., 2018. Temperature and pressure dependent Raman spectroscopy of plasma treated multilayer graphene nanosheets. Diamond and Related Materials, 84, pp.146-156.

[55]   Li, X., Li, J., Wang, K., Wang, X., Wang, S., Chu, X., Xu, M., Fang, X., Wei, Z., Zhai, Y. and Zou, B., 2016. Pressure and temperature-dependent Raman spectra of MoS2 film. Applied Physics Letters, 109(24).

[56]   Alula, M.T., Mengesha, Z.T. and Mwenesongole, E., 2018. Advances in surface-enhanced Raman spectroscopy for analysis of pharmaceuticals: A review. Vibrational Spectroscopy, 98, pp.50-63.

[57] Kiefer, W., 2010. Surface enhanced Raman spectroscopy: analytical, biophysical and life science applications. John Wiley & Sons.

[58] Terry, L.R., Sanders, S., Potoff, R.H., Kruel, J.W., Jain, M. and Guo, H., 2022. Applications of surface-enhanced Raman spectroscopy in environmental detection. Analytical Science Advances, 3(3-4), pp.113-145.

[59] Pilot, R., Signorini, R., Durante, C., Orian, L., Bhamidipati, M. and Fabris, L., 2019. A review on surface-enhanced Raman scattering. Biosensors, 9(2), p.57.

[60] Tran, T.H., Le, M.P., Pham, N.H., Nguyen, V.T., Do, D.B., Nguyen, X.T., Trinh, B.N.Q., Van Nguyen, T.T., Pham, V.T., Luu, M.Q. and Ngac, A.B., 2022. Highly efficient photo-induced surface enhanced Raman spectroscopy from ZnO/Au nanorods. Optical Materials, 134, p.113069.

[61] Zhang, M., Sun, H., Chen, X., Yang, J., Shi, L., Chen, T., Bao, Z., Liu, J. and Wu, Y., 2019. Highly efficient photoinduced enhanced Raman spectroscopy (PIERS) from plasmonic nanoparticles decorated 3D semiconductor arrays for ultrasensitive, portable, and recyclable detection of organic pollutants. ACS sensors, 4(6), pp.1670-1681.

[62] Ben-Jaber, S., Peveler, W.J., Quesada-Cabrera, R., Cortés, E., Sotelo-Vazquez, C., Abdul-Karim, N., Maier, S.A. and Parkin, I.P., 2016. Photo-induced enhanced Raman spectroscopy for universal ultra-trace detection of explosives, pollutants and biomolecules. Nature communications, 7(1), p.12189.

[63] Chapkin, W.A., McNerny, D.Q., Aldridge, M.F., He, Y., Wang, W., Kieffer, J. and Taub, A.I., 2016. Real-time assessment of carbon nanotube alignment in a polymer matrix under an applied electric field via polarized Raman spectroscopy. Polymer Testing, 56, pp.29-35.

[64]	Bunaciu, A.A., UdriŞTioiu, E.G. and Aboul-Enein, H.Y., 2015. X-ray diffraction: instrumentation and applications. Critical reviews in analytical chemistry, 45(4), pp.289-299.

[65]	Khan, H., Yerramilli, A.S., D'Oliveira, A., Alford, T.L., Boffito, D.C. and Patience, G.S., 2020. Experimental methods in chemical engineering: X-ray diffraction spectroscopy—XRD. The Canadian journal of chemical engineering, 98(6), pp.1255-1266.

[66]	Stanjek, H. and Häusler, W.J.H.I., 2004. Basics of X-ray Diffraction. Hyperfine interactions, 154(1), pp.107-119.

[67]	Pope, C.G., 1997. X-ray diffraction and the Bragg equation. Journal of chemical education, 74(1), p.129.

[68]	Hamilton, W.C., 1962. The structure of solids. Annual Review of Physical Chemistry, 13(1), pp.19-40.

[69]	Dahiya, M., Kumar, R., Kumar, D., Kumar, D. and Khare, N., 2021. Enhanced flux pinning properties of NaNbO3 nanorods added YBCO composite superconductor. Journal of Alloys and Compounds, 883, p.160840.

[70]	Bindu, P. and Thomas, S., 2014. Estimation of lattice strain in ZnO nanoparticles: X-ray peak profile analysis. Journal of Theoretical and Applied Physics, 8(4), pp.123-134.

[71]	Gautam, A.K. and Khare, N., 2023. Enhanced thermoelectric figure of merit at near room temperature in n-type binary silver telluride nanoparticles. Journal of Materiomics, 9(2), pp.310-317.

[72]	Picollo, M., Aceto, M. and Vitorino, T., 2019. UV-Vis spectroscopy. Physical sciences reviews, 4(4), p.20180008.

[73]	Cole, K. and Levine, B.S., 2020. Ultraviolet-visible spectrophotometry. In Principles of forensic toxicology (pp. 127-134). Cham: Springer International Publishing.

[74]	Rocha, F.S., Gomes, A.J., Lunardi, C.N., Kaliaguine, S. and Patience, G.S., 2018. Experimental methods in chemical engineering: Ultraviolet visible spectroscopy—UV-Vis. The Canadian Journal of Chemical Engineering, 96(12), pp.2512-2517.

[75] Daştan, K., Eneş, D., Kaplan, O., Dogan, A. and Çelebier, M., 2025. A Comprehensive Examination of UV-VIS Spectrophotometric Methods in Pharmaceutical Analysis Between 2015-2023. Combinatorial Chemistry & High Throughput Screening, 28(7), pp.1125-1132.

[76] Shahwan, T., Sirriah, S.A., Nairat, M., Boyacı, E., Eroğlu, A.E., Scott, T.B. and Hallam, K.R., 2011. Green synthesis of iron nanoparticles and their application as a Fenton-like catalyst for the degradation of aqueous cationic and anionic dyes. Chemical Engineering Journal, 172(1), pp.258-266.

[77] Guo, Y., Liu, C., Ye, R. and Duan, Q., 2020. Advances on water quality detection by uv-vis spectroscopy. Applied Sciences, 10(19), p.6874.

[78] Jubu, P.R., Obaseki, O.S., Nathan-Abutu, A., Yam, F.K., Yusof, Y. and Ochang, M.B., 2022. Dispensability of the conventional Tauc's plot for accurate bandgap determination from UV–vis optical diffuse reflectance data. Results in Optics, 9, p.100273.

[79] Khosya, M., Kumar, D., Faraz, M. and Khare, N., 2023. Enhanced photoelectrochemical water splitting and photocatalytic degradation performance of visible light active ZnIn2S4/PANI nanocomposite. International Journal of Hydrogen Energy, 48(7), pp.2518-2531.

[80] Hossain, M.S., Kabir, H., Rahman, M.M., Hasan, K., Bashar, M.S., Rahman, M., Gafur, M.A., Islam, S., Amri, A., Jiang, Z.T. and Altarawneh, M., 2017. Understanding the shrinkage of optical absorption edges of nanostructured Cd-Zn sulphide films for photothermal applications. Applied Surface Science, 392, pp.854-862.

[81] Rathje, E.M. and Adams, B.J., 2008. The role of remote sensing in earthquake science and engineering: Opportunities and challenges. Earthquake Spectra, 24(2), pp.471-492.

[82] Zhang, S., Zheng, J., Zhao, Z., Du, S., Lan, D., Gao, Z. and Wu, G., 2025. New prospects in built-in electric fields for electromagnetic wave absorption: from fundamentals to interdisciplinary applications. Advanced Functional Materials, p.e13762.

[83] Soler, M. and Lechuga, L.M., 2025. Label-Free Photonic Biosensors: Key Technologies for Precision Diagnostics. ChemistryEurope, p.2400106.

[84] Lakowicz, J.R. ed., 2006. Principles of fluorescence spectroscopy. Boston, MA: springer US.

[85] Pivovarenko, V.G. and Klymchenko, A.S., 2024. Fluorescent probes based on charge and proton transfer for probing biomolecular environment. The Chemical Record, 24(2), p.e202300321.

[86] Yang, X., Zhang, A.Y., Wheeler, D.A., Bond, T.C., Gu, C. and Li, Y., 2012. Direct molecule-specific glucose detection by Raman spectroscopy based on photonic crystal fiber. Analytical and bioanalytical chemistry, 402(2), pp.687-691.

[87] Vollmer, F. and Arnold, S., 2008. Whispering-gallery-mode biosensing: label-free detection down to single molecules. Nature methods, 5(7), pp.591-596.

[88] Paltusheva, Z.U., Ashikbayeva, Z., Tosi, D. and Gritsenko, L.V., 2022. Highly sensitive zinc oxide fiber-optic biosensor for the detection of CD44 protein. Biosensors, 12(11), p.1015.

[89] Oh, H.E., Eathorne, S. and Jones, M.A., 2022. Use of biosensor technology in analysing milk and dairy components: A review. International Journal of Dairy Technology, 75(4), pp.738-748.

[90] Thawany, P., Khanna, A., Tiwari, U.K. and Deep, A., 2023. L-cysteine/MoS2 modified robust surface plasmon resonance optical fiber sensor for sensing of Ferritin and IgG. Scientific Reports, 13(1), p.5297.

[91] Chen, S. and Lin, C., 2019. Sensitivity analysis of graphene multilayer based surface plasmon resonance biosensor in the ultraviolet, visible and infrared regions. Applied Physics A, 125(4), p.230.

[92] Nair, R.V. and Vijaya, R., 2010. Photonic crystal sensors: An overview. Progress in Quantum Electronics, 34(3), pp.89-134.

[93] Rizk, S., Abd-Elsamee, S., Marzouk, E.S.A. and Areed, N.F., 2025. Photonic crystal biosensor featuring an eye-shaped cavity for precise identification of cancerous cells. Scientific Reports, 15(1), p.23926.

[94] Farooq, M.S., Abdullah, M., Riaz, S., Alvi, A., Rustam, F., Flores, M.A.L., Galán, J.C., Samad, M.A. and Ashraf, I., 2023. A survey on the role of industrial IOT in manufacturing for implementation of smart industry. Sensors, 23(21), p.8958.

[95] Bagha, H., Yavari, A. and Georgakopoulos, D., 2021, November. IoT-based plant health analysis using optical sensors in precision agriculture. In 2021 Digital Image Computing: Techniques and Applications (DICTA) (pp. 01-08). IEEE.

[96] Zha, B., Wang, Z., Ma, L., Chen, J., Wang, H., Li, X., Kumar, S. and Min, R., 2024. Intelligent wearable photonic sensing system for remote healthcare monitoring using stretchable elastomer optical fiber. IEEE Internet of Things Journal, 11(10), pp.17317-17329.

[97] Souza, L.C., Neto, E.R., Lima, E.S. and Junior, A.C.S., 2021. Optically-powered wireless sensor nodes towards industrial internet of things. Sensors, 22(1), p.57.

[98] Mishra, A., Singh, P.K., Chauhan, N., Roy, S., Tiwari, A., Gupta, S., Tiwari, A., Patra, S., Das, T.R., Mishra, P. and Nejad, A.S., 2024. Emergence of integrated biosensing-enabled digital healthcare devices. Sensors & Diagnostics, 3(5), pp.718-744.

[99] Kumar, S., Rani, R., Dilbaghi, N., Tankeshwar, K. and Kim, K.H., 2017. Carbon nanotubes: a novel material for multifaceted applications in human healthcare. Chemical society reviews, 46(1), pp.158-196.

[100] Sharma, V., Priyanka, Verma, M., Kumar, D. and Gupta, A., 2025. Multiparametric Investigation of Chemically Treated and Untreated Sugarcane Bagasse Fiber-Reinforced Epoxy Composites With Wood Apple Shell as Filler: From Waste to Green Composite. International Journal of Polymer Science, 2025(1), p.2181735.

[101] Mahapatra, S.D., Mohapatra, P.C., Aria, A.I., Christie, G., Mishra, Y.K., Hofmann, S. and Thakur, V.K., 2021. Piezoelectric materials for energy harvesting and sensing applications: Roadmap for future smart materials. Advanced Science, 8(17), p.2100864.

[102] Kaur, G., Kaur, D., Sharma, V. and Kumar, D., 2024. Quantum dots for luminescence thermometers. In Luminescent Thermometers (pp. 63-78). CRC Press.

[103] Singh, B., Lin, H. and Bansil, A., 2023. Topology and symmetry in quantum materials. Advanced Materials, 35(27), p.2201058.

[104] Kumar, D., Rajayan, A.K., Rawal, I. and Pal, R., 2024. Organic–Inorganic Nanohybrids for Sensing and Optoelectronics Applications. In Functional Fluorescent Materials (pp. 187-198). CRC Press.

[105] Spanos, I., Stevens, C.J., Solymar, L. and Shamonina, E., 2023. Tailoring the dispersion characteristics in planar arrays of discrete and coalesced split ring resonators. Scientific Reports, 13(1), p.19981.

[106] Mohan Rao, S.J., Kumar, D., Kumar, G. and Chowdhury, D.R., 2017. Modulating the near field coupling through resonator displacement in planar terahertz metamaterials. Journal of Infrared, Millimeter, and Terahertz Waves, 38(1), pp.124-134.

[107] Deng, J., Hu, Z., Chen, Y., Chen, J., Wang, H., Li, K., Kivshar, Y. and Li, G., 2025. Nonlinear Optical Information Encoding with Grayscale Lithography Enabled Metasurfaces. Nano Letters, 25(18), pp.7450-7456.

[108] Banerjee, S., Amith, C.S., Kumar, D., Damarla, G., Chaudhary, A.K., Goel, S., Pal, B.P. and Chowdhury, D.R., 2019. Ultra-thin subwavelength film sensing through the excitation of dark modes in THz metasurfaces. Optics Communications, 453, p.124366.

[109] Bose, J.C., 1898. On the rotation of plane of polarisation of electric wave by a twisted structure. Proceedings of the Royal Society of London, 63(389-400), pp.146-152.

[110] Veselago, V.G. and Narimanov, E.E., 2006. The left hand of brightness: past, present and future of negative index materials. Nature materials, 5(10), pp.759-762.

[111] Pendry, J.B., Holden, A.J., Robbins, D.J. and Stewart, W.J., 1999. Magnetism from conductors and enhanced nonlinear phenomena. IEEE transactions on microwave theory and techniques, 47(11), pp.2075-2084.

[112] Smith, D.R., Padilla, W.J., Vier, D.C., Nemat-Nasser, S.C. and Schultz, S., 2000. Composite medium with simultaneously negative permeability and permittivity. Physical review letters, 84(18), p.4184.

[113] Kumar, D., Jain, R., Shahjahan, Banerjee, S., Prabhu, S.S., Kumar, R., Azad, A.K. and Roy Chowdhury, D., 2020. Bandwidth enhancement of planar terahertz metasurfaces via overlapping of dipolar modes. Plasmonics, 15(6), pp.1925-1934.

[114] Hosseininejad, S.E., Khalily, M. and Tafazolli, R., 2025. Time-modulated 1-bit amplitude-coded metasurface for space-frequency beam shaping. Scientific Reports, 15(1), p.10964.

[115] Banerjee, S., Abhishikth, N.L., Karmakar, S., Kumar, D., Rane, S., Goel, S., Azad, A.K. and Chowdhury, D.R., 2020. Modulating extraordinary terahertz transmissions in multilayer plasmonic metasurfaces. Journal of Optics, 22(12), p.125101.

[116] Rahman, M.M., Yang, Y. and Dey, S., 2025. Application of Metamaterials in Antennas for Gain Improvement: A Study on Integration Techniques and Performance. IEEE Access.

[117] Kumar, D., Devi, K.M., Kumar, R. and Chowdhury, D.R., 2021. Dynamically tunable slow light characteristics in graphene based terahertz metasurfaces. Optics Communications, 491, p.126949.

[118] Akram, S. and Israr, A., 2025. Passive Acoustic Metamaterials for Low Frequencies—Theories, Types, Testing, and Future Directions. Advanced Engineering Materials, 27(5), p.2402270.

[119] Kumar, D., Gupta, M., Srivastava, Y.K., Devi, K.M., Kumar, R. and Chowdhury, D.R., 2022. Photoinduced dynamic tailoring of near-field coupled terahertz metasurfaces and its effect on Coulomb parameters. Journal of Optics, 24(4), p.045101.

[120] Bertoldi, K., Vitelli, V., Christensen, J. and Van Hecke, M., 2017. Flexible mechanical metamaterials. Nature Reviews Materials, 2(11), pp.1-11.

[121] Hamdi, M.S., Bouali, A. and AbdelMalek, F., 2025. A machine learning approach for enhanced early detection of cancerous cells using optimized metamaterial graphene biosensors. Discover Sensors, 1(1), p.6.

[122] Singh, H., Sharma, A., Gupta, A. and Singhal, A., 2024. A polarization-insensitive metamaterial absorber for moisture-sensing applications of agriculture products. Microwave and Optical Technology Letters, 66(1), p.e33907.

[123] Barri, K., Zhang, Q., Kline, J., Lu, W., Luo, J., Sun, Z., Taylor, B.E., Sachs, S.G., Khazanovich, L., Wang, Z.L. and Alavi, A.H., 2023. Multifunctional nanogenerator-integrated metamaterial concrete systems for smart civil infrastructure. Advanced Materials, 35(14), p.2211027.

[124] Karmakar, S., Kumar, D., Varshney, R.K. and Chowdhury, D.R., 2020. Strong terahertz matter interaction induced ultrasensitive sensing in Fano cavity based stacked metamaterials. Journal of Physics D: Applied Physics, 53(41), p.415101.

[125] Liu, H., Ke, X., Shen, L., Cao, Y., Zhang, Y., Tian, L., Chen, J., Meng, X., Huang, P. and Zhang, G., 2025. Polarization-insensitive terahertz biosensing method based on toroidal dipole metasurface. IEEE Sensors Journal.

[126] Li, Z., Panmai, M., Zhou, L., Li, S., Liu, S., Zeng, J. and Lan, S., 2023. Optical sensing and switching in the visible light spectrum based on the bound states in the continuum formed in GaP metasurfaces. Applied Surface Science, 620, p.156779.

[127] Fang, J., Levchenko, I., Yan, W., Aharonovich, I., Aramesh, M., Prawer, S. and Ostrikov, K., 2015. Plasmonic Metamaterial Sensor with Ultra-High Sensitivity in the Visible Spectral Range. Advanced Optical Materials, 3(6), pp.750-755.

[128] Xin, S., Luo, S., Luo, Y. and Ye, L., 2025. Dual-band flexible plasmonic metasensors for ultrasensitive terahertz biomedical sensing. Sensors and Actuators B: Chemical, 432, p.137480.

[129] Bui, T.S., Dao, T.D., Dang, L.H., Vu, L.D., Ohi, A., Nabatame, T., Lee, Y., Nagao, T. and Hoang, C.V., 2016. Metamaterial-enhanced vibrational absorption spectroscopy for the detection of protein molecules. Scientific Reports, 6(1), p.32123.

[130] Rahman, M.A., Al-Bawri, S.S., Abdulkawi, W.M. and Islam, M.T., 2024. Miniaturized tri-band integrated microwave and millimeter-wave MIMO antenna loaded with metamaterial for 5G IoT applications. Results in Engineering, 24, p.103130.

[131] Kumar, D., Sharma, K., Kumar, M. and Kumar, R., 2024. Controlling the optical wavefronts for multiparametric sensing: Holography cum metamaterial centric perspectives. Optics & Laser Technology, 176, p.110954.

[132] Altıntaş, O., Aksoy, M. and Ünal, E., 2020. Design of a metamaterial inspired omega shaped resonator based sensor for industrial implementations. Physica E: Low-dimensional Systems and Nanostructures, 116, p.113734.

[133] Karmakar, S., Banerjee, S., Kumar, D., Kamble, G., Varshney, R.K. and Roy Chowdhury, D., 2019. Deep-Subwavelength coupling-induced fano resonances in symmetric terahertz metamaterials. physica status solidi (RRL)–Rapid Research Letters, 13(10), p.1900310.

[134] Park, J.G., Kim, B., Song, J.Y., Ko, K., Lee, H.K., Choi, D., Baek, S. and Park, S.M., 2025. Machine learning-driven optimization of locally resonant metamaterials for simultaneous vibration control and effective triboelectric sensing. Nano Energy, p.111224.

[135] Ahmed, S., Jiang, X., Wang, C., Kalsoom, U.E., Wang, B., Khan, J., Muhammad, Y., Duan, Y., Zhu, H., Ren, X. and Zhang, H., 2021. An insightful picture of nonlinear photonics in 2D materials and their applications: Recent advances and future prospects. Advanced Optical Materials, 9(11), p.2001671.

[136] Wu, J., Zheng, G. and Lee, L.M., 2012. Optical imaging techniques in microfluidics and their applications. Lab on a Chip, 12(19), pp.3566-3575.

[137] Federici, J.F., Schulkin, B., Huang, F., Gary, D., Barat, R., Oliveira, F. and Zimdars, D., 2005. THz imaging and sensing for security applications—explosives, weapons and drugs. Semiconductor science and technology, 20(7), p.S266.

[138] Hartwick, T.S., Hodges, D.T., Barker, D.H. and Foote, F.B., 1976. Far infrared imagery. Applied Optics, 15(8), pp.1919-1922.

[139] Gowen, A.A., O'Sullivan, C. and O'Donnell, C.P., 2012. Terahertz time domain spectroscopy and imaging: Emerging techniques for food process monitoring and quality control. Trends in Food Science & Technology, 25(1), pp.40-46.

[140] Kumar, V., Mukherjee, P., Valzania, L., Badon, A., Mounaix, P. and Gigan, S., 2025. Fourier synthetic-aperture-based time-resolved terahertz imaging. Photonics Research, 13(2), pp.407-416.

[141] Goodman, J.W., 2015. Statistical optics. John Wiley & Sons.

[142] Khare, K., Butola, M. and Rajora, S., 2015. Fourier optics and computational imaging (pp. 153-165). Chichester: Wiley.

[143] Moon, K., Do, Y., Park, H., Kim, J., Kang, H., Lee, G., Lim, J.H., Kim, J.W. and Han, H., 2019. Computed terahertz near-field mapping of molecular resonances of lactose stereo-isomer impurities with sub-attomole sensitivity. Scientific reports, 9(1), p.16915.

[144] Wang, X.K., Ye, J.S., Sun, W.F., Han, P., Hou, L. and Zhang, Y., 2022. Terahertz near-field microscopy based on an air-plasma dynamic aperture. Light: Science & Applications, 11(1), p.129.

[145] Ishimaru, A., 1978. Wave propagation and scattering in random media (Vol. 2, pp. 148-166). New York: Academic press.

[146] Sheng, P. and van Tiggelen, B., 2007. Introduction to wave scattering, localization and mesoscopic phenomena.

[147] Gigan, S., 2022. Imaging and computing with disorder. Nature Physics, 18(9), pp.980-985.

[148] Gigan, S., Katz, O., De Aguiar, H.B., Andresen, E.R., Aubry, A., Bertolotti, J., Bossy, E., Bouchet, D., Brake, J., Brasselet, S. and Bromberg, Y., 2022. Roadmap on wavefront shaping and deep imaging in complex media. Journal of Physics: Photonics, 4(4), p.042501.

[149] Cecconi, V., Kumar, V., Pasquazi, A., Gongora, J.S.T. and Peccianti, M., 2023. Nonlinear field-control of terahertz waves in random media for spatiotemporal focusing. Open Research Europe, 2, p.32.

[150] Mosk, A.P., Lagendijk, A., Lerosey, G. and Fink, M., 2012. Controlling waves in space and time for imaging and focusing in complex media. Nature photonics, 6(5), pp.283-292.

[151] Totero Gongora, J.S., Olivieri, L., Peters, L., Tunesi, J., Cecconi, V., Cutrona, A., Tucker, R., Kumar, V., Pasquazi, A. and Peccianti, M., 2020. Route to intelligent imaging reconstruction via terahertz nonlinear ghost imaging. Micromachines, 11(5), p.521.

[152] Cecconi, V., Kumar, V., Bertolotti, J., Peters, L., Cutrona, A., Olivieri, L., Pasquazi, A., Totero Gongora, J.S. and Peccianti, M., 2024. Terahertz spatiotemporal wave synthesis in random systems. ACS photonics, 11(2), pp.362-368.

[153] Kumar, V., Cecconi, V., Peters, L., Bertolotti, J., Pasquazi, A., Totero Gongora, J.S. and Peccianti, M., 2022. Deterministic terahertz wave control in scattering media. ACS photonics, 9(8), pp.2634-2642.

[154] Shen, Y.C., Gan, L., Stringer, M., Burnett, A., Tych, K., Shen, H., Cunningham, J.E., Parrott, E.P.J., Zeitler, J.A., Gladden, L.F. and Linfield, E.H., 2009. Terahertz pulsed spectroscopic imaging using optimized binary masks. Applied Physics Letters, 95(23).

[155] Shen, H., Gan, L., Newman, N., Dong, Y., Li, C., Huang, Y. and Shen, Y.C., 2011. Spinning disk for compressive imaging. Optics letters, 37(1), pp.46-48.

[156] Shrekenhamer, D., Watts, C.M. and Padilla, W.J., 2013. Terahertz single pixel imaging with an optically controlled dynamic spatial light modulator. Optics express, 21(10), pp.12507-12518.

[157] Stantchev, R.I., Sun, B., Hornett, S.M., Hobson, P.A., Gibson, G.M., Padgett, M.J. and Hendry, E., 2016. Noninvasive, near-field terahertz imaging of hidden objects using a single-pixel detector. Science advances, 2(6), p.e1600190.

[158] Stantchev, R.I., Yu, X., Blu, T. and Pickwell-MacPherson, E., 2020. Real-time terahertz imaging with a single-pixel detector. Nature communications, 11(1), p.2535.

[159] Stantchev, R.I., Li, K. and Pickwell-MacPherson, E., 2021. Rapid imaging of pulsed terahertz radiation with spatial light modulators and neural networks. ACS Photonics, 8(11), pp.3150-3155.

[160] Watts, C.M., Shrekenhamer, D., Montoya, J., Lipworth, G., Hunt, J., Sleasman, T., Krishna, S., Smith, D.R. and Padilla, W.J., 2014. Terahertz compressive imaging with metamaterial spatial light modulators. Nature photonics, 8(8), pp.605-609.

[161] Hashemi, M.R., Cakmakyapan, S. and Jarrahi, M., 2017. Reconfigurable metamaterials for terahertz wave manipulation. Reports on Progress in Physics, 80(9), p.094501.

[162] Li, W., Hu, X., Wu, J., Fan, K., Chen, B., Zhang, C., Hu, W., Cao, X., Jin, B., Lu, Y. and Chen, J., 2022. Dual-color terahertz spatial light modulator for single-pixel imaging. Light: Science & Applications, 11(1), p.191.

[163] Zhao, J., E, Y., Williams, K., Zhang, X.C. and Boyd, R.W., 2019. Spatial sampling of terahertz fields with sub-wavelength accuracy via probe-beam encoding. Light: Science & Applications, 8(1), p.55.

[164] Olivieri, L., Gongora, J.S.T., Peters, L., Cecconi, V., Cutrona, A., Tunesi, J., Tucker, R., Pasquazi, A. and Peccianti, M., 2020. Hyperspectral terahertz microscopy via nonlinear ghost imaging. Optica, 7(2), pp.186-191.

[165] Chen, S.C., Feng, Z., Li, J., Tan, W., Du, L.H., Cai, J., Ma, Y., He, K., Ding, H., Zhai, Z.H. and Li, Z.R., 2020. Ghost spintronic THz-emitter-array microscope. Light: Science & Applications, 9(1), p.99.

[166] Li, X., Li, J., Li, Y., Ozcan, A. and Jarrahi, M., 2023. High-throughput terahertz imaging: progress and challenges. Light: Science & Applications, 12(1), p.233.

[167] Kumar, V., Cecconi, V., Cutrona, A., Peters, L., Olivieri, L., Totero Gongora, J.S., Pasquazi, A. and Peccianti, M., 2025. Terahertz microscopy through complex media. Scientific Reports, 15(1), p.11706.

[168] Li, W., Qi, J. and Sihvola, A., 2020. Meta-imaging: From non-computational to computational. Advanced Optical Materials, 8(23), p.2001000.

[169] Sorathiya, V., Lavadiya, S., Parmar, B., Das, S., Krishna, M., Faragallah, O.S., Baz, M., Eid, M.M. and Rashed, A.N.Z., 2022. Numerical investigation of the tunable polarizer using gold array and graphene metamaterial structure for an infrared frequency range. Applied Physics B, 128(1), p.13.

[170] Chen, J., Huang, S.X., Chan, K.F., Wu, G.B. and Chan, C.H., 2025. 3D-printed aberration-free terahertz metalens for ultra-broadband achromatic super-resolution wide-angle imaging with high numerical aperture. Nature Communications, 16(1), p.363.

[171] Soldoozy, A., Rezaei, I., Zanjani, M.S. and Sadrnia, H., 2024. Meta-surface filter for visible frequency range based on meta-materials. Memories-Materials, Devices, Circuits and Systems, 7, p.100098.

[172] Hossain, A., Islam, M.T., Beng, G.K., Kashem, S.B.A., Soliman, M.S., Misran, N. and Chowdhury, M.E., 2022. Microwave brain imaging system to detect brain tumor using metamaterial loaded stacked antenna array. Scientific reports, 12(1), p.16478.

[173] Lio, G.E. and Ferraro, A., 2021, February. LIDAR and beam steering tailored by neuromorphic metasurfaces dipped in a tunable surrounding medium. In Photonics (Vol. 8, No. 3, p. 65). MDPI.

[174] Xie, Y., Shen, C., Wang, W., Li, J., Suo, D., Popa, B.I., Jing, Y. and Cummer, S.A., 2016. Acoustic holographic rendering with two-dimensional metamaterial-based passive phased array. Scientific reports, 6(1), p.35437.

[175] Jonkman, J., Brown, C.M., Wright, G.D., Anderson, K.I. and North, A.J., 2020. Tutorial: guidance for quantitative confocal microscopy. Nature protocols, 15(5), pp.1585-1611.

[176] Panchal, V., Yang, Y., Cheng, G., Hu, J., Kruskopf, M., Liu, C.I., Rigosi, A.F., Melios, C., Hight Walker, A.R., Newell, D.B. and Kazakova, O., 2018. Confocal laser scanning microscopy for rapid optical characterization of graphene. Communications physics, 1(1), p.83.

[177] Kumar, S., Saravanan, M.P., Kumar, D. and Venkatesh, R., 2022. Screen-printed film deposited using quasi 2-dimensional Bi2Se3 nanostructures for desalination membrane filler application. Journal of Environmental Chemical Engineering, 10(2), p.107128.

[178] Pierzynska-Mach, A., Cainero, I., Oneto, M., Ferrando-May, E., Lanzanò, L. and Diaspro, A., 2023. Imaging-based study demonstrates how the DEK nanoscale distribution differentially correlates with epigenetic marks in a breast cancer model. Scientific Reports, 13(1), p.12749.

Chapter 5

[1] Petit, C., & Sieffermann, J. (2021). Testing consumer preferences for iced-coffee: Does the drinking environment have any influence? Journal of Photonics Research, 18(2), 161-172. https://doi.org/10.1007/s12596-023-01321-8

[2] Kitayama, K., Notomi, M., Naruse, M., Inoue, K., Kawakami, S., & Uchida, A. (2019). Novel frontier of photonics for data processing—Photonic accelerator. APL Photonics, 4(9), 090901. https://doi.org/10.1063/1.5108912

[3] Satoshi Kawakami "Towards ultra-efficient photonic computer system from a computer architecture perspective", Proc. SPIE 13375, AI and Optical Data Sciences VI, 133750J (21 March 2025); https://doi.org/10.1117/12.3041837

[4] Fu Feng et al. (2023). Symbiotic evolution of photonics and artificial intelligence. Advanced Photonics, 7(2), 024001. https://doi.org/10.1117/1.AP.7.2.024001

[5] Shaker, L.M., Al-Amiery, A., Isahak, W.N.R.W. et al. Integrated photonics: bridging the gap between optics and electronics for enhancing information processing. J Opt (2023). https://doi.org/10.1007/s12596-023-01321-8

[6]   Khan, Taha. (2024, February 05). What to Know About
      Integrated Photonics in Data Centers. AZoOptics. Retrieved
      on June 03, 2025 from `https://www.azooptics.com/Article.aspx?ArticleID=2540`

[7]   Zhou, X., Yi, D., Chan, D.W.U. et al. Silicon photonics for
      high-speed communications and photonic signal processing.
      npj Nanophoton. 1, 27 (2024). `https://doi.org/10.1038/s44310-024-00024-7`

[8]   Photonics Manufacturing. (2024). Industrial Internet of Things
      & Photonics. Photonics Manufacturing Journal, 14(2), 67-82.
      Retrieved from `https://www.photonicsmanufacturing.org/sites/default/files/documents/industrial_internet_of_things.pdf`

[9]   Roy, S.K., Sharan, P. (2018). Photonic Crystal Based Sensor for
      DNA Analysis of Cancer Detection. In: Mishra, A., Basu, A., Tyagi,
      V. (eds) Silicon Photonics & High Performance Computing.
      Advances in Intelligent Systems and Computing, vol 718. Springer,
      Singapore. `https://doi.org/10.1007/978-981-10-7656-5_9`

[10] Roy, S. K. and Sharan, P.: Application of machine learning for
      real-time evaluation of salinity (or TDS) in drinking water using
      photonic sensors, Drink. Water Eng. Sci., 9, 37–45, `https://doi.org/10.5194/dwes-9-37-2016`, 2016

[11] Ranjeet Kumar Pathak, Sumita Mishra, Sandip Kumar Roy,
      Preeta Sharan, A two-stage detection methodology for thyroid
      cancer using photonic crystal: Logistic regression and artificial
      neural networks, Optik, Volume 321,2025,172148, `https://doi.org/10.1016/j.ijleo.2024.172148`

[12] P. Sharan, R. Mulimani and S. K. Roy, "A finite element analysis
      for dynamic strain measurement with enhanced sensitivity,"
      Workshop on Recent Advances in Photonics (WRAP), New Delhi,
      India, 2013, pp. 1-2, doi:10.1109/WRAP.2013.6917718.

[13] Alan E. Willner, Salman Khaleghi, Mohammad Reza Chitgarha, and Omer Faruk Yilmaz, "All-Optical Signal Processing," J. Lightwave Technol. 32, 660-680 (2014).

[14] Bogaerts, W., De Heyn, P., Van Vaerenbergh, T., De Vos, K., Kumar Selvaraja, S., Claes, T., ... & Van Thourhout, D. (2012). Silicon microring resonators. Laser & Photonics Reviews, 6(1), 47–73. https://doi.org/10.1002/lpor.201100017

[15] D. A. B. Miller, "Attojoule Optoelectronics for Low-Energy Information Processing and Communications," in Journal of Lightwave Technology, vol. 35, no. 3, pp. 346-396, 1 Feb.1, 2017, doi:10.1109/JLT.2017.2647779

[16] Soref, R. (2006). The past, present, and future of silicon photonics. IEEE Journal of Selected Topics in Quantum Electronics, 12(6), 1678–1687. https://doi.org/10.1109/JSTQE.2006.883151

[17] Jalali, B., & Fathpour, S. (2006). Silicon photonics. Journal of Lightwave Technology, 24(12), 4600–4615. https://doi.org/10.1109/JLT.2006.885782

[18] Shen, Y., Harris, N. C., Skirlo, S., Prabhu, M., Baehr-Jones, T., Hochberg, M., ... & Soljačić, M. (2017). Deep learning with coherent nanophotonic circuits. Nature Photonics, 11, 441–446. https://doi.org/10.1038/nphoton.2017.93

[19] Tait, A.N., de Lima, T.F., Zhou, E. et al. Neuromorphic photonic networks using silicon photonic weight banks. Sci Rep 7, 7430 (2017). https://doi.org/10.1038/s41598-017-07754-z

[20] Smit, M., Van der Tol, J., & Hill, M. (2012). Moore's law in photonics. Laser & Photonics Reviews, 6(1), 1–13. https://doi.org/10.1002/lpor.201100017

[21] Thomson, D., Zilkie, A., Bowers, J. E., Komljenovic, T., Reed, G. T., Vivien, L., ... & Smit, M. (2016). Roadmap on silicon photonics. Journal of Optics, 18(7), 073003. https://doi.org/10.1088/2040-8978/18/7/073003

[22] Reed, G. T., Mashanovich, G. Z., Gardes, F. Y., & Thomson, D. J. (2010). Silicon optical modulators. Nature Photonics, 4, 518–526. https://doi.org/10.1038/nphoton.2010.179

[23] Sun, C., Wade, M. T., Lee, Y., Orcutt, J. S., Alloatti, L., Georgas, M. S., … & Stojanović, V. M. (2015). Single-chip microprocessor that communicates directly using light. Nature, 528(7583), 534–538. https://doi.org/10.1038/nature16454

[24] Xu, Q., Schmidt, B., Pradhan, S., & Lipson, M. (2005). Micrometre-scale silicon electro-optic modulator. Nature, 435, 325–327. https://doi.org/10.1038/nature03569

[25] Roelkens G, Abassi A, Cardile P, Dave U, De Groote A, De Koninck Y, Dhoore S, Fu X, Gassenq A, Hattasan N, et al. III-V-on-Silicon Photonic Devices for Optical Communication and Sensing. Photonics. 2015; 2(3):969-1004. https://doi.org/10.3390/photonics2030969

[26] Shastri, B. J., Tait, A. N., Ferreira de Lima, T., Nahmias, M. A., & Prucnal, P. R. (2016). Neuromorphic photonics. APL Photonics, 1(5), 050803. https://doi.org/10.1063/1.4954694

[27] Chatterjee, K., Pastorczak, E., Jawulski, K., & Pernal, K. (2016). A minimalistic approach to static and dynamic electron correlations: Amending generalized valence bond method with extended random phase approximation correlation correction. *The Journal of Chemical Physics, 144*(24), 244111. https://doi.org/10.1063/1.4954694

[28] Wang, J., Sciarrino, F., Laing, A., & Thompson, M. G. (2020). Integrated photonic quantum technologies. Nature Photonics, 14, 273–284. https://doi.org/10.1038/s41566-019-0532-1

[29] Bhargava, S., Yavits, L., & Ginosar, R. (2020). Photonics-enabled edge computing. IEEE Communications Magazine, 58(1), 76–81. https://doi.org/10.1109/MCOM.001.1900473

[30] Y. Pan et al., "CDD: Coordinating Data Dissemination in Heterogeneous IoT Networks," in IEEE Communications Magazine, vol. 58, no. 6, pp. 84-89, June 2020, doi:10.1109/MCOM.001.1900473.

[31] Feldmann, J., Youngblood, N., Karpov, M. et al. Parallel convolutional processing using an integrated photonic tensor core. Nature 589, 52–58 (2021). https://doi.org/10.1038/s41586-020-03070-1

[32] Jost, J. (2006). *Partial differential equations* (1st ed.). Springer. https://doi.org/10.1007/b97312

[33] Miloš A. Popovíc, Tymon Barwicz, Michael R. Watts, Peter T. Rakich, Luciano Socci, Erich P. Ippen, Franz X. Kärtner, and Henry I. Smith, "Multistage high-order microring-resonator add-drop filters," Opt. Lett. 31, 2571-2573 (2006).

[34] M. A. Taubenblatt, "Optical interconnects for high performance computing," IEEE Photonic Society 24th Annual Meeting, Arlington, VA, USA, 2011, pp. 668-669, doi:10.1109/PHO.2011.6110726.

[35] Liu, Y., et al. (2021). High-speed and low-loss silicon photonic modulators for data center networks. IEEE Photonics Technology Letters, 33(2), 123–126. https://doi.org/10.1109/LPT.2020.3034763

[36] R. K. Pathak, S. Mishra, P. Sharan and S. K. Roy, "Nodule Detection in Infrared Thermography Using Deep Learning," 2022 IEEE 7th International conference for Convergence in Technology (I2CT), Mumbai, India, 2022, pp. 1-6, doi:10.1109/I2CT54291.2022.9824313.

[37] Nandhini, V.L., Suresh Babu, K., Roy, S.K., Sharan, P. (2021). Multichannel Biosensor for Skin Type Analysis. In: Patnaik, S., Yang, XS., Sethi, I. (eds) Advances in Machine Learning and Computational Intelligence. Algorithms for Intelligent Systems. Springer, Singapore. https://doi.org/10.1007/978-981-15-5243-4_57

Chapter 6

[1] Vaibhav S. Narwane, Angappa Gunasekaran, Bhaskar B. Gardas & Pinyarat Sirisomboonsuk (20 Dec 2023): Quantum machine learning a new frontier in smart manufacturing: a systematic literature review from period 1995 to 2021, International Journal of Computer Integrated Manufacturing, DOI: 10.1080/0951192X.2023.2294441.

[2] Tan, J. Y., Ker, P. J., Lau, K. Y., Hannan, M. A., & Tang, S. G. H. (2019). Applications of Photonics in Agriculture Sector: A Review. *Molecules*, *24*(10), 2025. https://doi.org/10.3390/molecules24102025

[3] Idier, H., Dehhaoui, M., Maatala, N., Kadi, K. A. E. (2024). Assessing the Impact of Precision Farming Technologies: A Literature Review. *World Journal of Agricultural Science and Technology*, *2*(4), 161-179. https://doi.org/10.11648/j.wjast.20240204.17

[4] Zakya H. Kafafi, Raúl Jose Martín-Palma, Ana Flavia Nogueira, Deirdre M. O'Carroll, Jeremy J. Pietron, Ifor D. W. Samuel, Franky So, Nelson Tansu, and Loucas Tsakalakos "The role of photonics in energy," Journal of Photonics for Energy 5(1), 050997 (12 October 2015). https://doi.org/10.1117/1.JPE.5.050997

[5] Wang, Z., Wei, Y., Liu, Z., Duan, G., Yang, D., & Cheng, P. (2022). Perfect Solar Absorber with Extremely Low Infrared Emissivity. Photonics, 9(8), 574. https://doi.org/10.3390/photonics9080574

[6] Anup M. Upadhyaya, Maneesh C. Srivastava, Preeta Sharan, and Sandip Kumar Roy "Silicon nanostructure-based photonic MEMS sensor for biosensing application," Journal of Nanophotonics 15(2), 026001 (26 April 2021). https://doi.org/10.1117/1.JNP.15.026001

[7] P. Sharan, A. Upadhyaya, S. Roy, D. Roy, "Design and Development of Plantar Pressure Measurement Device Using Optical Sensor", 2023 IEEE Photonics Conference (IPC).

[8] Roy, S.K., Sharan, P. Design of ultra-high sensitive biosensor to detect E. Coli in water. Int. j. inf. tecnol. 12, 775–780 (2020). https://doi.org/10.1007/s41870-019-00327-5

[9] VL Nandhini, KR Sandip, KS Babu, Detection of malignant tissue using metal dielectric interface based plasmonic biosensor, J. IJITEE 8,3,2019, https://www.ijitee.org/wp-content/uploads/papers/v8i6s4/F1274048654S419.pdf

[10] Roy, S.K., Sharan, P. (2018). Photonic Crystal Based Sensor for DNA Analysis of Cancer Detection. In: Mishra, A., Basu, A., Tyagi, V. (eds) Silicon Photonics & High Performance Computing. Advances in Intelligent Systems and Computing, vol 718. Springer, Singapore. https://doi.org/10.1007/978-981-10-7656-5_9

[11] Nandhini, V. L., K. Suresh Babu, Sandip Kumar Roy and Ketan Pandit, Photonic crystal based micro inter-ferometer biochip (PC-IMRR) for early stage detection of melanoma, Pertanika J Sci Technol 26 (3), 1505-1512 4, July 2018.

[12] D. Roy, Dr. P. Sharan, S. K. Roy, Optical Biosensor Design To Detect Mycobacterium Tuberculosis Bacteria, Journalof Advanced Research in Dynamical and Control systems 2 (Special -02), 2017.

[13] A Raganna, SH Bharathi, SK Roy, P Sharan, Rapid Detection of Drugs Abuse by Adapting Surface Plasmonic Micro Ring Resonator, International Journal of Signal Processing, Image Processing and Pattern, 3, 2017 https://www.ijitee.org/wp-content/uploads/papers/v8i6s4/F1274048654S419.pdf

[14] Roy, S. K. and Sharan, P.: Application of machine learning for real-time evaluation of salinity (or TDS) in drinking water using photonic sensors, Drink. Water Eng. Sci., 9, 37–45, https://doi.org/10.5194/dwes-9-37-2016, 2016

[15] Sriram G, Vivek M, Sandeep Kumar Roy and P. Sharan, "Spectral analysis of photonic crystal based bio-sensor using AdaBoost algorithm," 2015 International Conference on Communications and Signal Processing (ICCSP), Melmaruvathur, India, 2015, pp. 1806-1810, doi:10.1109/ICCSP.2015.7322834.

[16] S. Mishra, A. Prakash, S. K. Roy, P. Sharan and N. Mathur, "Breast Cancer Detection using Thermal Images and Deep Learning," 2020 7th International Conference on Computing for Sustainable Global Development (INDIACom), New Delhi, India, 2020, pp. 211-216, doi:10.23919/INDIACom49435.2020.9083722.

[17] A. Prakash, S. Mishra, S. K. Roy, P. Sharan, "Comparative Analysis of Anomaly in Hormonal Behavior in Hypothyroidism using Artificial Intelligence", Medlab Middle East 2020, Dubai, `https://www.medlabme.com/content/dam/Informa/medlabme/2020/scientific-posters/Aditya-Prakash.pdf`

[18] R. K. Pathak, S. Mishra, P. Sharan and S. K. Roy, "Nodule Detection in Infrared Thermography Using Deep Learning," 2022 IEEE 7th International conference for Convergence in Technology (I2CT), Mumbai, India, 2022, pp. 1-6, doi:10.1109/I2CT54291.2022.9824313.

[19] N. Roy, S. K. Roy and P. Sharan, "Effective Brain Tumor Segmentation for MRI Image Analysis using Dual Attention Network based YOLACT++," 2023 10th International Conference on Computing for Sustainable Global Development (INDIACom), New Delhi, India, 2023, pp. 10-15.

[20] Ibrar Jahan, M.A., Honnungar, R.V., Nandhini, V.L. et al. Deciphering the sensory landscape: a comparative analysis of fiber Bragg grating and strain gauge systems in structural health monitoring. J Opt (2024). `https://doi.org/10.1007/s12596-024-02001-x`

[21] P. Sharan, P. Deshmukh and S. K. Roy, "Mapping of aqua constituents using photonic crystal," 2013 IEEE Region 10 Humanitarian Technology Conference, Sendai, Japan, 2013, pp. 320-325, doi:10.1109/R10-HTC.2013.6669063.

[22] Ranjeet Kumar Pathak, Sumita Mishra, Sandip Kumar Roy, Preeta Sharan, A two-stage detection methodology for thyroid cancer using photonic crystal: Logistic regression and artificial neural networks, Optik, Volume 321,2025,172148, https://doi.org/10.1016/j.ijleo.2024.172148

[23] Nandhini, V.L., Suresh Babu, K., Roy, S.K., Sharan, P. (2021). Multichannel Biosensor for Skin Type Analysis. In: Patnaik, S., Yang, XS., Sethi, I. (eds) Advances in Machine Learning and Computational Intelligence. Algorithms for Intelligent Systems. Springer, Singapore. https://doi.org/10.1007/978-981-15-5243-4_57

[24] Hamamatsu Photonics Europe. (2024, September 19). Advancing Manufacturing: The Impact of Photonics Technology. AZoM. Retrieved on February 07, 2025 from https://www.azom.com/article.aspx?ArticleID=23856

[25] P. Sharan, R. Mulimani and S. K. Roy, "A finite element analysis for dynamic strain measurement with enhanced sensitivity," Workshop on Recent Advances in Photonics (WRAP), New Delhi, India, 2013, pp. 1-2, doi:10.1109/WRAP.2013.6917718.

[26] Sharan, P., Yasmeen, M.S., Nagesh, N. et al. Med-tech device security through advanced server cryptography. Int. j. inf. tecnol. (2024). https://doi.org/10.1007/s41870-024-02339-2

[27] S. K. Roy, M. Harshitha and P. Sharan, "A comparative study of saline and non-saline water in application of tomato yield by using photonic sensor," 2016 3rd International Conference on Computing for Sustainable Global Development (INDIACom), New Delhi, India, 2016, pp. 2733-2735.

[28] KS Priyanka, SK Roy, P Sharan, A Novel-Platform for the Detection of Magnesium in Seawater using Photonic Crystal based Ring Resonator, History 47 (216), 18-21, 2015.

[29] J. Lavanya, S. K. Roy and P. Sharan, "Design of optical sensor for detection of brininess of water," 2014 IEEE Global Humanitarian Technology Conference - South Asia Satellite (GHTC-SAS), Trivandrum, India, 2014, pp. 99-104, doi:10.1109/GHTC-SAS.2014.6967566.

[30] Roy, Sandip Kumar and Sharan, Preeta. "13 Image-based hibiscus plant disease detection using deep learning". Internet of Things and Machine Learning in Agriculture: Technological Impacts and Challenges, edited by Jyotir Moy Chatterjee, Abhishek Kumar, Pramod Singh Rathore and Vishal Jain, Berlin, Boston: De Gruyter, 2021, pp. 251-274. `https://doi.org/10.1515/9783110691276-013`

Index

© Dr. Preeta Sharan, Dr. Sandip Kumar Roy, Harshada J. Patil, Aryan Chaudhary, and Dr. Deepak Kumar 2026
Dr. P. Sharan et al., *Photonics in Industrial IoT: Transforming Manufacturing and Beyond*,
https://doi.org/10.1007/979-8-8688-2694-8

Free-Space Optics (FSO), 54
Fully photonic architectures, 179